LAW'S PRACTICAL WISDOM

Στον Ανδρέα, τη Μαρία, και τον Εμμανουήλ

Law's Practical Wisdom

The Theory and Practice of Law Making in New Governance Structures in the European Union

KATERINA SIDERI

University of Exeter, UK

Routledge
Taylor & Francis Group
LONDON AND NEW YORK

First published 2007 by Ashgate Publishing

Reissued 2018 by Routledge
2 Park Square, Milton Park, Abingdon, Oxon, OX14 4RN
711 Third Avenue, New York, NY 10017, USA

Routledge is an imprint of the Taylor & Francis Group, an informa business

A Library of Congress record exists under LC control number: 2006025027

ISBN 13: 978-0-815-39018-3 (hbk)
ISBN 13: 978-1-351-15412-3 (ebk)

Contents

List of Figures and Tables		*vii*
Acknowledgements		*ix*
1	**Introducing the Problématique of Law and New Governance: From *Phronesis* to *Compromise***	**1**
	Phronesis	3
	Elements of a Theory of Law Making	4
	Law Making and New Governance	5
	Conclusions	7
2	**Economy, Polity, and the European Experience**	**9**
	Innovation, Economy, and Society	12
	Innovation: Modern Theoretical Paradigms	19
	The Story of the European Union: Market Integration and the European Commission	22
	The Democratic Deficit and the European Demos	29
	Conclusions	32
3	**The European Commission and the Law Making Process: Compromise as a Category of Praxis**	**33**
	Schemas as Social Constructs	34
	Inside the European Commission: Rules of Interaction	36
	Compromise and Law Making Inside the European Commission	55
	Conclusions	58
	Appendix I	58
	Appendix II	59
4	**Procedural Rationality, Power, and the Bureaucratic Mode of Thinking**	**61**
	Proceduralization, Decentralization, and Internet Regulation	61
	Power, Capital, and the Interests of the European Administration	64
	Law, Code, and Internet Regulation	68
	Scarce Resources: Domain Name Allocation	71

Establishing the Difference between the Joint Partnership Model and the Self-Regulation Model 76
The Internet Action Plan and Soft Law: Setting the Vocabulary of the Debate 79
Conclusions 84

5 Ruptures in Established Practice 85

The Proposal for a Directive on the Patentability of Computer-Implemented Inventions: The Consultation 86
Patterns of Thinking about Intellectual Property: The European Commission 90
Framing with Legal Language 98
The Juridico-Administrative Rationality 100
Divergent Voices and Phronetic Ruptures 102
Conclusions 104

6 Elements of a Theory of Law Making in the European Union 107

Law, the Proceduralist Paradigm, and People's Democratic Common Sense 108
Power and Context: The Regulation of Everyday Activities 115
The Force of Law and Participation 118
Is Dialogue Possible? From Consensus and Bargaining to Compromise 119
Compromise and Law Making 121
Compromise and Power 123
Conclusions 125

Bibliography *127*

Index *141*

List of Figures and Tables

Figure 4.1	European Community S&T Policy 'Trialogue'	81
Figure 5.1	Opponents and Supporters of Software Patents: Some Statistics	91

Table 3.1	Decision Making Process in the EU: Proposal for a Council Framework Decision on Attacks against Information System	41

Acknowledgements

I would like to thank Tim Murphy and Colin Scott for reading earlier drafts of this book. I am grateful for comments by the anonymous reviewer of this book and the participants of various workshops and conferences held at the European University Institute, University of London, and Aix-Marseille III. I am especially indebted to Andreas Panagopoulos for engaging in a critical discussion of the key arguments. The assistance of the William Robson Memorial Fund at the LSE was invaluable in facilitating the writing of this book.

I was fortunate to see Chapters Three, Four, and Five published individually as journal articles. Chapter Three was published as 'The European Commission and the Law-Making Process: Compromise as a Category of Praxis', in *International Journal of Law in Context*, 1/4 (2005): pp. 155–82; Chapter Four was published as 'Questioning the Neutrality of Procedural Law: Internet Regulation in Europe through the Lenses of Bourdieu's Notion of Symbolic Capital', in *European Law Journal*, 10/1 (2004): pp. 61–86. I would like to thank the publishers of these journals for letting me reuse them in the book. Chapter Five was published as 'The European Commission, *Phronetic* Judgement and the Regulation of Computer-Implemented Inventions by Patent Law: A Critique of Decentralised Governance Techniques', in Michael Freeman (ed.), *Law and Sociology: Current Legal Issues 2005 Volume 8* (Oxford, 2006), pp. 325–360.

Finally, I would like to thank my family, and especially Andreas, my husband, for all their support and encouragement during the writing of this book. This would have never been completed without them.

Acknowledgements

Chapter One

Introducing the Problématique of Law and New Governance: From *Phronesis* to *Compromise*

Toute définition de la liberté donnera raison au déterminisme.

Henri Bergson, *Essai sur Les Données Immédiates de la Conscience*

The exercise of questioning the function of law in new governance structures implies the adoption of a wide definition of what counts as law. In the legal pluralist tradition, state law appears to coexist with autonomous normative orders produced by groups, networks, and social systems in an increasingly complex and globalized social world.[1] This approach radically revisits the conceptual boundaries of the notion of law, by casting a critical eye on the traditional hierarchy between formal law and social norms, in other words, between 'law' and 'non-law'. Legislation enacted by Parliaments is not the ultimate source of authority, as state law coexists in a heterarchical fashion with the proto-law of various communities, global networks of economic, cultural, academic, and technological nature.[2]

What is then the role of state law in such a fragmented world inhabited by autonomous systems, networks, and groups having their own codes of conduct regulating their behaviour? *Proceduralization* is directly related to these processes, denoting the relocation of governmental functions to the market or the civil society.

---

1 For a detailed exposition of legal pluralism, see Brian Z. Tamanaha, *A General Jurisprudence of Law and Society* (Oxford, 2001), 112–117.

2 There is extensive literature on the possibility to conceptualize state law (whose production is linked to the state apparatus) as coexisting with autonomous normative orders, emerging from the codes of conduct of social groups, and potentially presenting a source of resistance to the dominant ideology, see for example Jean Comaroff and John Comaroff, *Of Revelation and Revolution: Christianity, Colonialism, and Consciousness in South Africa* (Chicago, 1991). Anthropologists and sociologists have pointed out long ago that rules governing conduct need not emanate from the state, while the extensive literature on the constitutive role of law also embraces a heterarchical understanding, see for instance Eugen Ehrlich, *Fundamental Principles of the Sociology of Law*, trans. W.L. Moll (Cambridge, 1936). On the other hand, Simon Roberts reminds us that equating state law with informal legal orders may be problematic, as their function and mode of ordering remains distinctively different, see Simon Roberts, 'After Government? On Representing Law without the State', *Modern Law Review*, 68/1 (2005): 1–24. For a rich analysis of these points, see Tamanaha, *A General Jurisprudence of Law and Society*.

It may also indicate the partnership between the state and private actors with the aim of achieving public ends. Alternatively, it may suggest the shift from state regulation to community self-regulation, with state law establishing the general conditions of negotiation. Finally, it may point to the inclusion by governments of interest groups in the decision making process.[3]

Examples of the way such processes are institutionalized in the European Union can be found in the consultation that followed the proposal for a Directive on the patentability of computer-implemented inventions, and in the comitology and other advisory committees, which play an important role in the implementation of the European Union's Research and Technological Development Framework. Internet filters and technological fences, developed by the industry to block harmful material on the net and to prevent unauthorized copying, present us with more instances of industry self-regulation, where enforcement and coordination is retained by the European Commission.

There are various different theoretical articulations of proceduralization. For Habermas proceduralization interweaves with the notions of deliberative democracy and public sphere, the latter facilitating public participation and debate over key issues.[4] Law should provide structures enabling fair discussion and discursive opinion formation by equally entitled citizens, while, at the same time, it should be the outcome of deliberation, reflecting consensus that stems from shared practice. Rawls's liberal articulation of justice describes the process where constitutional consensus on basic rights and liberties can be established in a morally fragmented world. According to Teubner's formulation of proceduralization inspired by systems theory, law should avoid direct intervention; instead it should encourage communities to reflect over selected considerations by means of steering activity rather than imposing goals. In all these instances, the question of proceduralization links to the problem of governance in modern societies.

Governance depends on decisions relevant to who is governed, who participates in governing, and how power is dispersed amongst governing bodies. Law constitutes the relevant arrangements, hence reflects the sum of ways in which public purposes are authoritatively decided on and implemented,[5] with various actors being active in the shaping of their content. The move away from government to governance is marked by the simultaneous shift of attention from the formal legal order to informal ones; from representative democratic structures to deliberation and engagement of citizens in new governance structures; from command and control rules to procedural rules communicating local knowledge; from the sovereign state

---

3 Julia Black, 'Proceduralizing Regulation-Part I', *Oxford Journal of Legal Studies*, 20/4 (2000): pp. 597–614. However, what is exactly included in such reinvention of regulatory mechanisms is quite ambiguous, see Jody Freeman, 'Collaborative Governance in the Administrative State', *UCLA Law Review*, 45/1 (1996): pp. 18–98.

4 Jürgen Habermas, *The Structural Transformation of the Public Sphere: An Inquiry into a Category of Bourgeois Society* (Cambridge, 1989).

5 Richard H. Pildes and Cass R. Sunstein, 'Reinventing the Regulatory State', 62 *University of Chicago Law Review*, 62/3 (1995): pp. 1–129.

to the responsible citizen; from hierarchies to networks; from state imposed control and ordering of social relations to facilitation, mediation and freedom. This trend coincides with the challenge to the capacity of the institutions of democracy and political representation to correspond to the need to advance fairness, regulate markets, and secure participation of interested parties in decision making. The role of state law is also challenged, since it is viewed as having failed to deliver social justice. Law does not mirror social norms and custom, which find their way into the law making process through the mediation of academics and jurists drafting legal codes, or judges creating common law. Instead, law is generated by representatives of citizens and special commissions, and in this instance law emerges as a technical field of practice, with its own logic and function, often alien to people's concerns. Procedural law and new governance structures seek to remedy these problems.

In the light of the above, the book seeks to articulate a critique of our current understanding of the function of new modes of legal ordering and progressively propose a new framework to come to grips with law making. In a nutshell, the thesis advanced is that for one thing, when the state acts as a mediator or facilitator, when it provides enforcement structures, steers activity to make informal orders reflect over selected problems, or carries the fruits of agreement amongst interested parties, it always seeks to create obedient bodies. For another, I here adopt a wide definition of both the notions of state and legal orders, to examine the processes whereby a legal proposal is made and a legal measure is implemented, as these stages acquire considerable importance in new governance structures. The proposition here is that, for a sociological understanding of law making, it is equally important to consider the function of courts and Parliaments and the workings of forums of discussion, committees, and networks involved in the early and later stages of the law making process. In other words, law has two facets, the one feeding into the other: the stage where law appears as an instance of verticality, and order and the stage where it is created, negotiated, and applied by a multitude of agents. The study of law should include both stages, while being attentive to *phronesis* experience embedded in minds and legal texts.

Phronesis

Aristotle distinguishes amongst three different ways of arriving at truth: *episteme*, *techne*, and *phronesis*. Episteme concerns the possibility of developing universal explanatory frameworks. Techne is attentive to technical know-how. Finally, phronesis is concerned with prudent action, calling attention to practical knowledge and practical ethics.

Phronesis according to Aristotle is a virtue of those who manage households or states. Such individuals advance their own good, and the good of a tradition, on the basis of stocks of practical knowledge as to how a particular situation should be handled. Phronesis is a tacit skill, common sense, practical wisdom, such as the one possessed by a housewife in respect to the management of everyday activities in the household. This type of knowledge results from the accumulation of experience in a particular social setting. In other words, it presents us with practical understandings held by a layman ('honey helps wounds and burns heal'), contrasted with the knowledge of universal rules by a doctor ('a healthy wound bed assists the regrowth of tissue'). Similarly, this type of common sense reasoning is different from the knowledge of general principles about politics, law, and economy. It is a process of learning and acting by experience, which should underpin any inquiry of socio-political nature.[6]

Reason triggers the choice of our beliefs; however, action is underpinned by phronesis. This implies that although we may agree on the theoretical principles that should underlie the function of new modes of legal ordering, the application of these principles in practice will supersede this logic. This is because, the context of the particular circumstances involve the practical judgment of the situation by reference to a wider background of personal experience. This type of practical knowledge forms expectations, tacit understandings underpinning our judgment of what a situation requires, in both cognitive and ethical terms. In the context of the present study on the function of law in new governance, relevant tacit understandings include conceptions about the role of law, what counts as a good legal argument, who should be included in the making of laws, and what makes dialogue fruitful in forums of discussion.

In other words, the notion of phronesis, broadly conceived, is particularly important, as we can address questions such as: is the interpretation of law dependent on the social background of those engaged in its application? Legal procedures advancing deliberation, do they reproduce common sense understandings, such as the centrality of property and contract, and the importance of legal certainty and continuity? If yes, how is the illusion of objectivity created? How does this affect choices as to what topics should be subject to deliberation and whose voice is important to be heard?

Elements of a Theory of Law Making

In a nutshell, I here adopt a phronetic analysis of law making that is attentive to the question of who is involved in the production of law; it examines the typified impetus triggering the making, application, and interpretation of law; it comes to grips with law as a field of practice primarily concerned with reproducing its existence; it seeks to uncover the forgotten history carried in legal concepts, reminding us of the alternatives which became unthinkable; it inquires on the conditions under which tacit understandings embedded in legal rules are challenged and altered; it points to the importance of examining the particular, as opposed to the universal; finally, it incorporates the notion of power in the relevant analysis of the practical and the particular.

---

6 Αριστοτέλης, *Ηθικά Νικομάχεια* (3 τόμοι, Αθήνα, 1992).

In this instance, following Nietzsche, Foucault, and Bourdieu amongst others, the present study is skeptical to a rational understanding of the legal/political discourse, being devoted to a historical analysis of the relationship between truth and power, and incorporating a critique of reason as disguising domination. In the light of such an analysis, the focus here is also on the ways in which the ordering of social relations is exercised in indirect ways in legal rules.

Following this intuition, law making can be conceptualized as a flexible process, whose final product is crystallized in vertical legal rules, aiming at ordering social relationships by means of objectifying practices, and ensuring legal certainty and continuity. This view implies the recurrent movement from multiplicity and flexibility to order, while providing the possibility to conceptualize the opposite movement, from order back to difference. In this framework, the instance of law making in new governance structures, promoting proceduralization, engagement and dialogue, has three idiosyncratic characteristics: it brings to the foreground of analysis the notion of compromise as an anthropological category of praxis, it draws attention to the novel ways in which state power may be exercised, and finally, it requires examination of the conditions under which such novel reconfigurations of power may be challenged.

Law Making and New Governance

Legal texts and principles, and agents applying them or debating them, present the crystallization of experience. When agents apply legal principles, they apply these in the light of tacit understandings, experience accumulated in the course of interaction in work settings, or during receiving particular education and professional training.

Following this intuition, one of the main propositions of the book is that new governance structures may fulfill their promise to promote deliberation, and bring more democratic legitimacy into the lawmaking process in the EU, when compromise becomes a phronetic category of praxis. Compromise provides the theoretical tools to move away from the notions of consensus and bargaining. Consensus denotes reaching agreement on universal principles anchored in citizens' democratic common sense. Strategic bargaining advances a view of maximization of egoistic interests. Instead, the notion of compromise indicates the simultaneous operation of several truth claims in the law making process, and in this instance it loses its derogatory meaning. When it emerges as a category of praxis, dialogue and communication between different views of the world becomes possible, and order is always open to question. This is because legal rules encompass a temporary balance ordered by the force of the written text to temporarily objectify practices and simultaneously ensure legal certainty and continuity. Compromise as a category of praxis is socially constructed, as it emerges in a state of interdependence with strong ties. Only if we need the 'other' will compromise emerge, sacrificing personal ends, while taking into consideration other alternative views for the sake of acting jointly. The elaboration of this proposition will be taken up in Chapter Three of the book, where a case study on the European Commission seeks to uncover tacit understandings regulating the conduct of officials engaging in the production of a legal proposal or the implementation of a legal measure.

In this instance, value systems are always open to restructuring, and the sociology of law becomes attentive to the process of actualization of power relations in a field of possibilities. Hence, the notion of compromise provides the theoretical tools to come to grips with the relationship between deliberation and the force of law; it inquires on the discursive formation of statements embedded in law, while considering the ideas and practices never actualized; it considers agents as active participants constructing the social world; it seeks to discover the process of formation of forms of ordering, which are always open to restructuring and reform. This can be accomplished if the question of what justice is, is accompanied by a query about why, when, and who wants justice, implying an analysis on the subtle ways in which power may be exercised. This point links to the *problématique* concerning the bureaucratic mode of thinking.

In decentralized law making structures it appears that the role of administrations is strengthened. As already noted, having expanded the boundaries of law to relocate its operation as being scattered throughout the social milieu, led to debating the nature and role of state law. If the legitimacy of state law depends upon its consistency with social norms, then it should not order social relations but should seek to facilitate inclusion, promote participation, and communicate local knowledge. This expansion implies the shift of the focus of attention from parliaments and courts to forums of discussion and networks, with the administration establishing the general conditions of negotiation; coordinating the creation of networks furnishing the raw material feeding into legislative proposals; securing enforcement in self regulatory regimes; steering activity on the part of autonomous groups of actors to make them reflect upon selected problems.

It is wrong however to conceive their role as being limited to the mere execution of the legal mandate. Moving beyond the concepts of impartiality and neutrality, the analysis of chapter four of the book seeks to illustrate the indirect ways, often operating beyond the conscious level, in which administrations strive to maximize their position as major think tanks. When providing for the impartial management of practical affairs, administrations recognize some social problems, while simultaneously neglecting some others. They appreciate some solutions, while disregarding alternatives. They reproduce socially accepted stereotypes, often deeply embedded in the dominant rhetoric of policy and legal analysis, which go without saying. As Foucault reminds us, normalization and the production of docile bodies is a property of disciplinary power, reproduced in technical administrative assessments and regulation. To this effect, Chapter Four will consider the employment of technological fences by the industry to protect their intellectual property rights. The chapter will also concentrate on domain name allocation by the Internet Corporation for Assigned Names and Numbers (ICANN), and on the regulation of harmful and illegal content on the Internet.

However, such an analysis is not meant to trap social relations in the melancholy of irreversible relations of domination. True, a phronetic approach reminds us that the faith in the efficacy of law making in new governance structures reproduces historically contingent assumptions, such as the belief in scientific objectivity, in the responsible emancipated rational agent able to regulate itself, in law's impartiality and neutrality, and in the potential of consensus building amongst agents with a free will. In the same spirit, legal rules carry a forgotten history, as Chapter Two of the book will seek to illustrate, in the course of examining the political and legal traditions of the European Union, and engaging in a brief historical overview of the political economy of innovation. Nevertheless, as Chapter Five of the book will endeavour to show, ruptures in the normal flow of events and the increase in the capacity and will of social groups to change the world, may trigger the need to reconsider dominant patterns of praxis, promoting novel understandings. To this effect, Chapter Five will consider the proposal for a Directive on the patentability of computer-implemented inventions, which failed to be adopted. The aim here is to examine the conditions under which law and social norms come into fruitful contact.

Uncontested tacit knowledge and stereotypes embedded in legal documents can be brought onto the conscious level and be challenged. In this instance, embedded 'commonsensical' taxonomies open to embrace different forms of experience, alternative types of culturally informed understandings about what counts as justice. Law and the practical wisdom it embraces can then be altered, and communication amongst different views of the world becomes possible. Yet, these new, revolutionary visions will always present us with new attempts to control conduct and impose the right way to conceptualize justice.

If one accepts that power is at the heart of social relations, then we do away with a view of society and law as moving towards a refined state of affairs untouched by vulgar antagonisms. If one accepts that power is a *modus vivendi*, the study of law should be prepared to come to grips with social phenomena by means of flexible concepts and frameworks of analysis. In the same spirit, recognizing the dual nature of law, as in ordering and compromising, objectifying and negotiating, stabilizing and accommodating, implies the need to study the function of law as in both the process of debating and applying order, and the product of this process encapsulated in the final legal text. The notions of power, phronesis, and compromise are useful tools in this direction, and are indispensable to any effort to develop a theory of law making in new governance structures. Chapter Six of the book will consolidate my theoretical propositions in this direction.

Conclusions

Law's Practical Wisdom critically examines some of the assumptions underlying our understanding of the function of new modes of legal ordering and governance. It recasts the problem of rationality, objectivity, and consensus building, to draw attention to the indirect ways power is exercised in decentralized rules. It further focuses on the invisible avenues through which the notions of free will and consensus are curbed under the weight of practice, reproducing unuttered cognitive frames. It finally enquires on whether modes of facilitation and inclusion conceal new means of ordering by the administration. The empirical substantiation of the argument is premised on case studies from the European Union, long troubled by the question of democratic deficit, presenting us with fine examples of social complexity, which require solutions beyond traditional command and control rules. Progressively the book proposes elements for a theory of law making in the EU, being attentive to the ideas of domination, inequality, difference, and last but not least, compromise.

Chapter Two

Economy, Polity, and the European Experience

History is more or less bunk. It's tradition. We don't want tradition. We want to live in the present and the only history that is worth a tinker's damn, is the history we made today.

Henry Ford, Interview in *Chicago Tribune*, 15 May 1916

The object of the this chapter is to trace the assumptions underpinning the idea that law making in new governance structures presents us with the possibility to do away with the gripping effect of command and control rules. It may appear that there was some kind of inevitability in promoting flexible governance structures in Europe. The Union's democratic deficit, the challenge to the capacity of hierarchically organized law and governance systems to effectively order economic and social relations, technological innovation, internationalization, and new economic conditions, can all be said to have led to the need to debate the role of law. True, the discussion on the democratic deficit of the European Union brought to the foreground the need to rethink political participation, and new technological improvements were decisive in uniting markets as well as positioning the European Commission as a key player; however, there are various competing paradigms to conceptualize the above processes.

Against this background, the aim of this chapter is twofold. First, it seeks to show that definitions are the result of specific socio-economic circumstances. Hence, conducting a historical overview of the diverse experiences, and competing theoretical paradigms leading to the genesis of an object of study, is an exercise aiming at examining the set of different statements constructing it. This is important, as we are constantly reminded that things could have been different, since under different socio-economic circumstances a different set of statements could have informed the genesis of a new field of study.[1]

Such an analysis is a powerful tool to introduce ruptures, as it does not only bring attention to the discourses feeding into the emergence of a new object of analysis, but also to the potentialities that were never actualized, in other words to the discarded possibilities. Engaging in such an enquiry requires being able to move

[1] Pierre Bourdieu, 'Rethinking the State: Genesis and Structure of the Bureaucratic Field', *Sociological Theory*, 12/1 (1994): 1–18; Michel Foucault, *The Archaeology of Knowledge*, A.M. Sheridan Smith (translator), (London, 1972); Friedrich Nietzsche, *On the Genealogy of Morals*, D. Smith (translator and introduction) (Oxford, 1996).

among different disciplines, and deal with never ending sources. This is certainly a difficult task given the limits of space imposed here. It also injects in the analysis the inevitability of being selective as to the themes chosen to unfold the present narrative. A related problem inherent in such an exercise is that overgeneralizations seem to be unavoidable.[2]

The choice of the common thread tying together the unfolding of diverse narratives is crucial. The starting point to unfold the analysis here is the observation that the stages of formation of legislative proposals, and implementation of legal rules, acquire considerable importance in new law making structures. They present us with an instance when the symbolic violence of the state, as manifested in top-down command and control rules, is sought to be counterbalanced by means of including in the law making process autonomous individuals, networks, and social systems. This observation is valuable, as it is underlied by the idea of an objective and neutral administration able to coordinate the participation of civil society and steer activity on their part, with the aim to make them reflect upon selected social problems. In other words, the building blocks of the idea that new governance structures can provide for horizontal rule making, is the concept of objectivity in law, administrative neutrality, and responsible individuality.

Concerning the objectivity of legal rules, the present analysis will not engage in a general exposition of the relevant philosophical arguments. Instead, it will proceed in giving a practical example of the argument promoting the view that legal rules crystallize context-dependent understandings. To this effect, the chapter will broadly examine the diverse theoretical frameworks informing the notion of innovation, as elaborated by various political economists. The aim is to show that legal rules as enacted nowadays reflect *one* particular way to come to grips with innovation, its importance, and its development. However, this does not preclude the existence of alternative conceptual paradigms. This is a point whose empirical elaboration will be further taken up in Chapter Five of this book.

One may be tempted to ask what factors led to the choice of the concept of innovation, in order to make the point that legal rules are culturally contingent. The reason is that innovation is a concept that cuts across many areas, such as health and life sciences, the environment, competition, research, and intellectual property rights relevant to biotechnology and software. This has been acknowledged in the EU, and every impact assessment conducted for European legislation (for instance environmental issues) has to take into account the importance of the dimension of innovation.[3] The case studies I have included further illustrate this point, since the

---

2 As this chapter discusses broad themes, about which there is extensive literature, I have kept footnote references to a minimum.

3 For more on this, see Communication from the Commission on Impact Assessment COM(2002) 276 final. The introduction states:

> The Commission intends to launch impact assessment as a tool to improve the quality and coherence of the policy development process. It will contribute to an effective and efficient regulatory environment and further, to a more coherent implementation of the European

concept of innovation appears to have spurred debate as to the scope and content of regulatory law in various instances. Indeed, innovation and the information society were the ideological luggage for liberalizing markets in the 1980s, a process that appears to have boosted the powers of the European Commission, as it used its quasi-legislative powers to issue the liberalization Directives, and its quasi-judicial powers in the process of competition law enforcement, when taking decisions on individual cases and imposing fines on individual firms.[4] Nevertheless, in order to present the alternative choices available to the dominant rhetoric concerning innovation, it is important to concentrate on the experience of the nineteenth and twentieth century, to consider the ways in which liberalism, economic theory, and conceptions as to the virtues of new technologies and competition interweaved and consequently came under radical doubt, as early as in 1760, but also later in the First World War and during the depression of the 1930s.

However, understanding how the above perspectives acquired meaning in the context of the European Union requires examination of its political and legal traditions. To this effect, the analysis here will also concentrate upon the importance of market integration, expertise, and ordoliberalism as offering powerful paradigms influencing the early attempts to integrate markets in Europe. The argument is that these frameworks are still relevant for us today, in order to come to grips with the role of the European Commission in providing expertise and interest intermediation. Moreover, ordoliberalism shaped an understanding of regulatory law as being neutral and objective, implementing the mandate of constitutional principles, and indirectly intervening in the economy. A different focus is on sudden technological advances and globalization, which gave rise to new understandings as to the merits of cooperation, providing the operating context of all of the above ideas. For an intellectual framework to successfully become dominant, it has to find its efficacy in this real world, and in particular historical circumstances favouring a certain way of thinking.

Finally, I will consider how the above mentioned processes interweaved with the problem of democratic deficit in the European Union, as triggered by the reality of an enlarged European Union of 450 million citizens, internationalization, multiculturalism, and the Enlightenment belief that we can create our own future

---

strategy for Sustainable Development. Impact Assessment identifies the likely positive and negative impacts of proposed policy actions, enabling informed political judgments to be made about the proposal and identify trade-offs in achieving competing objectives. It also permits to complete the application of the subsidiarity and proportionality protocol annexed to the Amsterdam Treaty.

Annex 2 Paragraph 4.1 considers the importance of taking into account innovation and technological development.

[4] The European Commission has quasi-legislative, supervisory, executive (for instance administering the budget) and quasi-judicial powers. It is entrusted with the task of preparing legislative proposals, for the various legislative procedures see Paul Craig and Grainne de Búrca, *EU Law: Text, Cases, and Materials*, (Oxford, 2003).

by means of subjecting tradition to critique. The last point links to the belief in that dialogue can help society evolve on the basis of human reason, safely protected from vulgar antagonisms and prejudice.

Innovation, Economy, and Society

In 1733, John Kay, a 29-year-old inventor, was awarded a patent for his new machine for opening and dressing wool, the Flying Shuttle. The widespread adoption of this invention motivated Sir Richard Arkwright to conceive a new device in 1770, the Cotton Jenny, providing for the more efficient spinning of yarn. By the 1780s, new machinery was invented to card and comb the wool supplying the new spinning machines, and by the turn of the century, the production of cloth had been fully mechanized. The cottage industry of English textiles flourished, and exports rose sharply.[5]

The idea of using machines was being introduced into other industries, a prominent example being the construction of the Bridgewater Canal by the Duke of Bridgwater in 1759, which was important for the transportation of coal by boat from his coalmines at Worsley to Manchester,[6] and James Watt's Steam Engine invented in 1765. Those events brought about the industrial revolution, which began in England and spread around Europe. They marked the genesis of the idea that innovation is important for economic growth, whilst linking economic progress with the freedom to trade. Early attempts to conceptualize the relationship amongst these notions are presented by Smith, Babbage, and Rae.[7]

Back in 1776, Adam Smith did away with the notion of mercantilist protectionism, to argue that prices can be determined by means of competition, as then they would change responding to market conditions. The classical view of economics emphasized the role of risk-taking and of the innovative entrepreneur, and took into account the importance of the technology and organization of firms (division of labour) in the process of competition, while it assumed that the division of labour facilitates technological innovation.[8]

---

[5] Raymond Kurzweil, *The Age of Intelligent Machines* (Cambridge, 1990), 2; David S. Landes, *The Unbound Prometheus: Technological Change and Industrial Development in Western Europe from 1750 to the Present* (Cambridge UK, 1969).

[6] Kurzweil, *The Age of Intelligent Machines*.

[7] The choice of these authors is influenced by Rosenberg's work, see Nathan Rosenberg, *Exploring the Black Box: Technology, Economics and History* (Cambridge UK and NY, 1994), where he analyses the work of thinkers such as Charles Babbage, Karl Marx, and Joseph Schumpeter. My choice of John Rae's work was influenced by Anthony Brewer, 'Economic Growth and Technical Change: John Rae's Critique of Adam Smith', *History of Political Economy*, 23/1 (1991): 1–12. Many other thinkers brought attention to the importance of innovation, but I limit my references to authors whose work is primarily associated with it.

[8] Adam Smith, *The Wealth of Nations* (London, 1999), especially see, Book I, Chapter 1, 'Of the Division of Labour'; Nathan Rosenberg, 'Adam Smith on the Division of Labour:

Charles Babbage[9] wrote some 60 years after Smith, when the industrial revolution was a far more mature phenomenon, and technological progress was rapidly advancing. Rosenberg argues that Babbage is the first observer calling attention, in an explicit way, to the causal links between economic forces and inventive activity. Indeed, Babbage took the idea of the division of labour, and twisted it to argue that technical change is a consequence, as well as a cause, of the division of labour. Hence, he observed that investing in improving machines is important for economic success. According to Babbage, this is because as the application of the division of labour tends to produce cheaper articles, it increases the demand, and gradually results in large capital being invested in factories, as new machines automating all stages of production are introduced. Moreover, skilled workers, who can use these machines, are hired, and engineers, who can fix the machines on the spot, are employed. Finally, the addition of a machine to light the factory at night using gas is built, and an accountant's department is added. This would have to have clerks to pay the workmen, communicate with the agents who purchase the raw produce, and sell the manufactured article.

The division of labour in this instance produces cheaper articles as it:

> is not merely the precise amount of skill purchased, which is necessary for the execution of each process, but throughout every stage – from that in which the raw material is procured, to that by which the finished produce is conveyed into the hands of the consumer – the same economy of skill prevails. The quantity of work produced by a given number of people is greatly augmented by such an extended arrangement; and the result is necessarily a great reduction in the cost of the article, which is brought to market.[10]

Babbage parallels the function of the division of labour in a factory with mental division of labour:

> We have seen, then, that the effect of the division of labour, both in mechanical and in mental operations, is that it enables us to purchase and apply to each process precisely that quantity of skill and knowledge which is required for it: we avoid employing any part of the time of a man who can get eight or ten shillings a day by his skill in tempering needles, in turning a wheel, which can be done for sixpence a day; and we equally avoid the loss

---

Two Views or One?', *Economica*, 32/126 (1965): 127–139 citing Adam Smith, *Wealth of Nations*.

[9] Babbage was a pioneer mathematician, engineer, and political economist. He is sometimes referred to as the father of computing, as his Difference Engine No. One was the first successful automatic calculator, and remains one of the finest examples of precision engineering of the time. For more information see the webpage of the Charles Babbage Institute at http://www.cbi.umn.edu/exhibits/cb.html (webpage visited on 22 September 2005).

[10] Charles Babbage, *On the Economy of Machinery and Manufactures* (London, 1963), Chapter 20 'On the Division of Labour', point 269; Nathan Rosenberg, 'Babbage; Pioneer Economist', in Nathan Rosenberg, *Exploring the Black Box*, citing Babbage, *On the Economy of Machinery and Manufactures*, 191 and 260.

> arising from the employment of an accomplished mathematician in performing the lowest processes of arithmetic.[11]

However, the relationship between technological innovation and the division of labour is not a one way one, but cyclical. This is because, the division of labour results in capital accumulation, capital is used to promote innovation, and innovative activity produces more capital. Very importantly, innovation is not only the result of a genius mind, but most of the time is brought about by means of minor improvements accomplished in the workplace.

At the same time, Scottish John Rae in his *New Principles* totally reversed Smith's causality that the division of labour results in the invention of machines. In sum, Rae's analysis is centred on the role of invention as the primary factor behind economic growth. Without denying the importance of capital accumulation, Rae argued that the motor behind this process is technological progress, and pointed to the creative power inherent in inventive activity. Thus, he suggested that governmental legislation may be required, promoting science.[12]

Smith treated the invention of machines as a result, not a cause, of the division of labour, Babbage observed that the one feeds into the other, while Rae reversed the causality and attributed to technological innovation a primary role. Albeit the difference of opinion as to the level of importance conferred to machines, innovation was thought to be a factor to be taken into account when discussing economic progress. However, the experience of the early days of industrial revolution was also marked by the inexorable relationship between the science of economics and liberalism.

The Socio-Political Context

The freedom to pursue economic conduct became the cornerstone of liberal thinking.[13] Economic freedom was viewed as a right, and law was understood as

---

[11] Ibid., Babbage. The division of labour inside a factory represents its domestic economy. Thus, Babbage argues that there is no point in introducing laws restricting machinery exports, to avoid providing foreigners with machinery that will threaten England's competitive advantage:

> It is contended that by admitting the exportation of machinery, foreign manufacturers will be supplied with machines equal to our own. But in order to succeed in a manufacture, it is necessary not merely to possess good machinery, but that the domestic economy of the factory should be most carefully regulated.

[12] For an introduction to Rae's thinking see, Brewer, 'Economic Growth and Technical Change'; Syed Ahmad, 'Smith's Division of Labour and Rae's "Invention": A Study of the Second Dichotomy with an Evaluation of the First', *History of Political Economy*, 28/3 (1996): 95–107.

[13] David J. Gerber, *Law and Competition in Twentieth Century Europe: Protecting Prometheus* (Oxford and New York, 1998), 17. The literature on liberalism is extensive. On the nineteenth century liberalism see Ernest K. Bramsted and John K. Melhuish (eds), *Western Liberalism: A History in Documents from Locke to Croce* (London, 1978); Massimo

being entrusted with its protection. Therefore, the political and economic component interweaved, as individuals would have the freedom to influence the laws governing their conduct, and at the same time possess the necessary freedom of choice as to what to produce and how to produce it.

The bourgeoisie acquired new rights and freedoms; and the ruling elite in Europe also largely embraced the new ideas. By the mid-1870s European economies flourished and technological and transportation advances were important developments driving economic growth.[14] At the same time, the modes of production were altered, as factories grew in size, employing hundreds or thousands of workers, management emerged as a new profession, funding by banks became increasingly important, and trade was internationalized, with artisans facing competition from manufactured goods.[15] As a result, a new social class was created, whose members were people who had to change their traditional way of life and leave their communities.[16] However, laws protecting workers arrived late.[17]

Salvadori, *The Liberal Heresy: Origins and Historical Development* (London, 1977); Guido de Ruggiero, *The History of European Liberalism* (Gloucester, 1981), especially see 'What Liberalism Is', 347–69.

14 David R. Weir, 'Life under Pressure: France and England, 1670-1870', *Journal of Economic History*, 42/1 (1984): 27–47; Donald N. McCloskey, 'The Industrial Revolution 1780–1860: A Survey', in Joel Mokyr (ed.), *The Economics of the Industrial Revolution* (London, 1985); Landes, *The Unbound Prometheus*, Chapters 1 and 2.

15 Of course, there were considerable divergences in Europe as to the means of financing businesses. In the UK, up until the late nineteenth century, most of the firms were family firms, and were financed by family finance and loans. On the other hand, in Germany banks played an important role in financing businesses. On the German banking system see Robert Franz, 'The Statistical History of the German Banking System', *Miscellaneous Articles on German Banking*, US Senate Document 508 (Washington DC, 1910).

16 Landes, *The Unbound Prometheus*. According to Landes, in 1912 in England, 12 per cent of people were employed in agriculture, while in 1951, this number dropped to 5 per cent. However, in France, in 1789, around 55 per cent of the population were farmers, and interestingly, in 1866, at the heyday of the first industrial revolution, the same number still applied, while in 1950 it only dropped to one third of the population. Landes argues that one of the reasons for this is the high tariffs introduced to imported goods back in the nineteenth century. It is beyond the scope of this chapter to engage in a comparative appreciation of the effects of industrialization in different European countries. The aim is simply to sketch the general characteristics of industrialization.

17 For instance, see the 1847 Ten Hours Act and the 1874 Factory Act, which, in contrast to earlier attempts, could be more adequately enforced. Several intellectual movements reacted to social injustice. *Utopian Socialists, Fabian Socialists*, and the *French Saint Simonians* were all concerned with this. On these issues see, Keith Taylor, *The Political Ideas of the Utopian Socialists* (London, 1982); Lisanne Radice, *Beatrice and Sidney Webb: Fabian Socialists* (London, 1984); Amand Bazard, Emile Barrault and Prosper Enfantin, *The Doctrine of Saint-Simon: An Exposition; First Year, 1828–1829*, G. Iggers, (translator) (New York, 1972). As regards Utopian Socialists, Robert Owen was one of the members of this intellectual school. He was a factory owner in Scotland, introduced shorter working hours, safer working conditions and sick pay, and was involved in advancing the cause of limiting

However, the aftermath of the great depression in the 1870s, which came as a result of the crash of the Vienna stock market, disastrous harvests, and increases in wheat sales from North America, was that in times of economic upheaval business would join forces with the government to keep prices up, increase their size, organize in cartels, and demand the imposition of taxes in imported products.[18]

As a result, liberalism, economic theory, and conceptions as to the virtues of new technologies and open markets, were all under radical doubt. At the theoretical level, there were various responses to the inadequacies of classical economic theory. The German historical school, neo-classical economics, and Marxism, all attempted to suggest novel theoretical paradigms.[19] Neo-classical economics and Marxism in particular, took into account the role of technological innovation in the process, albeit the former only positioned it in the periphery of its analytical framework, while the latter attributed to it a prominent role.

Casting a Critical Eye

The neo-classical school of thought established in England offered a new understanding of economic phenomena. Although currently neo-classical economics encompasses a variety of approaches, the following paragraph will very briefly summarize some common threads. Competition is viewed as a state of affairs, and the abstract model of perfect competition is used to describe rivalry as being dependent on a demand and cost equilibrium, determining which firm survives and which fails. Firms are conceived to be profit-maximizing agents, rationally choosing to enter or exit a market according to a set of observed profit opportunities. Firms then select an output where marginal costs equal the market price. As long as profit opportunities appear to exist, firms will continue to enter the market. When too many firms enter the market, this will lead to increased production, and lower prices and profits. If profits are very low, this will result in companies going out of business. This in turn means that the remaining companies will be better off, as a competitive equilibrium is achieved. Thus, in the long run, firms choosing to remain will produce at the minimum efficient scale. Since a demand and cost equilibrium is the

---

child labour. Owen built settlements, called 'Villages of Cooperation', in both the US and the UK, which were agricultural communities offering employment, schools for children and adults, and safer working conditions. Saint-Simon envisaged a society, where an elite of philosophers, scientists, and artists would be engaged in governing and opinion shaping on the basis of 'rational' Christianity. Finally, Fabian Socialists' main position was that social reforms would be accomplished through a strong representative democracy, and the right to vote. A full discussion on these positions falls outside the scope of this chapter.

18 Gerber, *Law and Competition in Twentieth Century Europe*, 25–7.

19 Ibid. The previous discussion on liberalism and industrialization did not touch on the very important issue of imperialism. Imperialism links to industrial revolution, as the colonies provided new markets and cheap raw material, see John R. Ward, 'The Industrial Revolution and British Imperialism, 1750–1850', *The Economic History Review*, 47/1 (1994): 44–65. Again, due to limits of space I cannot possibly elaborate on these issues here.

prerequisite of competition, the neo-classical focus is on the effects of competition and on market structure (perfect competition, monopolistic competition, oligopoly, and monopoly).

There are two points emerging from the previous discussion: first, there is a circular effect between the notions of market equilibrium and utility maximization. This is because, when individuals maximize their utilities, they bring about the economic condition of equilibrium, and the economic equilibrium itself is the required condition under which the maximization of the utilities of all individuals can be accomplished. This is why perfect competition is good for entrepreneurs and for the society as a whole.[20] Second, according to the neo-classical production theory, firms make rational optimization decisions based on the calculation of profits. To engage in such calculations, information on prices is crucial, while the development of new technologies is marginally important. Accordingly, technological change is an exogenous dimension in the neo-classical models.

Marx conceptualized technological innovation in a different way, attributing to it a central role in his analysis of economic phenomena. His position is generally underlied by the assumption that phenomena under observation acquire meaning only under specific socio-economic circumstances. Hence, terms, such as value, money, and profit, do not have meaning outside the context of a capitalist society. Moreover, human history in the capitalist world is the product of struggles, which come about as a result of the contradiction between the forces of production and the relations of production. The upshot of this is that class struggles are the fundamental force injecting dynamism in the making of history.

At the same time, Marx attaches great importance to technological factors. Technological advance is thought to be the motor behind the process of competition amongst firms, as firms are constantly driven to adopt new technologies. This process results in rising productivity, but the flip side of it is unemployment. Nonetheless, the innovative potential of technologies is not indefinite. For this reason, Marx hypothesizes that eventually the economic growth of the capitalist world will cease. The solution is to choose a different economic order, otherwise depressions are unavoidable.[21]

He analyses two major stages in the history of technology: the *Manufacturing System*, based on the division of labour, and the *Modern Industry*, based on machines incorporating scientific knowledge. In this framework, full productive possibilities will be realized when machines are employed in the production of other machines.[22] Marx also argues that businesses were prone to grow in size, as capitalists would accumulate capital, and then invest it in new machines, resulting in the production of more capital, thus identifying a cyclical effect between innovation and capital

---

20 The utilitarian discourse as developed by Bentham and Mill would require an extensive analysis beyond the scope of this chapter.

21 Nathan Rosenberg, 'Marx as a Student of Technology', in Nathan Rosenberg, *Inside the Black Box: Technology and Economics* (Cambridge, 1982), 34–51.

22 Ibid.

accumulation. Rosenberg mentions that Marx's analysis borrows much from Babbage on this point. Marx himself makes explicit reference to the latter author in volume III of *Capital*, where he draws attention to the fact that the introduction of technological improvements is a central preoccupation of capitalists, which effectively means that a machine has a short life expectancy. As a result of this, a capitalist will have to make a new investment, and then will have to recoup it as soon as possible, a process that may prove to be rather difficult.[23]

Transitions

Indeed, the late nineteenth century turned out to be a difficult time for European economies. Marxists gave gloomy predictions as to the possible effects of economic turmoil. Nonetheless, at the same time, a new wave of innovations made its appearance. Electrical science and internal combustion power provided new opportunities, and marked the beginning of the second industrial revolution and the rise of new industries.[24]

Specifically, inventions, such as the dynamo in the late nineteenth century, allowed electric power to become the leading generating force of factories. This technological improvement, taking the place of the steam engine, permitted factories to work with greater efficiency and at a lower cost, improving the economic growth of the capitalist world.[25] Initially, this technological improvement was at the cost of thousands of jobs. However, the lower production costs enabled capitalists to invest heavily in the new technology, a process, which was not completed until after the Second World War, when new jobs were created.

The beginning of the twentieth century was marked by another major event: the First World War. It was then that Europe witnessed the collapse of three empires, Germany, Austro-Hungary, and Russia. Weapons of mass destruction, such as chemical gas, were used, while machine guns, airplanes, and submarines were employed in great numbers. More than ever before, it was made clear that the army possessing the most technologically advanced weaponry had a huge advantage over others, and the capacity to wreck havoc on entire regions in Europe.

The First World War changed European politics. In Britain, in 1918 the electorate expanded to include women property owners aged over 30 years old, and in 1922 the Labour Party became the second largest party in the House of Commons. Still, times

---

[23] Ibid. Rosenberg notes that Babbage quotes a *Report of the Committee of the House of Commons on the Wool Trade* (1806), which asserts that large factories can afford the risks and experiments to generate technological change that are not feasible for the '*little master manufacturer*'. On these issues generally see Nathan Rosenberg, 'Karl Marx on the Economic Role of Science', *Journal of Political Economy*, (1974) 82/4: 713–28.

[24] Landes, *The Unbound Prometheus*.

[25] Nathan Rosenberg, *Technology and the American Economic Growth* (New York, 1972); Paul David, 'The Computer and the Dynamo: A Historical Perspective on the Productivity Paradox', *The American Economic Review Papers and Proceedings*, 80/2 (1990): 355–61.

were hard for European economies in the 1920s and 1930s.[26] The Great Depression of the 1930s resulted in high unemployment in Europe, and workers faced despair as factories closed.

Protectionism, strong control of capital movement, and fixed exchange rates were introduced to domestic economies. It was then that the foundations were laid for the modern welfare state, as post-war Keynesian economic thought reacted to the inequalities produced by capitalist economies. To this effect, full employment and social rights of citizenship were to be secured by the state. At the same time, the 1930s nourished new technologically creative ideas in the western world. The application of chemical and electrical science, and advances in the generation and delivery of power were some of the events that gave birth to the third industrial revolution.[27]

Innovation: Modern Theoretical Paradigms

The events described in the previous section demonstrated one thing: technological progress can be a good and an evil at the same time. Joseph Schumpeter, who first wrote on the relationship between technology and economy as early as 1911, lived to see the upheaval emerging from the transition from a technology having saturated its potential to a new technological paradigm. By 1930, technology had already arrived in three clusters, all of them defining an era, but transition from the one to the other proved to be difficult.[28]

Schumpeter reconciled both these facets by arguing that, although instability is endemic to capitalism, transitory periods are difficult but temporary. He thus offered an alternative model to the orthodox neo-classical paradigm, positioning technological innovation at the heart of economic analysis. In the 1940s and 1950s Fabricant, Abramovitz, and Kendrick in the US studied the relationship between economic growth and technological advances, establishing a school of thought that is still prominent today. In the 1960s, some neo-classical economists took the importance of innovation on board, arguing that state intervention aiming at promoting science can be justified if understood as a public good. Finally, Rosenberg and Kline offered a different framework, where innovation is conceived as a learning process.

The previous sections argued that innovation is important for the economy and society. I here consider the above-mentioned different paradigms, with a view to show the diverse options available to law and policy as to the ways innovation may be fostered.

---

[26] The literature on the reasons and consequences of the Great Depression in Europe is vast. For an interesting review see Patricia Clavin, *The Great Depression in Europe, 1929–1939* (Basingstoke, 2000). For a view on the implications for Britain see John Stevenson and Chris Cook, *Britain in the Depression* (London and New York, 1996).

[27] Landes, *The Unbound Prometheus*.

[28] The exact phases and what happens within them are subject to debate. I adopt Landes' chronology, ibid.

Schumpeter and the Technological Imperative

Schumpeter was strongly influenced by Marx's analysis.[29] He reiterated that technological change is 'the fundamental impulse that sets and keeps the capitalist engine in motion'.[30] He thus understood economic activity as functioning according to a technological teleological imperative, as, for firms to survive, they must engage in technological innovation. Unlike Marx, Schumpeter argued that new technologies continuously come into existence, forming a sequence of techno-economic paradigms, it being a process resulting in the destruction of the old techno-economic structure, and the emergence of a new one. He terms this process 'creative destruction', and understands it as being one of the operating principles of capitalism. Transitions may be difficult for entrepreneurs, but in the face of uncertainty firms engage in new types of investment generating new innovations.[31]

Schumpeter reacted to the neo-classical static model of competition to argue that competition should be viewed as a dynamic event, and not as a state of affairs, focusing on the behaviour of firms, and not on market structure, as otherwise economic theory would fail to come to grips with reality, and in particular with technological innovation. The reason for this is that technological progress is possible in what neo-classical economists describe as an inefficient economic environment, as innovation may be brought about in concentrated markets, since it requires considerable resources. What would then be the role of law in this process? If governments intervene to reduce the profits of winners, this may reduce the incentives to innovate.[32, 33]

---

29 Nathan Rosenberg, 'Schumpeter and Marx: How Common a Vision?', in Roy M. MacLeod (ed.), *Technology and the Human Prospect* (London, 1986), 197–213; John E. Elliott, 'Marx and Schumpeter on Capitalism's Creative Destruction: A Comparative Restatement', *Quarterly Journal of Economics*, 95/1 (1980): 45–68; George Catephores, 'The Imperious Austrian: Schumpeter as Bourgeois Marxist', *New Left Review*, 205/1 (1994): 3–30.

30 Joseph A. Schumpeter, *Capitalism, Socialism and Democracy*, (London, 1943), 83.

31 Schumpeter predicted that capitalism would be replaced by socialism:

> The capitalist process not only destroys its own institutional framework but it also creates the conditions for another ... The outcome of the process is not simply a void that could be filled by whatever might happen to turn up; things and souls are transformed in such a way as to become increasingly amenable to the socialist form of life ... In both of these respects Marx's vision was right, ibid., at 162.

The argument to this conclusion is found in Chapters 11–14.

32 Joseph A. Schumpeter, *The Theory of Economic Development: An Inquiry into Profits, Capital, Credit, Interest, and the Business Cycle* (New Brunswick, 1983), 61–7 and 90–94.

33 In the same spirit the proponents of the Chicago school argue that market foreclosure and monopoly power is short lived, when markets are competitive. Therefore, competition policy should not only base its analysis on the notion of market share, as production efficiency may require large firms, and as such a highly concentrated industry can be efficient. Moreover, monopoly power may be an incentive to engage in innovation, so governments should be careful not to take away this incentive, David B. Audretsch, William J. Baumol and Andrew

It is important to note here that Schumpeter saw innovation as the introduction of decisively new products. He defined the process of technological change as in *invention*, where new technical or scientific principles are elaborated, *innovation*, where an invention is developed in the form of a commercial product or process, and *diffusion*, where products and processes spread in the relevant market.

Innovation as a Process and as a Good

Neo-classical economics also took on board the importance of innovation, and the literature on the subject is extensive. One aspect of the relevant research focused on the question of what public policies should be adopted in order to foster technological innovation. In this model technology is equated with science; therefore, the argument is that if a market failure is identified, public financing may be required. For instance, fundamental scientific research may attract such financing, as the knowledge produced at this stage may be conceived as a public good.

Yet, the importance of innovation is also acknowledged by a different theoretical paradigm: the chain-linked model of innovation as developed by Rosenberg and Kline.[34] This framework of analysis stands critical to both the understanding of innovation as science and the separation between innovation and diffusion processes, by emphasizing the role of tacit knowledge in production. Following this line of thinking, Rosenberg and Kline argued that innovation is not a linear process but one involving many interactions, as innovation does not only depend on the discovery of new scientific principles, but also on different forms of knowledge, for example production know-how at the level of workforce.[35]

Hence, innovation is not conceived as being an isolated event, but as being influenced by the wider environment. Firms are thought to be active participants in learning, as every firm has its own culture consisting of routines and ideas of best practice, which influences the ways in which new scientific ideas come about. In this framework, the role of institutions, understood as firms, universities, research institutes, and technology transfer agencies, is highlighted, since they are seen as constituting a form of collective memory, embedded in organizational practices determining how new information is processed.[36] To this effect, it is important to provide incentives and put in place procedures enabling the sharing of knowledge and participation. Policies should not concern themselves with the production of a particular product (for example microelectronics), but should promote education,

---

E. Burke, 'Competition Policy in Dynamic Markets', *International Journal of Industrial Organization*, 19/1 (2001): 613–34.

[34] Stephen J. Kline and Nathan Rosenberg, 'An Overview of Innovation', in Ralph Landau and Nathan Rosenberg (eds), *The Positive Sum Strategy: Harnessing Technology for Economic Growth* (Washington DC, 1986), 275–305.

[35] Ibid.

[36] John Peterson and Margaret Sharp, *Technology Policy in the European Union* (Basingstoke, 1998), 48.

put in place processes aiming at establishing consensus as to the development and implementation of technologies, and support experimental behaviour.

The Story of the European Union: Market Integration and the European Commission

By the 1960s Europe had experienced two world wars and successive clusters of innovations, the last being marked by the invention and use of the transistor and the electric circuit on a chip. Technological progress transformed the mode of living and thinking about the world.

On the theoretical level, competing economic paradigms lent themselves to the understanding of the importance of innovation in different ways; innovation could be conceived as being both the product of scientific research produced in laboratories and the result of minor modifications introduced by skilled workers in the workplace on the basis of tacit knowledge.

All these developments called attention to two fundamental understandings: first, innovation is good for the economy and for the society. Second, there are various ways to promote it. For example, promoting innovation can be done either directly by financing certain sectors of the economy and by giving property rights such as patents, or indirectly, by promoting collaboration, education, experimental behaviour, and the exchange of knowledge.

However, understanding how the above perspectives acquired meaning in the context of the European Union requires examining its political and legal traditions. To this effect, the following section will consider the process of market integration, as understood through the lenses of Jean Monnet's *technocracy discourse*, promoting expertise, elites, and functional intermediation. I here also discuss the influence of *ordoliberalism* in the early days of the European Community, as it presents an alternative model of regulatory law, based on the deployment of neutral and objective procedures indirectly intervening in the economy. Finally, I consider the historical conjunction of events leading to efforts to create the common and single market in Europe, to finally link this to the discussion concerning the democratic deficit of the European Union.

Ordoliberalism and Market Integration

The early days of European integration were considerably influenced by ordoliberalism, a school of thought established in Germany in the 1930s. The proponents of this theory, the ordoliberals, challenged the Western and Soviet economic models, by seeking to equally constrain private and public power, in the face of the catastrophic experience of the Weimar period in Germany.[37]

---

[37] Gerber, *Law and Competition in Twentieth Century Europe*, 239. Walter Eucken, Franz Bohm, and Hans Grosmann-Doerth are the founding members of the Freiburg school in the 1930s.

Eucken, one of the founders of this school of thought, challenged the historical method prominent in Germany at the time, as he considered that the simple contemplation of facts is not enough to adequately describe economic reality. Any empirical observations should serve as the basis for the deduction of abstract principles, with the aim of building ideal types for a particular society. To this effect, the method of 'isolating abstraction', the abstraction of especially significant characteristics should be employed. *Ordnungstheorie* or 'thinking in orders' is a concept interweaving with isolating abstraction. Eucken recognizes two fundamental economic orders: the transaction economy, characterized by economic freedom, and the centrally administered economy, characterized by organized economic activity. Choosing between one of these fundamental orders requires adopting adequate measures to implement its operating principle. This is because, when elements from the two orders are mixed, then this could result in an economic catastrophe. For example, governmental intervention should not be introduced to a system of transaction economy, whose effective function is based upon the notion of economic competition. In other words, these two orders are thought to be incompatible, and explaining economic failures requires recognizing this.[38]

Nevertheless, ordoliberals argued that the legal system should indirectly regulate a market economy. In particular, they claimed that societies need an economic as much as a political constitution, thus linking the legal to the economic system. If the desired order is a transaction market economy, then an economic constitution should be put in place to safeguard basic principles, such as private property and contractual freedom, while regulatory principles, such as competition law, should implement the basic principles. Competition law in particular was central to the ordoliberal vision, since the system of market economy would be ineffective if firms raised barriers to entry or fixed prices.[39]

Thus, ordoliberal thinking endorsed the basic liberal mandate, which provides that economic freedom is a right, and law should safeguard it. However, governmental power and private power were viewed as being equally potentially dangerous. The law was seen as safeguarding against abuses of power by both the sovereign and private forces. Central to this was the assumption that law is neutral and objective, functioning to put in place the structural conditions allowing the smooth function of the economy, hence its *indirect* character in regulating the economy.[40]

Gerber notes that many Germans associated with, or sharing an appreciation of, ordoliberalism were influential at the early stages of formation of the EU economic policy. In particular, Hallstein was one of the founders of the European Economic

---

[38] Robert Delorme, 'Ordnungstheorie and the Theory of Regulation Compared from the Standpoint of Complexity', in Agnès Labrousse and Jean-Daniel Weisz (eds), *Institutional Economics in France and Germany* (Berlin, 2000), citing Walter Eucken, *The Foundations of Economics* (London, 1950).

[39] Gerber, *Law and Competition in Twentieth Century Europe*, 250, citing Walter Eucken, Edith Eucken, and Paul Hensel, *Grundsätze der Wirtschaftspolitik* (Tübingen, 1990), 251.

[40] Ibid., 240–41, and 248, citing Franz Böhm, *Die Ordnung der Wirtschaft als Geschichtliche Aufgabe und Rechtsschöpferische Leistung* (Stuttgart, 1937), 7–9.

Community (EEC) Treaties, and served as the first President of the European Commission. He had been a law professor in Germany, being deeply influenced by the ideas of Eucken, and being closely acquainted with Bohm and Kronstein, two prominent members of the Freiburg school. Gerber argues that Hallstein was clearly pursuing ordoliberal goals during the early attempts to integrate markets in Europe.[41] Moreover, von der Groeben, also sympathetic to ordoliberal ideas, was one of the two drafters of the Spaak report, upon which the Treaties of Rome were based.[42] Finally, Muller-Armack also exerted an important influence in early policy making. He was the founding father of the social market economy circle of intellectuals, a movement closely associated with ordoliberals.[43] He was working for the German government, with responsibility for Community matters.

Although the creation of a common market in Europe has different underpinnings, as we will see in the following sections, the pursuit of European integration was well suited to the ordoliberal vision of a competitive market economy, with neutral and objective rules safeguarding against the abuse of power.

The Common Market

The first attempt to integrate markets in Europe was in 1952, when the European Coal and Steel Community (ECSC) was established by France, Germany, Italy, and the Benelux countries (Belgium, Netherlands, and Luxemburg). This first form of cooperation came as a reaction to the havoc that the Second World War inflicted upon Europe. The text of the Treaty was based on a proposal by the French foreign minister, Schuman, was drafted by Monnet, a key figure in French politics, and was underlied by the endeavour to deter disputes over scarce resources, such as coal and steel.[44]

The institutions put in place were: the *High Authority*, the main executive body, consisting of nine independent appointees of the six Member States (MS); the *Assembly*, comprising of national Parliament delegates; the *Council*, whose members

---

41 Ibid., 263–4, citing Walter Hallstein, *Europe in the Making* (London, and New York, 1972), 28:

> what the Community is integrating is the role of the state in establishing the framework within which economic activity takes place.

42 Ibid., 263.

43 Ibid. There are differences between Müller-Armack's position and ordoliberals. Müller-Armack thought that social policies (such as taxation and minimum wages) should be provided for, while for Eucken social justice would be the consequence of a competitive order, see Michael Wohlgemuth, 'Unification, European Integration, Globalization: The German Social Market Economy at the Crossroads', in Katrik Roy and Jörn Sideras (eds), *Domestic Institutions and Empowerment in an Integrating World Economy: A Global Perspective* (Cheltenham UK, 2004).

44 Craig and de Búrca, *EU Law*, 7–10.

were representatives of national governments; the *Court of Justice*, to interpret the provisions of the Treaty.[45]

The Treaties of Rome represented a later effort to foster cooperation on a larger scale. Spaak, the Belgian minister of Foreign Affairs, was the chair of an intergovernmental committee, which prepared a report proposing the creation of the European Atomic Energy Community and the European Economic Community. The report was soon approved by the six ECSC members, which subsequently asked Spaak to draw the Treaties. These were signed in 1957, and are similar to the institutional pattern introduced to the ECSC. For the first time, the notion of a regulated common market was employed, aiming at promoting market integration and eliminating tariffs and barriers to entry.

The common market would share the Assembly and the Court of Justice with the ECSC, but a separate Council of Ministers and a separate executive body, the Commission, were put in place. Institutional rebalancing was required though, as the new common market would include economic activity in general, and not only activity emerging from the coal and steel sectors. Therefore, the Council would have to approve all legislative proposals by the European Commission, but the latter body, set at a supranational level, was entrusted with the task of policy initiation, was the 'watchdog' of the Treaties, and the negotiator of international agreements on its behalf.[46]

Nonetheless, it would be wrong to consider that the first efforts to integrate markets in Europe were underlined by consensus as to the merits of the liberal mandate to foster economic competition. Many Europeans saw economic integration as the way to generate economic wealth, since national markets were too small to support economies of scale. Close to this was the idea that firms would then have the necessary size to compete internationally. Thus, economic integration was seen as the necessary prerequisite to compete with the Americans.[47]

A theoretical framework, which was particularly influential in the early days of the Community, can be found in what has been termed as the Jean Monnet approach. The following section will focus on this.

Monnet and the Technocracy Discourse of the Early Days of the Community

Monnet was a key figure in French politics after the Second World War. In 1945 the *Monnet Plan* provided that key sectors of the French economy, such as transportation, coal, electricity, steel, and agricultural mechanization, would have to undergo reconstruction until 1950. The key institution was the *Commissariat General du Plan*, which was a small and flexible administration attached to the Prime Minister's office, coordinating technical studies and organizing the consultation of all parties involved. Committees of civil servants, the industry, scientific institutions, all

[45] Ibid., 10–12.
[46] Ibid., 12.
[47] Gerber, *Law and Competition in Twentieth Century Europe*, 348.

presented opinions and tried to reach consensus incorporated in a Plan. This was not binding, but the government would choose whether to adopt it and how to implement it. This process came to be known as *planification.*[48]

Featherstone traces the origins of the Monnet Plan back to the French *dirigiste* tradition of central governmental planning.[49] This term interweaves with the notion of a strong, esteemed, cohesive, and above all autonomous from societal influences bureaucracy, with prestigious schools being entrusted with the production of the administrative elite.

Indeed, the Monnet Plan both stressed the importance of expertise and was *dirigiste*, in the sense that it favoured specific sectors of the economy. It also exhibited corporatist elements,[50] as it provided that policy making would be formed by bringing together interested parties.[51] Understanding the rationale underlining the Monnet Plan in France is important, as it casts light on the ideas influential during the early steps of the Community. This is because the first attempts to integrate markets in Europe bear the traces of the Monnet approach.[52]

As we saw, the ECSC was assisted by an Assembly, which had little power, mainly advisory and supervisory, while the High Authority was entrusted with

---

48 Saul Estrin and Peter M. Holmes, *French Planning in Theory and Practice* (London, 1983).

49 Kevin Featherstone, 'Jean Monnet and the Democratic Deficit in the European Union', *Journal of Common Market Studies*, 32/2 (1994): 149–70, 155.

50 For an introduction to corporatism see Peter J. Katzenstein, 'The Historical Origins of Democratic Corporatism', in Peter J. Katzenstein, *Small States in World Markets: Industrial Policy in Europe* (Ithaca NY, 1985).

51 Featherstone, 'Jean Monnet and the Democratic Deficit in the European Union'.

52 Michelle Cini, *The European Commission: Leadership, Organization and Culture in the EU Administration,* (Manchester and New York, 1996). Jean Monnet was president of the High Authority of the ECSC from 1952 to 1955. Jean Monnet's approach is associated with 'functionalist integration', see Sonia Mazey, 'European Integration: Unfinished Journey or Journey without End?', in Jeremy Richardson (ed.), *European Union: Power and Policy-Making* (London, 2001), 27–50. At 28, the author characterizes European integration as basically functionalistic, but also as being underpinned by ambiguity:

> The 'Community method' of functional integration advocated by Jean Monnet was an ingenuous device; crucially it enabled the (federalist inclined) founding fathers of European integration to side-step the politically intractable barrier of national sovereignty. Then, as now, there was no consensus over the precise form that European cooperation should take. The founding Treaties of the European Communities did not resolve this issue; rather they represented an ambiguous compromise between intergovernmentalists and European federalists involved in the post-war debate on European co-operation. The former viewed the European Coal and Steel Community (ECSC), the European Economic Community (EEC) and the European Atomic Energy Community (EURATOM) created by the Treaties, as functional agencies charged only with the coordination of national, economic strategies in designated sectors. However, European federalists hoped that these agencies would, over time, provide the basis for a more comprehensive kind of political integration.

regulating the limited areas of policy falling within its supranational competences. This body was structured along the lines of the French administration.[53] Nevertheless, Monnet preferred small and flexible structures. He asserted that the supranational competencies of the High Authority could be best exercised by small teams, 'as a few hundreds of European civil servants would be enough to set thousands of national experts to work'.[54] Moreover, the permanent staff would have to be assisted by national experts, who would spend small periods of time in the High Authority. The same rationale was carried over to the new institution, the European Commission, which was put in place to support the creation and regulation of a common market, as propagated by the Treaties of Rome. As Cini argues:

> the discourse underpinning the new European Commission was that of the High Authority. This was a discourse that emphasized the importance of efficiency, expertise, elites and functional interest intermediation-one that had little to say on the subject of democratic accountability and democratic representation: one which we might call a 'technocracy discourse'.[55]

The Single European Act

The creation of a European common market encountered great resistance, as member states, such as France, were not ready to give up sovereign control of resources to a supranational entity.[56] Despite the above, things changed in the 1980s, and the Single European Act (SEA) entered into force in 1987. It sought to progressively move Europe from a customs union to a single market within a five year period. To this effect, the SEA removed barriers to the free movement of people, goods, services, and capital. All MS happily accepted the new prospect of economic cooperation. One reason for this may be that there was a widespread feeling in Europe that the global challenge was too big to be undertaken independently, especially in the field of new technologies.[57] Another explanation may be that there were considerable ambiguities as to the main objectives of the Treaty, and as to the means to attain these. Britain

---

53 Featherstone, 'Jean Monnet and the Democratic Deficit in the European Union'.

54 Edward G. Page, *People Who Run Europe* (Oxford, 1997), 5.

55 Michelle Cini, 'Organizational Culture and Reform: The Case of the European Commission under Jacques Santer', *EUI Working Paper EC* (1996/00/25).

56 The 1960s signified an intergovernmental turn in the history of the European Union. De Gaulle in France supported the *Luxembourg Accords*, which stated that when majority voting was required in the Council, if a national interest was at stake, discussion would continue until unanimity is reached. This in essence meant that unanimity became the norm and majority voting the exception, a development that marked a return to intergovernmentalism, see Craig and de Búrca, *EU Law*, 13.

57 This line of thinking is repeated in many documents produced by the European Commission, see for example the Communication from the Commission to the Council, the European Parliament, the Committee of Regions and the Economic and Social Committee COM (1998) 718 on the Competitiveness of European Enterprises on the Face of Globalization – How It Can Be Encouraged. On the attempts of Europe to catch up with new developments in

for example conceived the SEA as a liberal charter, whereas some commentators questioned the feasibility of fulfilling economic objectives without addressing social issues, as the two necessarily interweave.[58]

Yet, despite differences, consensus was established as to the virtues of economic cooperation, as market integration would confer the economies of scale required to compete internationally. In the midst of these developments in the 1980s and 1990s, the European Commission established itself as a regulator, with efficiency, expertise, elites, and functional interest intermediation being the core characteristics of its role. This was particularly the case when it used Articles 81[85], 82 [86] and 86 [90] of the EC Treaty[59] to liberalize the telecommunication markets in Europe.

---

the high-tech industry see Wayne Sandholtz, *High-Tech Europe: The Politics of International Cooperation* (Berkeley, 1992).

58 Craig and de Búrca, *EU Law*, 21.

59 These Articles are the fundamental articles of EU competition law. Under Article 81, the Treaty prohibits agreements, undertakings, decisions or practices, which may or in fact affect trade within the European Common Market. However, 81[85] (3) provides for the exemption of an activity from the prohibitions of the article, if the activity 'contributes to the production or distribution of goods or to promoting technical or economic progress'. Yet, restrictions to competition must give consumers a 'fair share of the resulting benefit', and must be 'indispensable to the attainment of objectives'. Article 82 [86] prohibits a market actor from abusing a dominant position within the common market 'in so far as it may affect trade between member states'. Article 86 [90] applies the prohibitions of Articles 81[85] and 82 [86] to 'public undertakings and undertakings to which member states grant special or exclusive rights'. However, Article 86 [90] (2) provides that market actors 'entrusted with the operation of services of general economic interest', shall benefit from a derogation of competition articles if application would obstruct the performance of the particular task assigned to them. Article 86 [90] (3) provides that the European Commission should ensure the application of the provisions of Article 86 [90] and shall, where necessary, address appropriate Directives or Decisions to Member States. In 1985, in *British Telecommunications* OJ L 360/363 (1985), the European Court of Justice (ECJ) decided that competition applied in the telecommunication sector, and that the European Commission had the exclusive right to decide on any derogation to be granted. The court affirmed that the 'provision of a public network' could be considered as an activity of general economic interest, thus qualifying exemption under Article 86 [90] (2) derogation, nevertheless recommended that Article 86 [90] (2) should be narrowly interpreted.

As for the power to issue Directives under this Article, the controversial element is that they present an exceptional instance when the European Commission exercises quasi-legislative powers. The decision making process stops at the level of the College of Commissioners, as these Directives do not have to go through the Council/Parliament. This is the legal context that underpinned the European Commission's legislative initiative to draft the Terminal Equipment Directive and the Competition in Services Directive in 1988, as provided in Article 86 [90] (3). The European Commission considered a step-by-step liberalization and maintained exclusive rights for the provision of infrastructure and voice telephony with the prospect of liberalizing them eventually after having opened services and equipment to competition first. The Telecommunication Services Directive was challenged in the European Court of Justice (ECJ) by several member states, but the court confirmed both the legality of

Recent developments aimed at strengthening cooperation include the introduction of common currency, the Enlarged Union of 450 million citizens, and the attempt to agree upon a European Constitution. However, all three developments faced resistance, and brought once again to the foreground the problem of democratic legitimacy of the European Union.

The Democratic Deficit and the European Demos

The problem of democratic legitimacy refers to the weak powers conferred to the European Parliament, the obscure decision making processes underlying the functioning of the European Commission, the lack of accountability and direct control of the Council, and the lack of a European democratic demos.[60] The latter is indicated by the poor turnout of the general public in European elections, the 'no' vote to the Euro by the Danish referendum, and the rejection of the European Constitutional Treaty in 2005 in referendums held in France and Netherlands. The 'Maastricht judgment' rendered by the German Federal Constitutional Court in 1994 elaborated on the relationship amongst democracy, democratic deficit, and demos.[61] The court held that although ratification of the Maastricht treaty was compatible with the German Constitution, it retained the power to review the constitutionality of community law, and in particular its compatibility with the fundamental principles of the German Constitution.

The reason for this is the democratic deficit of the European Union. Since democracy reflects the will of the people, and as there is not a European demos, then it would be undemocratic for the European Union to extend its powers in a way incompatible with the fundamental principles of the German Constitution, as the latter *is* the expression of the will of the people. This is the 'No Demos Thesis' according to which the absence of a European demos requires the intervention of Member State institutions.[62]

Nevertheless, this approach presupposes that a democratic demos derives its cognitive frame of reference from within the boundaries of nation states. In other words, citizenship and nationality presuppose each other. For Grimm, a common language is of absolute importance for the effective function of demos; hence

---

the Competition in Services Directive and the European Commission's power to issue such directives and initiate action if MS do not comply. It has been argued that by issuing the Directive liberalizing the terminal equipment supply market, and by opening data and value added services to competition under Article 86 [90] of the Treaty, the European Commission avoided the possibility of the Council delaying these developments for years, due to disagreement amongst its members.

60 A *demos* is a group of people with close ties allowing for engagement in democratic discourse.

61 *Brunner v. The European Union Treaty*, [1994] 1 CMLR 57.

62 Joseph H.H. Weiler, 'Does Europe Need a Constitution? Reflections on Demos, Telos and the German Maastricht Decision', *European Law Journal*, 1/3 (1995): 219–58.

linguistic boundaries of nation states present the main obstacle to the creation of a transnational public discourse.[63] Weiler and Habermas strongly disagree with this ethnocentric view of demos. Ethnicity, history, language, and religion can be separated from the political dimension of demos. Weiler in particular argues for a conceptualization of multiple overlapping identities, cultural and civic, national and supranational *demoi* instead of *demos*, in simultaneous operation:

> The national is Eros: reaching back to the pre-modern, appealing to the heart with a grasp on our emotions, and evocative of the romantic vision of creative social organization as well as responding to our existential yearning for a meaning located in time and space. The supranational is civilization: confidently modernist, appealing to the rational within us and to Enlightenment neo-classical humanism, taming that Eros.[64]

Habermas also separates the cultural from the political dimension of demos. Accordingly, one of Habermas's solutions to the problem of democratic deficit and societal fragmentation is constitutional patriotism.

> A previous background consensus, constructed on the basis of cultural homogeneity and understood as a necessary catalyzing condition for democracy, becomes superfluous to the extent that public, discursively structured processes of opinion and will formation, make a reasonable political understanding possible, even among strangers. Thanks to its procedural properties, the democratic process has its own mechanisms for securing legitimacy; it can, when necessary, fill the gaps that open in social integration, and can respond to the changed cultural composition of a population by generating a common political culture.[65]

In other words, despite difference, the peoples of Europe can find common ground in their civic traditions. In the postnational era, the EU can provide a space of experimentation of discursive deliberation in search of the common thread to overcome isolation and fragmentation, further presenting a challenge to the monopoly of nation states over the production of identity and culture.

The emergence of the idea of civic demos certainly reflects the realities of internationalization. What is more, in attacking artificial cultural boundaries imposed by state definitions, while simultaneously calling for the authentic and spontaneous expression of identity and belongingness, it is inspired by the Kantian moral philosophy, which views moral obligations as stemming not from simply following established ethical norms, but from the rational endeavour to determine

---

63 Dieter Grimm, 'Does Europe Need a Constitution?', *European Law Journal*, 1/3 (1995): 282–302.

64 Joseph H.H. Weiler, 'To Be a European Citizen – Eros and Civilization', *Working Paper Series in European Studies Special Edition*, Spring 1998, 36; Also see Neil MacCormick, 'The Maastricht-Urteil: Sovereignty Now', *European Law Journal*, 1/3 (1995): 259–66.

65 Jürgen Habermas, *The Postnational Constellation: Political Essays* (Cambridge, 2001), 73.

ourselves what these norms should be.[66] In other words, we should seek to rise above prejudice, to engage in civic dialogue, and discover the idea of humanity. In this sense, the notion of civic demos is attentive to fundamental Enlightenment ideas, such as the capacity to create our own future while subjecting tradition to critique. This resonates with the belief in dialogue and in a society that can evolve on the basis of human reason.

Although the vocabulary of Enlightenment rationalism presented a revolution and a way out of religious and social prejudice, having now crystallized in the dominant way of thinking in social sciences, it seeks to hide its inability to adequately describe the social world. Habermas and Weiler advance the vision of a progressive society, strong democracy, and authentic identity, while ignoring the often invisible ways power relations are exercised, the unuttered stereotypes reproduced in everyday practice, and the perplexing ways in which the public interweaves with the private sphere. Foucault's genealogies sought to come to grips with the reality of power, when he described how an object of study reveals possibilities, which happened to be actualized, and conceals potentialities, which turned out to have been discarded.

The analysis in the sections relevant to the history of the diverse ways to theorize innovation illustrates this point. As explained, innovation can be promoted directly by means of financing particular sectors of the economy, and by giving monopoly rights, such as patents. Alternatively, it may be promoted indirectly, by means of fostering collaboration and exchange of information. As Chapter Five will argue, the dominant way for lawyers to think about innovation is in terms of intellectual property rights, as property is one of the conceptual cornerstones of the modern legal system. The proposal for a directive introducing patent protection in computer-implemented inventions in the EU, which was never adopted because of disagreement as to its terms and scope, illustrates how difficult it is for lawyers to think about innovation in terms of collaboration, and cast doubt on the virtues of the proprietary model. In this instance, stereotypes reproducing the dominant way of thinking about innovation render other solutions unthinkable. I will come back to this point in detail in Chapter Five of this book, but what is relevant for us here is the observation that legal texts and principles are context dependent, and individuals engaging in their production are not always rational, but reinforce the dominant rhetoric in their field, while simultaneously seeking to maximize their position as effective regulators by means of regenerating established practice.

Similarly, the orthodox way to think about participation in new governance structures in the EU is by means of dialogic communication and exchange, in a state of affairs where vulgar antagonisms remain unuttered. Still, this is not the only way to think about new governance structures. Conflicts and struggles do not need to be unarticulated in order to achieve democratic participation.[67] On the contrary, they can be conceived as the healthy way to achieve dialogic reflection, sensitive to a

---

66 Weiler, 'To Be a European Citizen – Eros and Civilization'.

67 Albert O. Hirschman, 'Social Conflicts as Pillars of Democratic Market Society', *Political Theory*, 22/2 (1994): 203–18.

flexible and ever changing social reality. Following this intuition, the function of law in new governance structures should be conceptualized on the basis of a framework attentive to the ideas of domination, inequality, and difference.

Machiavelli, Nietzsche, Foucault, and Derrida insisted on an analysis of the diverse ways in which power pertains social relations. Nietzsche viewed beauty as '*a sign of the habituation and pampering of the victorious*', and '*what is ugly as the expression of many defeats*'.[68] Foucault's analysis of technologies of the self follows the same spirit, as the object of study of governmentality concerns the indirect techniques aiming at controlling individuals.[69] One way to achieve this is by means of elevating subjects to the status of responsible individuals. Free will and self-determination justify the withdrawal of the state; however, at the same time the state invents new ways to exercise control. These last points resonate in the analysis of all the chapters of the book.

Conclusions

Ordoliberalism required that law indirectly influences the economy by means of providing an objective and neutral framework of rules. This vision was significant in shaping conceptions of cooperation in the foundational period of the EU, and in later years. Moreover, the foundational years were characterized by a discourse emphasizing the importance of efficiency, expertise, elites, and functional interest intermediation. This technocracy discourse positioned the European Commission as a neutral regulator, mediating amongst interested parties and providing expert knowledge.

However, this approach also triggered the debate on the democratic deficit of the European Union, which further led to discussion on the need to advance new governance structures, enabling the formation and participation of the European demos (or demoi) in the law making process. This particular solution to the problem of democratic deficit is based on a number of assumptions, such as the one that stipulates that rational individuals possess the inherent capacity to rise above prejudice and critically question the monopoly of nation states to create identities, by means of engaging in fruitful dialogue in common search of authenticity. However, this view does not seriously address the importance of incorporating in the relevant framework of analysis the notion of power. Power resides in legal rules promoting one particular vision of innovation and discarding alternative ones, in the notions of objectivity and neutrality, in everyday exchange inside administrations. Power is a *modus vivendi*; it cannot be tamed, civilized, or neutralized. It is essential to democracy and a requisite for life, as the following chapters will seek to illustrate.

---

[68] Friedrich Nietzsche, *The Will to Power*, W. Kaufmann and R.J. Hollingdale (translators), W. Kaufmann (ed.) (New York, 1974), points 462 and 712.

[69] Michel Foucault, 'Technologies of the Self', in Luther H. Martin, Huck Gutman and Patrick H. Hutton (eds), *Technologies of the Self: A Seminar with Michel Foucault* (London, 1988).

Chapter Three

The European Commission and the Law Making Process: Compromise as a Category of Praxis

> To perceive means to immobilize. We seize, in the act of perception, something, which outruns perception itself.
>
> Henri Bergson, *Essai sur les Données Immédiates de la Conscience*

The general question of how the social environment informs the shaping of substantive and procedural aspects of law has long been at the heart of academic debate. From an anthropological perspective, answering this question requires conceptualizing the legal order as being embedded in society, and following Comaroff and Roberts, the emphasis may shift from studying the formal rules of adjudication to coming to grips with the processes shaping the resolution of disputes and development of norms.[1] Furthermore, in the light of the social constructivist stance, it is suggested that the study of legal processes should also include the examination of beliefs, perceptions, and identifications. This has been termed as the cognitive approach.

The cognitive turn was a major intellectual development of the twentieth century, and its theoretical insights initiated debate in various disciplines, such as philosophy, psychology, linguistics, anthropology, and social theory.[2] The present case study adopts this approach to examine tacit understandings regulating the conduct of officials of the European Commission, who engage in the production of a legal proposal, or in the implementation of a legal measure. This is because the arguments in a legal file are the result of the complex interaction amongst many persons and many different services of the European Commission. Such interaction may be successful, or less successful, depending on how contentious a legal file is, but it is underlied by certain understandings, particular norms of conduct, as to how things are get done. In uncovering shared understandings, the chapter examines modes of cooperation in working parties and shared files, promotion procedures and

---

1 Jean Comaroff and Simon Roberts, *Rules and Processes: The Cultural Logic of Dispute in an African Context* (Chicago, 1981).

2 For a review see Rogers Brubaker, Mara Loveman, and Peter Stamatov, 'Ethnicity as Cognition', *Theory and Society*, 33/1 (2004): 31–64.

mobility, while reputation, how it is valued and acquired, is a theme that runs across all relevant sections.[3]

Schemas as Social Constructs

Schemas[4] can be universal, idiosyncratic (characteristic to individuals), or culturally constructed, and as such distinctive to groups of people.[5] It is this third category of schemas that concerns us here, as the focus of the relevant analysis is on the cultural characteristics of law making inside the European Commission. In particular, the analysis is attentive to practical knowledge dependent on specific cultural and historical conditions, and on practical reason linking to the initiation of action.

The position taken here is that action is not always bound by rules, but experts, having first associated what the right way to respond in respect to a particular class of experiences is, proceed to recognize similarities between new situations and accumulated experience, and act accordingly. This follows Aristotle's contention that *phronesis*, as in tacit knowledge encapsulated in practice, is an important type of knowledge, a position also adopted in philosophy,[6] cultural studies,[7] and anthropology.[8]

In sociology, this understanding of schemas strongly resembles Bourdieu's notion of habitus, Garfinkel's ethnomethodological approach, and Goffman's interactionism. According to the interactionist tradition, the individual mind can exist only in relation to other minds,[9] and individuals create the social world by

---

[3] Hugh Heclo and Aaron Wildavsky, *The Private Government of Public Money: Community and Policy inside British Politics* (London, 1981).

[4] It is beyond the scope of this chapter to elaborate on the distinction between categories, social categories, stereotypes, and cognitive schemas. For an overview of differences see Brubaker, Loveman, and Stamatov, 'Ethnicity as Cognition'.

[5] Goodwin R. D'Andrade, 'The Cultural Part of Cognition', *Cognitive Science*, 5/3 (1981): 179–95.

[6] Hans-Georg Gadamer, *Philosophical Hermeneutics* (Berkeley, 1976); Hans-Georg Gadamer, *Reason in Age of Science* (Cambridge, 1986); Hans-Georg Gadamer, *Truth and Method* (New York, 1994); Michel Polanyi, *Personal Knowledge: Towards a Post-Critical Philosophy* (London, 1958); Michel Polanyi, *The Tacit Dimension*, (New York, 1967); *John Searle, Intentionality: An Essay in the Philosophy of Mind* (Cambridge, 1983).

[7] Robert Bellah, Richard Madsen, William Sullivan, Ann Swindler, and Steven Tipton, *Habits of the Heart* (Berkeley, 1996).

[8] Elizabeth Rice, 'On Cultural Schemata', *American Ethnologist*, 7/2 (1980): 152–71; Naomi Quinn, 'Culture and Contradiction: The Case of American Reasoning About Marriage', *Ethos*, 24/3 (1996): 391–425.

[9] George H. Mead, *Mind, Self, and Society from the Standpoint of a Social Behaviourist* (Chicago, 1934).

means of reproducing it in the course of interaction.[10] Bourdieu's theory of practice and ethnomethodology take the interactionist position further. Agents do not merely respond to an objectively given social world, but there is constant communication between minds and structures, the one transforming the other.[11]

Bourdieu's understanding of cognitive schemas as 'habitus' presents us with an elaborate effort to study the ways in which symbolic forms of authority are embedded in mental structures. In the same spirit, Geertz argued that '*in the political centre of any complexly organized society there is both a governing elite and a set of symbolic forms expressing the fact that it is in truth governing*'.[12] Similarly, legal semiotics and the philosophy of language have shown how a legal document derives authority from invoking mental categories of social perception.[13] These have a double function of acting both as frames of interpretation and promoting images of authority and power. For instance, sustaining the image of law as objective and neutral is crucial in maintaining its legitimacy, further supported by the acts of codification,

---

[10] Herbert Blumer, *Symbolic Interactionism: Perspective and Method* (Englewood Cliffs NJ, 1969).

[11] It should be noted that the notion of 'structure' is notoriously difficult to define, and may be used in contradictory ways in sociology and anthropology. For the latter, it may be equivalent to culture, while, for the former, structure tends to be determining, and culture derived from it, on these issues see William H. Sewell, 'A Theory of Structure: Duality, Agency and Transformation', *American Journal of Sociology*, 98/1 (1992): 1–29. The present analysis takes on board Bourdieu's thesis that structures and schemas reproduce each other, as structures have to be legitimized, may be resisted, and subjected to change. However, Bourdieu's concept of habitus has been criticized as implying rigid determinism, leaving no place to accommodate the notion of social change and collapsing into objectivism, since the rationale behind agents' actions is found in the internalization of objective structures in the bodies of individuals. The position adopted here is that habitus is the catalyst between minds and social structures, processing information in a way that allows regulated improvization, interpretation, and appreciation of the possibilities embedded in structures, bridging the gap between micro and macro approaches. Such an understanding conforms to DiMaggio's claim that the challenge to cognitive approaches is to conceptualize the interaction between minds and structures, and adequately responds to the criticism addressed to the cognitive approach, as presenting us with static categories of thought, preventing a creative conceptualization of how the social world evolves, see Paul J. DiMaggio, 'Culture and Cognition', *Annual Review of Sociology*, 23/1 (1997): 263–87; Paul J. DiMaggio, 'Why Cognitive (and cultural) Sociology Needs Cognitive Psychology' in Karen. A. Cerulo (ed.), *Culture in Mind: Toward a Sociology of Culture and Cognition* (New York, 2002). For a lengthier analysis see Frédéric Vandenberghe, 'The Real is Relational: An Epistemological Analysis of Bourdieu's Generative Structuralism', *Sociological Theory*, 17/1 (1999): 32–68.

[12] Clifford Geertz, *Local Knowledge: Further Essays in Interpretive Anthropology*, (New York, 1983).

[13] Jack M. Balkin, 'The Promise of Legal Semiotics', *Texas Law Review*, 69/3 (1991): 1845–58; Richard Delgado, 'When a Story is Just a Story: Does Voice Really Matter?', *Virginia Law Review*, 76 (1990): 95–111.

formalization, systematization, and the grammatical persistence of passive and impersonal constructions in legal texts.[14]

The notion of schemas sits comfortably with the ethnomethodological idea that mundane interaction requires participants to 'fill in' information from their stocks of tacit knowledge. This is why Garfinkel studied the practical reasoning underpinning the decision making process of jury. The importance of the relevant exploration lays in the understanding that such common sense knowledge is based on particular conceptions of fact and what counts as a reasonable argument, in other words lay knowledge reproducing social practices. Jurors have stocks of knowledge, which consist of the categorization of context specific information applicable to particular situations, pointing to typified action making the social world (and members of it) reasonable.[15]

To summarize, a cognitive approach assumes that human beings sort experience into useful clusters of information to make sense of the world. When studying organizations such as courts, or, as in the present case, the European Commission, a cognitive approach is committed to uncovering schemas of perception and appreciation bounding decisions made by individuals such as officials and judges, while at the same time reproducing beliefs and practices that often go without saying.

In the light of the above, the suggestion in what follows is that the process of crystallization of a legal argument by the European Commission can be elucidated if studied with a view to uncovering patterns of praxis developed in the course of interaction amongst officials.

Inside the European Commission: Rules of Interaction

The European Commission is a fascinating field site for anthropological research. It is a powerful institution of the European Union, where various nationalities, political and administrative cultures, mix. At the same time, the European Commission frequently triggers popular stories about being an elite bureaucracy, remote from the desires of the peoples of Europe, often escaping accountability for its actions even now after the 1999 reform aiming at implementing new policies of transparency and openness.

---

[14] Pierre Bourdieu, 'La Force du Droit: Eléments pour une Sociologie du Champ Juridique', *Actes de la Recherche en Sciences Sociales*, 64/9 (1986): 3–19.

[15] Garfinkel, *Studies in Ethnomethodology*. Such an approach has been adopted in respect to patent disputes in Alberto Cambrosio, Peter Keating, and Michael Mackenzie, 'Scientific Practice in the Courtroom: The Construction of Sociotechnical Identities in a Biotechnology Patent Dispute', *Social Problems*, 37/3 (1997): 275–93. The authors examined transcripts and judicial opinions from a patent trial. Their research focused on the construction of socio-technical identities and knowledge as to what counts as an invention.

A number of authors have conducted research on the cultural characteristics of the European Commission.[16] Abélès, Bellier, and McDonald considered the use of language, hierarchies and personnel policy, and north-south differences. Abélès and Bellier in particular concluded that there was a multitude of competing cultures because of the diverse nationalities and languages, but also noted the existence of departmental identities and a culture of compromise emerging exactly as a result of abundant difference. On the other hand, Shore's work on the European Commission's organizational culture concluded that it is a system of political bargaining and informal networking, encouraging nepotism.[17]

Following Durkheim, the view taken here is that in order to study the existence of shared patterns of praxis, it is important to consider the extent to which civil servants interact. Work activities depending on differentiated yet complementary tasks attach agents to their work group. However, if one accepts that an organization is something more than the sum of its individual parts, then interaction results in civil servants accumulating and sorting experience into useful clusters of information to make sense of the world inside the European Commission, as ethnomethodology taught us. Without these, any social group is bound to degenerate.

In the light of the above, the aim here is to uncover cognitive schemas shared by officials inside the European Commission by means of employing a micro-interactionist study of the informal, everyday practices. As already mentioned in the previous section, such shared practices have a double function of acting both as frames of interpretation and promoting images of authority and power, as to how a legal proposal should look, and who should be involved in its making. They may become a 'bodily hexis'[18] attached in the physical expression of individuals. They may manifest themselves in turn takings and new paragraphs added in texts, in the particular way in which an internal note is written, or in repetitions during interviews.

This approach is inspired by the ethnomethodological research agenda that contends that documentary interpretation of official and unofficial documents can be used to interpret behaviour. Moreover, fieldwork should consist of closely

---

[16] Marc Abélès, Irène Bellier, and Maryon McDonald, 'Approche Anthropologique de la Commission Européenne' (Brussels, 1993), unpublished report for the European Commission); Irène Bellier, 'Une Culture de la Commission Européenne? De la Rencontre des Cultures et du Multilinguisme des Fonctionnaires', in Yves Mény, Pierre Muller, and Jean-Louis Quermonne (eds), *Politiques Publiques en Europe* (Paris, 1995); Irène Bellier, 'La Commission Européenne: Du Compromis Culturel à la Culture du Compromis', *Revue Française des Sciences Sociales* 46 (1996): 431–52; Michele Cini, *The European Commission. Leadership, Organization and Culture in the EU Administration* (Manchester and New York, 1996); Maryon McDonald, 'Accountability, Anthropology and the European Commission', in Marilyn Strathern (ed.), *Audit Cultures: Anthropological Studies in Accountability, Ethics and the Academy* (London, 2000); Chris Shore, *Building Europe: The Cultural Politics of European Integration* (London, 2000).

[17] Shore, ibid., p. 173.

[18] Bourdieu, 'La Force du Droit'.

observing situated activities in their natural settings and discussing them in the course of interviews with officials. The present analysis of data collected in the course of interviews with officials at various levels in the hierarchy, concentrated on identifying repetitions, themes occurring and re-occurring in the interviews,[19] and on searching indigenous categories, which are subsequently contrasted with analytical categories.[20] The interviews were conducted in three rounds with civil servants from various Directorates Generals of the European Commission, and various levels at the hierarchy. The first round of interviews from the third were separated by a two-year period of time, as the author initially identified various important themes, but had to further clarify issues before refining the final conclusions.

The research concentrates on language and hierarchies and on studying how officials work in shared files and committees; reputation, how it is valued and earned, is also a focal theme. Although the following sections examine the legislative context of initiating a legal proposal, the focus is also on the role of the European Commission in various committees, formal and ad hoc, and on promotion and mobility rules, in order to uncover patterns of interaction.

The Formal Organizational Characteristics of the European Commission

Formalism and hierarchy are omnipresent, denoting the Franco-German influence on the institution. The terminology used is similar to the one employed in a French Ministry. The organizational divisions of a Directorate General (hereinafter DG), *direction générale, direction* and *sous direction*, follow the French tradition. Moreover, the institutions of the *cabinet*, *body of advisers* and *aides to the Commissioner*, and the ranks (*conseiller*, *directeur*, *chef de cabinet*), all reflect French ministerial organization, which has also been adopted by many Southern European countries.[21]

Passing the *concours* (competitive entry examinations) is required in order to be employed by the European Commission. This is similar to the one introduced to France a century ago.[22] According to Stevens and Stevens the French influence is evident in the emphasis put on hierarchy, codification, centralization, the principles of permanence and independence, and the creation of an *esprit de corps* amongst the *élite* of officials, while the German traits can be found in employee participation in work councils and in the autonomy of individual Commissioners.[23]

---

19 D'Andrade, 'The Cultural Part of Cognition'.

20 Robert Bogdan and Stephen J. Taylor, *Introduction to Qualitative Research Methods. The Search for Meaning* (New York, 1984); Michael Q. Patton, *Qualitative Evaluation and Research Methods* (California, 1990). It is important to say that the author spent three months as a trainee in the European Commission, and has knowledge of work routines. This had considerable bearing on the kind of questions addressed to interviewees (semi-structured interviews), and helped gaining their trust.

21 Edward C. Page, *People Who Run Europe* (Oxford, 1997), p. 7.

22 Ibid.

23 Anne Stevens and Handley Stevens, *Brussels Bureaucrats? The Administration of the European Union* (Basingstoke, 2001).

Hierarchies are rigid when it comes to the approval of the drafts and proposals prepared by a civil servant (*fonctionnaire*). An official needs the approval of many persons for her drafts, as these will have to go through the Head of Unit, or sometimes the Head of Sector, the Director, the (deputy) Director General, the person in the cabinet of the Commissioner responsible for a *fonctionnaire*'s file, and the Commissioner. Moreover, officials are always dependent on the Legal Service and the Secretariat General. This is because formal approval of procedures by the Legal Service is required, while both the Secretariat General and the Legal Service report directly to the President of the European Commission.[24]

The life of a file inside the European Commission is also prescribed in formal rules. File allocation is done by the Head of Unit, while this is only decided at the level of the cabinet of the President of the European Commission in the event more than one DG considers that a particular file falls within its competence. Once a file is within the responsibility of a DG (or the joint responsibility of more DGs), it then sends a questionnaire to Member States (MS), and on the basis of the information it collects, it sets a working party, whose members are representatives of MS, the industry, and other interested parties.[25] Parallel to this, other DGs are consulted, but such interservice consultations are formalized, as there is a special informatics instrument (CISNET) for it. The relevant dossier moves around DGs with an attached note on it, which requires comments to be given within certain time limits. Meetings with lobbyists are managed on an informal basis.

Initiative in identifying a new legal problem may come from various levels of the hierarchy, but this should be undertaken in the light of general strategic priorities set by the Commissioner, such as 'competition should work in recently liberalized markets, and in sectors that were never monopolized, but are heavily regulated by Member States'. Within this framework, a Director can decide to launch a consultation (sector inquiry), and focus on cases (for instance Belgian architects). The Director should then speak to the Director General and the Commissioner to receive their agreement, and then move onto organizing hearings in order to prepare a policy paper. Afterwards, discussions with the professionals concerned are initiated: 'we want you to organize and clean up your house. We will not take action next year, but if there are still infringements we will be tough'.[26] Then, the proposed legislation goes through interservice consultation and is amended if necessary. It is then checked by the Legal Service and approved by the Commissioners' cabinets. Once the proposal is ready, the Secretariat General puts it on the agenda for a forthcoming Commission meeting. There, the responsible Commissioner explains to the College

---

24 Since the Legal Service and the Secretariat General report directly to the President of the European Commission, it is through these services that he can potentially keep an eye on European Commission's activities. Nonetheless, as Cini notes, the old days of the active, and at times interventionist Secretariat General, are over, see Cini, *The European Commission*.

25 Interview with a Head of Unit DG Information Society, conducted on 22 January 2002.

26 Interview with a Head of Unit DG Competition, conducted on 10 June 2004.

why this legislation is being proposed. If there is agreement, the College adopts the proposal, and the document is sent to the Council and the European Parliament for their consideration. If there is disagreement, the President of the Commission asks Commissioners to vote. If a majority is in favour, the proposal is adopted. Once adopted, according to the principle of collegiality, it has the unconditional support of all the members of the Commission.[27]

Blurring Hierarchical Relations: Negotiating and Cooperating in a Microcosm of Unclear Hierarchies

If one chooses to move beyond formal structures in order to understand how people are really related, how obligations are repaid, how reputations are built, and what the norms regulating the above are,[28] a different set of observations would be valuable in revealing indigenous categories of praxis. Therefore, understanding decision making as being the ordered orchestration of formal procedures giving birth to a proposal or a draft, simply misses the point. There is a more complicated reality underpinning the process of initiating a piece of legislation. The reason for this is that a civil servant working for the European Commission is called to negotiate and cooperate with various other persons. Good personal relationships with the hierarchy, and in particular with the Director of the DG, the Director General, or colleagues in the cabinet of the Commissioner, can prove to be very useful in the event a proposal is blocked.

This is because through these people there may be important exchanges of information. The exchange of information, in the sense of exchange of views, justifies the importance of balancing the formalism of prescribed rules and hierarchies with the need to allow some flexibility in the way the final arguments are crystallized. Much of the working time of officials is dedicated to drafting information notes to the Commissioner, to whom they report. Such notes have to be written before any decision is finalized. Most of the Directorate Generals have *jour fixe* meetings with the Commissioner in order to follow the most important notes, focusing on the ones that imply various legislative choices. However, the practice varies strongly from one DG to another and from one Commissioner to another.

When the cabinet of a Commissioner receives a note, it is common that the cabinet contacts the person who drafted it, to ask for clarifications and background information:

> The colleagues of the cabinet call me, and ask what I think about various points. And if I have this information it is important that I send it by email to the Director General and the cabinet. And it is important that you do it in a transparent way.[29]

---

[27] However, in practice the principle of collegiality does not fully apply in respect to contentious proposals, as the following sections will illustrate.

[28] Heclo and Wildavsky, *The Private Government of Public Money.*

[29] Interview with a Head of Unit DG Competition, conducted on 12 June 2004.

Table 3.1 Decision Making Process in the EU: Proposal for a Council Framework Decision on Attacks against Information System

Private Com (2002) 173	2002/0086/CNS
Proposal for a council framework decision on attacks against information systems	
Private Fields Of Activity:	
Justice and Home Affairs	
Legal basis:	
Commission:	Traité/UE/art 29, 30 par 1, 31, 34 par 2
Procedures:	
Commission:	Consultation procedure
Type of file:	
Commission:	Proposal for a Decision
Comments:	
This proposal does not relate only to acts directed at Member States. It also applies to conduct on the territory of the European Union, which is directed against information systems on the territory of third countries. This reflects the Commission's commitment to tackle attacks against information systems at a global as well as European Union level.	
Private 19-04-2002	Adoption By Commission
Primarily responsible	DG Justice and Home Affairs
Jointly responsible	DG Information Society
Optional consultation	European Parliament
Addressee for formal act	Council
Responsible	Erkki Liikanen; Antonio Vitorino
Documents:	COM/2002/173/FINAL IP/2002/601/_
Procedures:	Consultation procedure
Type of file:	Proposal for a Decision
Legal basis:	Traité/UE/art 29, 30 par 1, 31, 34 par 2
Numero Celex	52002PC0173

Source: COM (2000) 385, 2000/0189/COD.

The meetings of the *chefs de cabinet* are every week, and consist of hours of exchange of information. For those who want to form an informed opinion, it is important to have collected an array of different views from different avenues. A responsible member of the cabinet would send back any 'closed notes', notes that do not provide for alternatives. At a more informal level, chats are also significant for the cabinet of a Commissioner, as in this way a *fonctionnaire* may provide direct background information, not 'censored' by the Director General for example. Such chats are concerned with collecting information about people and their qualities, departments and their work, winners and losers in conflicts. They are important as they form expectations, warn about people, and point to good working practices.

The Director General is one of the most important avenues through which the cabinet and Commissioner may receive information. Therefore, if one's proposal is blocked, for example by the Head of Unit, then it may be possible to convince the Director General as to the importance of presenting an alternative view to the Commissioner or the cabinet. Therefore:

> good relations with the Director General may also prove useful as, in the event the Director or Head of Unit are unaware of this, they may consider the risk of blocking your proposal. Therefore, very important meetings are those in which your Director General participates, and for whom you have prepared the briefings.[30]

However, it is unusual for a *fonctionnaire* to try to directly reach the cabinet or the Commissioner. This may be perceived as disloyal to the Service and against team spirit. Contacting the Director General directly is understood in the sense that the latter person has an interest in hearing the advantages and disadvantages of as many opinions as possible, and as a result she may choose to discuss an array of views with the Commissioner or the cabinet. It does not offend the image of the DG, by means of revealing to outsiders that there are internal problems of coordination and communication amongst the different levels of the hierarchy.

In fact, when two colleagues strongly disagree on a point, they are expected to resolve the issue by meeting with the Director General. However, this is not always the case, and conflicts may reach a climax:

> We agreed in November on the Framework Decision, and we had been working since April, and then somebody destroyed everything for no good reason. Now, I have to talk to one member of the cabinet and try to convince him to speak to the Commissioner.[31]

In this instance, a *fonctionnaire* may try to mobilize the cabinet to 'sell' a proposal directly to the Commissioner, who then might want to speak to the Director General, circumventing opposition from lower in the hierarchy.

A *fonctionnaire* who knows her place will avoid doing this. Things should be kept in line with the views of other colleagues, as it is important to present the image of the particular DG, and the European Administration in general, as strong and successful, since a *fonctionnaire*'s career and reputation is also dependent on this.[32] Such an attitude may be perceived as a way to do things through the back door, and as such an unfair way to present one's view, while discarding the views of others.

---

30 Interview with an administrator DG Competition, conducted on 24 January 2002.

31 Interview with a Head of Unit DG Information Society, conducted on 22 January 2002.

32 Interview with an administrator DG Research, conducted on 8 June 2005.

Hence, one's reputation as a team player may be harmed. Nevertheless reputations are also built on the basis of one being an assertive and aggressive negotiator, and the balance to be kept is delicate. This was a theme constantly occurring during interviews. The following section on transdepartmental dialogue will seek to further elucidate this point.

Transdepartmental Dialogue

After allegations of mismanagement, nepotism, and fraud, which led to the resignation of the Santer Commission in 1999, a reform was launched by the Prodi Commission, which was supervised by Commission Vice President Neil Kinnock. Its central aim was to better plan and organize the way the European Commission carries out its work by setting clear priorities and guaranteeing the availability of necessary resources. The European Commission has long been associated in European citizens' minds with an obscure and unaccountable centre of decision making. The reform was partly concerned with addressing these issues, and the 2000 White Paper on Reforming the Commission explicitly states that its main preoccupation is to provide a quality service to citizens and taxpayers, promoting a culture of service.[33]

The situation relevant to interservice collaboration on files, where several DGs would have to be consulted, has also been revisited. The DGs of the European Commission are caught in constant communication and collaboration. Although one DG has prime responsibility for a file, it also has to consult other DGs. As already mentioned, casehandlers do not have to decide when and who to consult on their drafts. Interservice consultations are formalized, as there is a special informatics instrument (CISNET) for it.

While transdepartmental dialogue is an important component of decision making, it may prove problematic. This has been recognized by the European Commission in its report with the title 'Designing Tomorrow's Commission'.[34] The report stated that European Commission departments currently devote 5.7 per cent of intramural human resources to internal consultations. This comes to 1,280 men per year, with 880 men per year being in the administrator and manager category (as opposed to assistants and contract agents).[35]

---

[33] White Paper on Reforming the Commission COM(2000) final.

[34] Commission of the European Communities (1999) Report by the Inspectorate-General, 'Designing Tomorrow's Commission – A Review of the Commission's Organization and Operation', available at http://europa.eu.int/comm/reform/decode/screening_en.pdf.

[35] Before the Prodi reform the basic staff categories were four: A, B, C and D. A grade entrants could join the European Commission either without professional experience (at A8 level) or with a minimum of two years' experience (A7/A6 level). In order to sit some A7/A6 competitions, candidates needed a specialized degree in law, economics, accounting, or statistics and relevant professional experience. Note that a *Head of Unit* was an A3, a *Director* was an A2 and a *Director General* was an A1. Candidates for B grade posts must have successfully completed a course of advanced secondary education, and obtained a final

However, the report recognized that coordination is not as effective as it could be:

> due to a lack of clarity as regards the split of responsibilities between departments, the over-assertiveness by departments in some cases, and authoritarianism on the part of certain team leaders in others, which has the effect of distorting interdepartmental consultations and creating certain organizational problems which slow down response times.[36]

Therefore, it proposes that there should be a clear separation of responsibilities and that the lead department and the other departments consulted should be given autonomy and responsibility. To this effect, the Secretariat-General is now given a greater role to play, with a view to promote a culture of cooperation.

The importance of securing collaboration is aggregated in view of the need to integrate environmental considerations into key European Union policies, as required by Article 6 of the Amsterdam Treaty. For example, the environmental dimension is integrated in the mandate of the research funding programme of the European Commission (FP6), especially in respect to energy, transport, and agriculture. It is also incorporated into the priorities of various DGs such as DG Agriculture, Enterprise, Development, Energy and Transport and should be taken into account in EU cooperation with developing countries.[37] Very importantly, the European Commission seeks to ensure that its decision making is subject to an assessment of environmental impact. Projects such as SEAMLESS and SENSOR, funded by the Commission, aim at designing computer models for the assessment of alternative

---

certificate or diploma. They must also have had at least two years' experience in a field related to the activity being applied for. Staff in category B were mainly responsible for executive tasks, and participated in every area of EU activity. Staff in category C were mainly responsible for secretarial and clerical work, while Category D staff were engaged in manual or service duties (Report by the Inspectorate-General of 7 July 1999). With the Prodi reform, the situation has changed, as the basic categories for officials are reduced from four to two function groups, and a single pay scale with 16 grades (each with five seniority steps). The old B and C categories are now called assistants; the old A category is replaced by the administrator function group, while Heads of Unit, Directors, and Director Generals are called managers. Contract agents will gradually replace the D category. The transition period from the previous system to the new one was due on 1 May 2005.

36 Inspectorate General Report 1999. Interestingly, the report further mentions that some DGs have expressed their concern in reference to their relations with Member States' private offices, as they considered that there is interference by them in the internal management of DGs.

37 Communication from the Commission to the Council and the European Parliament on 'Europe's Environment: What Directions for the Future? The Global Assessment of the European Community Programme of Policy and Action in Relation to the Environment and Sustainable Development, Towards Sustainability', COM(1999) 543 final; Communication from the Commission to the Council and the European Parliament on '2004 Environmental Policy Review', COM(2005) 17 final.

agricultural and environmental policy options, and environment-friendly land use for sustainable development in Europe.

These computerized tools are expected to be used by the European Commission before the stage of implementation, to make an assessment as to the potential impact of policies (such as the common agricultural or rural development policies) to sustainable development. Sustainability Impact Assessment (SIA) implies that, for instance, to evaluate the benefit of developing infrastructure in a particular region, it is required to engage in the simultaneous examination of the impact on the environment, biodiversity, and employment. This may be expected to reshape in fundamental ways the interaction between different DGs, and involves management decisions at different levels of governance following the principle of subsidiarity. What is crucial for the purpose of the present analysis is that it brings the problem of cooperation amongst DG into the foreground.

It is true, coordination may prove to be difficult, but in other instances meetings would run smoothly, resulting in a fruitful exchange. Conflicts can be for two main reasons: personal conflicts and policy conflicts, as some issues are more contentious than others. This depends on the controversial nature of the file concerned. A very technical, politically neutral file would not normally be problematic. A politically sensitive file may be changed considerably, and in some cases, it may be completely blocked. Different DGs may approach and understand an issue from a totally different angle, as it was the case with the debate surrounding the issue of data retention.

The DGs involved in the data retention file were DG Justice and Home Affairs, DG Internal Market, and DG Information Society:

> We (DG Information Society) are 'the sausage', trying to compromise things in respect to issues that relate to privacy and the Internet ... What happens is that, on the one hand, you have the 'law enforcement' people, and on the other hand, Internet service providers and telecom operators in a strange position. Although telecom operators used to retain data themselves, since they are often victims of fraud (but of course nobody knew that, as it is an illegal act), they do not want laws [concerning data retention] to impose on them obligations. Then you have the civil rights people, who claim that this is a surveillance situation. I want to find a compromise solution, maybe accept that providers need some data to be retained, what data depends on the business model. If this practice [data retention] is legitimized by law, then the law should not impose heavy obligations on them.[38]

Negotiations can be very intense. Certainly, it is a matter of pride to have one's opinion taken into account. Various internal notes prove this point. At the level of Heads of Units, conflicts, as depicted in such notes, can be very intense and most

---

[38] Interview with a Head of Unit DG Information Society, conducted on 22 January 2002. In May 2002, the Parliament passed the Communications Data Protection Directive (EU 2002/58/EC) 351 to 133, despite an aggressive campaign by civil liberties groups. The Directive provides that unsolicited email (spam) is outlawed, Internet-fed identification programs (cookies) are tolerated if people are informed of them, and EU governments can order the retention of customer data beyond useful billing purposes.

of the time the message is 'you did not take me into account', while at the level of Directors Generals the tone changes and is far softer. After all, having won a battle will increase one's bargaining power in the next conflict. However, even if primary responsibility rests with one DG and other DGs are only consulted, a capable official understands the importance of trying to reach agreement. A report produced by the Secretariat General states that the leading department is responsible for involving and taking into account the legitimate interests of other departments, and that it is *a duty* to participate in a cooperative spirit, following the policy mandate of the Commission, and the strict priorities set to DGs. However, this statement presents us with another instance where the formal mandate of a report conflicts with native patterns of action; cooperation is in practice achieved, as success and securing present and future outcomes depend on it.

When a DG has principal responsibility for a file, while other DGs are consulted, the influence of the latter comes from the fact that the Commission is a collegial body. The principle of collegiality points to collective decision making and responsibility. All Commission decisions have to be submitted to the College of Commissioners with an attachment of the opinions of the other DGs consulted. However, it is important to note that, in principle, decisions are taken by consensus, and it is rare that vote takes place. If the President accepts or demands that there is a vote, decisions are taken according to simple majority. This may be problematic, as some Commissioners may be absent during this time. In respect to contentious proposals, this in practice means that a potential positive vote is not taken into account, and as a result, the proposal may be withdrawn. This is why in such instances the date of the meeting of the Commission is subject to careful consideration, in order to verify the presence of Commissioners. Of course, informal contacts and telephone calls are important, so as to secure support or find a compromise solution.[39]

However, the principle of collegiality also implies that a casehandler can block the input produced by consulted DGs, but then the risk is taken that the cabinet of the Commissioner in charge of the consulted DG would raise the issue and try to block the decision at the level of the College of Commissioners.[40] It is therefore important to engage in a dialogue with colleagues or at least try to minimize the points of disagreement:

> If you disagree with a colleague from another DG and primary responsibility rests with us [DG Competition], you should be careful to avoid putting anything on paper. Then the antagonism is crystallized. It is important not to do this, as this may prejudice the quality of the relationship for a long time, and you do not want this to happen, as you may need these people in the future. I avoid producing any document signed by the Director General

39 Interview with a Director DG Internal Market, conducted on 14 June 2004.

40 When a vote takes place, the President of the Commission can play a crucial role, as she may choose to intervene in order to maintain or withdraw a contentious proposal. Prodi for instance would not easily support controversial proposals, especially after the resignation of the Santer Commission. Interview with an administrator, Secretariat General, conducted on 12 June 2004.

> at this stage. I want to move them gradually to a point where an acceptable solution is agreed. Bilateral meetings and informal discussions are very important to do this. It is very important that you know when to crystallize intentions, not to do it too early. This is a decision that involves an assessment as to what you think you can decide yourself, and what you need to inform the hierarchy.[41]

In cases where transdepartmental dialogue is required, mundane administrative practices relating to where files are kept may be very important. This is because such details can be quite contentious, since they imply who *controls* the file.[42] Although interservice consultation is a frequent phenomenon, most of the time other DGs are only consulted, and one DG has the lead responsibility. Hence, shared files are not the rule, but the exception. Even in this case, the control is not really shared, since one of the two DGs has the master copy, and on technical and drafting issues it is not possible to block the colleague holding this. In order to avoid this unbalance, DGs may decide to divide the articles, to avoid one of them having the whole master copy.

In reference to the exact location of keeping files inside a DG, the system varies strongly. This is also because security considerations vary from one DG to another. At DG Competition casehandlers kept their files in their office, a practice that reflects the fact that *rapporteurs* have important independence in this particular DG. However, the files regarding infringement procedures were kept by the secretary, possibly because access to files and appeals procedures against the European Commission were relatively frequent, and the European Commission would then have to transmit the file to the court. In the Merger Task Force, secretaries make copies of all documents for the casehandlers. In other DGs again practices vary considerably.

In the course of interservice consultations, the casehandler sets the agenda of meetings with other DGs, and conflicts may be viewed as the healthy result of trying to balance many views, allowing the College of Commissioners to make informed decisions. Individual DGs have different priorities, still the College of Commissioners should take a balanced decision in the light of the overall policies of the Commission. For instance DG Environment, Competition, and Enterprise often disagreed exactly because of the interests they represent. However, consultations may take time also because of bad personal relationships or games of power amongst DGs. DG Competition has a difficult relationship with DG Enterprise on the issue of airline industry regulation:

> They think that they have a say, this is because the mission of DG Enterprise became unclear; it is not the time of national champions. They have a thousand people working there. They promote the interests of the industry, which is not the general view here. You know in advance what the other person is going to say, and then the dialogue is not fruitful. Of course, they realized that if they wanted to be heard they would have to bring

---

41 Interview with a Head of Unit DG Competition, conducted on 15 June 2004.

42 Cini, *The European Commission.*

> value added. Otherwise, they would never have the legitimacy to voice opinions and they would fight the battles and lose. At some point, they changed the person in charge and things improved. They now bring sector expertise, and this is valuable.[43]

Interservice consultations must be launched via the Head of Unit and signed by the Director. A casehandler's reputation and good relationship with these persons can thus prove crucial. For example, because of strong criticism by other DGs, a Director may decide to stop initiatives of her officials, to avoid starting a 'war' on the subject. On the other hand, if it is the case of a 'turf battle', a Director may try to protect the competences of the DG.

Overall, cooperation is facilitated by the fact that, due to the mobility of civil servants, it is likely that the persons involved know or have heard of each other.

Mobility

Page's analysis is of interest, as he concludes that there is considerable mobility in senior posts. His data indicate that 61 per cent of his sample had previously worked in another Directorate General.[44] In a Communication from Vice President Kinnock to the European Commission,[45] the above figures seem to hold true for today's situation.

According to the data in this communication, about 1,000 officials of all grades change DG or department each year. The figure for 1999 is 1,058 out of approximately 20,000 officials working for the European Commission. For the period between 1990 and 1999, the number of officials who changed posts in the context of interdepartmental mobility amounted to 8,669. Nevertheless, this number excludes mobility within a DG, as accurate numbers do not exist. In general, mobility is considerable, and the Kinnock communication sought to formalize this trend by means of setting benchmark periods: as a rule, all officials should consider changing jobs once they have spent at least two, but not more than five years in the same post. A reasonable period for a new official to remain in her first post would be three years. Nonetheless, individuals aged 55 and above, who wish to remain in their post, may do so.[46] Finally, as regards to officials in top management posts, such as Director Generals and Directors, they *have to* regularly move.[47] The principle of rotating

[43] Interview with a Head of Unit DG Competition, conducted on 15 June 2004. However, it is interesting to note that administrators from other DGs also complain that it is difficult to cooperate with DG Competition, interview with an administrator DG Enterprise, conducted on 22 June 2004.

[44] Page, *People Who Run Europe*, p. 35.

[45] Communication from Vice President Kinnock to the European Commission on 'Guidelines on Mobility' SEC 2002 146, p. 3. It is important to note that mobility is voluntary, with one exception: the case of sensitive posts, where officials have special expertise or handle sensitive information.

[46] Ibid., p. 6.

[47] Ibid.

senior posts after five years was introduced after the Santer Commission resigned, and the idea behind it was to reduce the control of certain Member Sates on particular departments, and to allow staff to build their careers upon broad experience.

Mobility is in principle not related to promotion, as officials keep their grades when moving to different DGs or another Unit in the same DG. An exception to this is the designation of Directors and Director Generals. This is considered a promotion, because the title corresponds to a specific grade and salary. In general, vacant positions are advertised on the intranet describing the grade/profile expected. Everyone can apply, but for someone to be transferred to another Unit, her Head of Unit has to consent. The only case of transfer without consent happens in the case of restructuring parts of Units (for example when Units merge), so, since files 'move', officials have to move with them.[48]

Heclo and Wildavsky contend that transfers between departments are vital for the administration's bond of unity and cohesion.[49] By means of transfers, individual DGs can benefit from outside expertise and tackle isolation. In the same spirit, the Prodi reform advocates the importance of increased decentralization. The complexity of files requiring interservice consultation also brings collaboration into the foreground. Mobility is crucial to achieve this, as individuals have knowledge of how other departments work, what their priorities are, and what people are like. Personal relationships and predictability of situations make collaboration easier. This last point is also valid in respect to promotions.

Promotion

Promotions used to be based on seniority rather than merit. However, when Jacques Delors was President of the European Commission (1985–95), this changed, as a reform of rules governing promotion procedures took place:[50]

> The reform was undertaken in the name of flexibility, as it would allow the capable to go up in the hierarchy faster than the others. However, in reality the reform aimed at controlling the people who occupy the A3 post (Heads of Unit), so as to ensure their willingness to respect and serve the ideals that underlie the political mandate of the Commissioner. Having the right contacts and ideas is important in order to become a Head of Unit. But, before the reform, A level *fonctionnaires* would inevitably one day become Heads of Unit, as going up the hierarchy was prescribed in administrative rules, with no involvement of political figures, such as the Commissioner. This actually resulted in some Head of Units not always being receptive to some of the Commissioner's ideas.[51]

---

48 Interview with an administrator DG Research, conducted on 29 May 2002.

49 Heclo and Wildavsky, *The Private Government of Public Money*, p. 81.

50 Geoffrey Edwards and David Spence (eds), *The European Commission* (London, 1997).

51 Interview with a Head of Sector DG Competition, conducted on 23 January 2002.

With the entering into force of the new Staff Regulations on 1 May 2004, staff policy, including recruitment, promotions, and retirement, has been significantly revised:

> The aim is to create an independent, sustainable, and top-quality European public service, making the Commission into an organization that sets world-wide standards.[52]

According to the 2003 Reform Progress Review,[53] the changes aim at better linking merit to career development. The new appraisal system takes on board training, mobility, and officials' ability to achieve fixed objectives. The criteria against which any assessment will be made are ability, efficiency, and conduct, as laid down in the Staff Regulations. Every year a Career Development Report (CDR) will have to be produced by staff on the basis of intensive dialogue with immediate superiors, and there are additional priority points, which DGs will be able to use to make special bonus awards of up to ten points for individual officials. Any assessment of special merit requires the involvement of the Director General, and an appeals system is in place within individual DGs.

As for Directors and Director Generals, a system of 360 degree appraisal is introduced (focusing on feedback from self, superiors, peers, and subordinates), to be conducted every two years. Commissioners will also be involved in the final appraisal.[54] Moreover, linear pay progression is introduced, meaning that the salary at a higher grade would always be equal to or higher than the salary in the previous grade. Finally, the number of grades in the new career system is increased, and the number of seniority posts decreased. The rationale behind this is to offer the possibility of an increased number of promotions, creating incentives for improvement of performance.[55]

With the Staff Reform, all staff members not only have specific responsibilities, and appraisal reports are written according to these, but also individual DGs have to produce an 'Annual Management Plan' (AMP), which again sets out objectives to be achieved and monitors progress.[56] Moreover, the reform requires a new activity-based management (ABM) approach, clearly defining the Commission's priorities and ensuring the availability of human and financial resources. ABM requires 'detailed management information on costs, resources and results, and necessitates continuous processes of monitoring of assessment and prioritization'.[57] It implies

---

52 http://europa.eu.int/comm/reform/2002/chapter02_en.htm#3, (webpage visited on 25 February 2005).

53 Commission of the European Communities, Reform Progress Review, COM(2003) 40 final/2.

54 Commission of the European Communities 'An Administration at the Service of Half a Billion Europeans: Staff Reforms at the European Commission, State of Play', Spring 2002.

55 Reform Progress Review, p. 27.

56 Ibid.

57 Communication from Vice-President Kinnock to the European Commission, p. 24.

that each Director General develops with her DG an Annual Management Plan for all activities, and that she has the autonomy to design management and control systems, subject to that minimum standards and performance standards are set for individuals and subunits.[58]

The Union Syndicale Fédérale, which is one of the three principal trade unions of the European public service, produced in 2000 a working paper critical of these changes. The reasons are that appraisals will disrupt work and create excessive paper load, lead to a potential abuse of power by Director Generals and the human resources department of DGs, and finally, the points system for individuals and quotas system for DGs may lead to the transformation 'of evaluations to a collective haggling and make them ineffectual'.[59] The UFS accepts the importance of linking merit to promotions, however, criticizes the new career system, as it may result in the creation of an 'elite emerging from permanent competition among individuals, contrary to team spirit necessary for the missions of the commission'.[60]

According to Levy it will be normal for individuals and DGs to emphasize achievements, conceal failures, and shift responsibilities to other DGs, or even the Council and the College of Commissioners. Levy notes that there is already evidence that this is happening, as the first annual reports produced claim that 70–75 percent of DGs managed to achieve minimum standards. In these reports, when DGs had to present reasons for not fully achieving the reforms, they blamed the lack of staff, lack of guidance, and lack of control over the Member States and decentralized agencies.[61] It appears that the USF's warning that the reformed appraisal system may lead to collective bargaining of appraisals and competitive behaviour among individuals, or even amongst DGs, between the College of Commissioners and DGs, and between cabinets and DGs, is an important possibility.

Just like the Delors reform of the 1980s, the Prodi reform is undertaken in the name of flexibility, aiming at allowing the capable to be promoted quickly on the basis of merit. However, being evaluated by the hierarchy, peers, and colleagues may very well mean that building a good reputation becomes increasingly important. In other words, fulfilling expectations and adhering to shared patterns of conduct as to how one should behave in the course of working on a legal file, becomes more significant. However, it is a mystery sometimes how reputations are built or shattered.

---

58 Ibid., p. 25.

59 Union Syndicale Fédéral, The Reform: Working Paper of the USF of 7 March 2000 on the Advisory Document of 18 January 2000.

60 Ibid, p. 9.

61 Roger Levy, 'Critical Success Factors in Public Management Reform: The Case of the European Commission', *International Review of Administrative Sciences*, 69 (2003): 553–66.

Reputation

A civil servant with a good reputation is a person who is a team player, confident and assertive, with a good drafting hand, motivation, political judgment, negotiating skills, and realism, all at the same time. However, it is not really through a logical process that reputations are formed. It is the result of things one knows, heard, or was told. When it comes to recruitment and mobility of civil servants for example, a candidate's curriculum vitae will be thoroughly examined, but after all, most candidates speak five languages and have considerable qualifications. What makes the difference and affects final decisions is a number of factors, which are very difficult to define.

In this instance, reputations travel amongst services and units, as what people say about others' qualities is important. Learning about one's personal qualities, such as the ability of the person in question to be a team player and cooperate with others, is important. After all, decisions inside an organization such as the European Commission are about limiting risk. Risk aversion requires that the choice of a person is underlied by the simultaneous consideration of personal qualities and the ability to do the job. For instance, it is important for the members of staff involved in recruitment to like the person and the ideas that she promotes, since they will find themselves having to cooperate with the person in question. This implies that, as in every organization, choices in respect to recruitment and mobility will also be motivated by the need to reinforce, replicate, and reproduce the culture of the staff involved in middle (Heads of Unit) and high management level.

This is a culture that requires a *fonctionnaire* not only to have experience, a good drafting hand, and intelligence, but also to know her place and conform to the unwritten rules of the game, summarized in the triptych: effectiveness in problem solving, common sense/political judgment, and information collector/team player. A *fonctionnaire* faces complex problems, which have to be solved quickly. Common sense and political judgment are invaluable to this effect, as a perfectly drafted legal argument may very well be politically impossible.

In this instance, common sense is important in order to draw the practical distinction between what can be done and what cannot be done. Effectiveness requires that the detail of the relevant problems is reduced to the minimum, simultaneously accommodating the necessary. The ability to be flexible and receptive is important, as cooperating with others minimizes conflicts, hence the importance of being a team player. Very importantly, cooperating, or, to use a better expression, being in constant communication with others, implies that the person in question will be able to furnish valuable information as to developments in other Units, DGs, or the cabinet. The European Commission is a small world, and officials are in touch with one another, exchanging views and information on the informal level. The complexity of issues dealt with by the DGs requires this, as in this way an informed view is shaped, and the chances of a draft being blocked are minimized.

Therefore, delivering relevant information helps build a good reputation. This can be done via informal avenues (chats, exchange of emails, and internal notes copied to a large number of colleagues) or more formal channels, such as meetings. This is why it is important to participate in meetings such as *ad hoc* interservice meetings organized on specific files (these refer to interdepartmental meetings), or horizontal issues (where many units from a DG may work together, one example being the meetings organized at DG Competition on collective dominance and access to networks). Weekly meetings are also significant in this respect. These are organized by the Head of Unit and serve the purpose of coordination and keeping everybody informed about the work carried out in the Unit. During these meetings, everybody has to report about the tasks performed in the previous week, and the ones that would be performed in the near future. Releasing important information shedding light onto a different aspect of a particular file is crucial.

Having served in a cabinet is definitely an indicator that one knows people and has the ability to collect and process important information. Cabinet members are important, as they deal directly with people in key positions. Every cabinet and every Director General have their own dynamic. The cabinet's job is to show the Commissioner another point of view by the one cast by the DG, to make recommendations and simultaneously explain drawbacks, to give advice and open options. In the course of this process, not only one builds a reputation of a person who is 'able to do the job', but also of a person who knows people and has access to important information.

In short, a *fonctionnaire* who knows her place should promote a culture of delivery and the interests of the organization, by means of securing regulatory output. Securing regulatory output requires that the administration collects as much information as possible in order to effectively put the social world in legal categories and minimize the potential of conflicts and embarrassments, when the proposal reaches the College of Commissioners or the Council/Parliament. However, there is a fragile balance to be held between promoting the image of being a flexible team player, and at the same time the image of a person who has informed views, brings information to the DG, and has influence.

The way to keep this delicate balance is subject to a learning process, through which a *fonctionnaire* will, to a certain extent, copy what others do. For instance, a junior *fonctionnaire* should not say more than she is expected to say, as this would show disrespect to the hierarchy and could be interpreted as a sign of lack of prudence and judgment. Or, as explained earlier, a Head of Unit should not try to contact the Cabinet and the Commissioner directly to convince them to speak to the Director General when a proposal is blocked, as circumventing the Director General means that things are done through the back door. Creating enemies by means of promoting risky initiatives is not desirable, as the Unit or the DG may be exposed. If somebody makes an improper public comment, disclosing sensitive information, everybody is exposed.

DGs increasingly have to deal with specialized and complex files requiring the collection of as much information as possible about local needs. The above analysis denotes that personal achievements and specialization are important to build a good reputation, but not enough. Bringing in information about local needs is a virtue, and this can be further enhanced by means of sitting in or having contacts with committees and specialized groups. National networks can also be important. French nationals for example are thought to be very well networked, although the people who have graduated from the elite French Universities, the *Grandes Ecoles*, present an interesting example of a network within a network, which is further hierarchically organized (*Ecole Supérieur, Ecole Normale*, and *Ecole Polytechnique*).

Committees and Groups

The degree of officials' active participation in committees and groups depends on the type of group concerned and, of course, on the subject matter. There are formal internal committees like the 'Communications Committee' (Cocom), which exercises its function through advisory and regulatory procedures in accordance with the Council Comitology Decision. The Cocom furthermore provides a platform for the exchange of information on market developments and regulatory activities. Similarly, in DG Agriculture only in respect to the management of the common fisheries policy, there are three such committees: the Committee on Structures for Fisheries and Aquaculture, the Committee for Fisheries and Aquaculture, and the Committee for Fisheries Products.[62]

Furthermore, there are groups, which serve as meeting points between national authorities and the European Commission, such as the European Regulators Group for electronic communications networks and services (ERG). This has been set up by Decision 2002/627/EC to encourage cooperation and coordination between national regulatory authorities and the Commission. The first meeting was held in Amsterdam on 23 January 2003. On average, the ERG meets every other month. Similarly, in DG Environment, following the EU legislation on sources of noise, a 'noise steering group' was established, comprising of representatives of MS, local authorities, industry, and NGOs.

Alternatively, there are many forums of discussion where interested parties are invited to participate, and which are run, but not controlled, by the European Commission (for instance the Cybercrime Forum has been hosting discussions on cybercrime and data retention). There are also internal task forces, where representatives of various DGs sit. A small interservice task force may have five participants. In general, the European Commission is surrounded by myriads of committees providing advice on both the development and implementation of legislation.[63]

---

[62] Council Regulation (EC) No 1260/1999; Council Regulation (EC) No 2371/2002; Council Regulation (EC) No 104/2000.

[63] See Chapter Four of this book, and Technological Options Assessment (STOA) Programme PE 167 327/Fin.St.

Compromise and Law Making Inside the European Commission

It is true that the European Commission is a blend of various cultures, nationalities, languages, and working styles. This certainly has an effect on how the organization thinks and pursues its interests. However, the argument here is that one important common cognitive schema, anthropological category of praxis, regulating life inside the European Commission is *compromise.*[64] The remaining of this section will engage in the theoretical articulation of this idea, in the light of the previous analysis on the processes of exchange underpinning the initiation of a legal document.

As mentioned earlier, the present analysis of data collected in the course of interviews with officials at various levels in the hierarchy, concentrated on identifying repetitions, themes occurring and reoccurring in the interviews, and on searching indigenous categories to subsequently contrast these with analytical categories. For instance, although hierarchies inside the European Commission are strict, they may be blurred for the sake of allowing flexibility and information flows. Mobility and promotion rules are meant to strengthen accountability, but in reality their consequence may be that an official conforms to expectations and becomes dependent on what others think, which has a further effect on how reputations are built. In respect to interservice consultations, one would expect that since other departments are only consulted, their opinion would not count, as it is non-binding. However, in practice, officials are very careful not to prejudice a relationship for long, as cooperation may also be required in the future. Moreover, the theory is that a civil servant is a well-educated person, independent, and with a good drafting hand, but the reality is that belonging to networks of information is very important, as securing regulatory outcomes is dependent on the availability of information in view of the increasing complexity of relevant issues. For this reason, tasks inside an administration become the responsibility of various individuals and departments, requiring the collection of information from interest groups, networks and experts.

In addition, the independence of civil servants is affected by rules concerning mobility and recruitment, which elevate the importance of appraisals by peers and hierarchies. This is because it appears that reputation and how it is earned, becomes increasingly dependent on how *others* evaluate performance. In this instance, following Goffman's analysis, civil servants also express themselves in ways reflecting what is thought to be a *proper* way of expression, conforming to expectations and compromising their individuality. Finally, the relational character of working inside the European Commission is further illustrated in everyday practices, such as the development of a meta-language. Words have been inserted in the French and English vocabulary having no meaning outside the context of the European Commission, such as *égalité des chance*, 'agenda', and 'speaking brief'.[65] This practice denotes the coexistence of different nationalities, languages, and

---

[64] Also see the special edition on *compromise* published in *Social Science Information* 43/2 (2004): 131–330, and in particular Mohamed Nachi's contributions.

[65] Irène Bellier, 'La Commission Européenne'.

working styles. It seems that the abundance of difference leads to certain osmosis in order to achieve cooperation.

The effect of these processes is that the stages of forming a legal proposal and implementing a legal measure reflect a compromise position, ordered by the authority of the written text to temporarily objectify practices, and at the same time guarantee formality, the rule of law, legal certainty and continuity, by means of providing for the rational prediction of outcomes. Officials have to achieve outcomes, and to do this they put the social world in legal categories on the basis of collected information. The collection of information through diverse avenues is important in order to minimize the potential of conflicts and embarrassment. Such information is incorporated in the making of a legal text, and the production of relevant regulatory output bolsters the image of the European Commission as a powerful organization. The tools of technical competence are employed, for example, specific legal language, reliance on precedent, codification, and objectification of practices by means of the grammatical persistence of impersonal and passive constructions in legal texts. Securing regulatory output further requires following routines and categories of praxis organizing the social world, while the details of individual cases are fit into organizational practices. Compromise as a category of thought regulates exchange and regenerates practices and images of authority as to the particular way the efficient production of regulatory output will be achieved, and as to the way in which the power to fit the social world in legal categories will be exercised. In other words, it reproduces understandings as to who should be involved in the making of a legislative proposal and how opposing views should be treated.

However, I here wish to depart from the notion of responsible individual who acknowledges the importance of compromise in sustaining social relationships. The argument here is that what creates the need to compromise is the division of labour inside and outside the European Commission, that is the need to collect information from as many sources as possible and cooperate with many other individuals. In other words, since the production of a legal measure presupposes the 'other' we *need* to recognize the 'other' in the light of the need to produce outcomes. If one accepts that structural conditions of interdependence may give rise to compromise, the proposition that logically follows is that interdependency also reflects the need to conform to shared expectations, shared patterns of praxis reproducing acceptance and belonging. Unity and collaboration is fostered and individuality is compromised in the course of trying to build a good reputation, form a respectable opinion, and be recognized by peers as important team members. In this instance, compromise as a category of praxis emerges for the sake of belonging.

The analysis here is not meant to promote the view that here is a single category of themes regulating the initiation of a legislative proposal. The argument is that compromise as a category of praxis is a major theme, which may function alongside other categories shaped by nationality, educational background, and professional training. For instance, nationality and how it may affect decision making has been a contentious issue. The very concept of *Commissioner* is a good starting point, as, although they are appointed by major parties in their MS, their role is to both serve the European interest and provide a channel of communication between the Government in their country and the European Commission.

Then, there is the difference between cabinets and DGs. McDonald's anthropological analysis shed light onto how cabinets are perceived by *fonctionnaire*s as being the ones with power and prestige, since they have the final say in drafts and proposals produced by the officials. They are also most certainly the place where national affiliations and national loyalties will be found, as they have regular contacts with national lobbyists, national administrations, and the permanent representations of MS in Brussels.[66]

On the individual level, it would be wrong to forget that most European Commission officials come from a national educational, administrative, and political system. As Christiansen notes, officials, with a 'European' educational formation (as a result of being educated at the College of Europe, the European Institute of Public Administration, or the European University Institute), are a small albeit growing minority.[67] Generally, the link with national administrative systems has been the subject of a number of recent studies.[68] Moreover, it appears that schemas derived from professional background may also be institutionalized in Units or even whole DGs.[69] However, the argument that Units, DGs, and officials as individuals may hold diverse cultural values, does not rule out the proposition that there are patterns of praxis embedded in modes of cooperation valid for the European Commission as a whole.

---

66 McDonald, 'Accountability, Anthropology, and the European Commission'. According to McGowan, on the level of Commissioners' cabinets there is a specialist, for example a competition specialist, who may try to protect the national interests of the Commissioner's home country. The specialists meet twice a week, and these meetings are called special chefs meetings. The recommendations from these meetings are referred to the weekly meetings of the chefs de cabinets. If agreement is reached among the chefs de cabinet, then the College of Commissioners usually accepts their recommendation. In this way decision making is linked to the overall framework of EU policy, Lee McGowan, 'Safeguarding the Economic Constitution. The Commission and Competition Policy', in Neil Nugent (ed.), *At the Heart of the Union: Studies in the European Commission* (Basingstoke, 2000).

67 Thomas Christiansen, 'Tensions of European Governance: Politicized Bureaucracy and Multiple Accountability in the European Commission', *Journal of European Public Policy*, 4/1 (1997): 73–90.

68 Michael Egeberg, 'Organization and Nationality in the European Commission Services', *Public Administration*, 74/3 (1996): 721–35. Irène Bellier, 'La Commission Européenne: Hauts Fonctionnaires et Culture du Management', *Revue Française d'Administration Publique*, 70/1 (1994): 253–62; Jarle Trondal, 'The Parallel Administration of the European Commission: National Officials in European Clothes?', *Arena Working Papers*, 2001/25.

69 Luis Jourdain, 'La Commission Européenne et la Construction d'un Nouveau Modèle d'Intervention Publique', *Revue Française des Sciences Sociales*, 46/2 (1996): 496–520. See also Chapter Five of this book.

Conclusions

Acculturation within a group implies the existence of coherent patterns of appropriate conduct, which should be performed, consciously or not, being embedded in cognitive structures. This approach does not present us with static categories of thought. Schemas are conceived as the catalyst between minds and social structures, processing information in a way that allows regulated improvisation, interpretation, and appreciation of the possibilities embedded in structures. To substantiate an argument in this direction, the present enquiry considered patterns of interaction inside the European Commission, concentrating on rules governing promotion and mobility, working in shared files and committees, with reputation, how it is earned and valued, underlining all relevant analysis.

The previous section concluded that compromise is an important category of praxis, reproducing understandings as to who should be involved in the making of a legal measure and how opposing views should be treated. Compromise then becomes a cognitive lens, as a legal proposal becomes less about saying the right thing and more about reflecting a temporary balance, bound to change again, especially now in view of the new decentralized governance structures promoting the engagement of interested parties in the decision making process.

In short, the need to collect information, identify problems, categorize findings, produce regulatory output, is what underlies the workings of every administration. However, these operating principles acquire particular meaning in the context of *compromise* or other categories of praxis stemming, for instance, from professional background. This is why there is a 'European administration' or a 'European way of doing things', in other words a European way of identifying problems, collecting information, and categorizing.

Appendix I

Introducing further decentralization and increasingly empowering Commission departments mean that better coordination and planning will be required. This need is all the more pressing given that Commissioners are to be housed in the same buildings as their departments, that many of the jobs handled cover a variety of disciplines, that responsibilities are fragmented and assigned to increasingly specialized departments and that strict priorities have to be applied to the activities and policies of the Commission. Consequently, internal coordination needs to be strengthened around the following three objectives:

1. promoting a real culture of cooperation (internal team spirit) where coordination is a matter for everyone and action is taken to guide, channel and foresee events as early on in the process as possible, with the emphasis increasingly on substance rather than form;
2. ensuring compliance with the guidelines set out by the President and with the policy priorities subsequently adopted by the Commission, strict priorities

being set for the Directorates-General and departments and taking into account available and/or necessary resources;
3. ensuring that the work done is consistent overall and that documents are of a high standard.

The competent department is primarily responsible for internal coordination, first, since it designs and launches the initiatives which fall within its area of responsibility and which must faithfully reflect the priorities set by the Commission and second, since it organizes and chairs the relevant interdepartmental working parties and any other networks or thematic discussion groups. The competent department is in particular responsible for involving from the outset the other departments directly concerned and for taking account of their legitimate interests. They in turn have a duty to participate in the work of coordination in a cooperative spirit.

Inter alia, the Secretariat-General will:

- check whether appropriate mechanisms are necessary to ensure coordination between departments in particularly difficult or strategically important cases;
- automatically inform the weekly meeting of Directors-General and heads of department of any matters likely to be appearing on the agendas of forthcoming Commission meetings so that their substance can be examined and so as to report on progress so far as regards their preparation;
- regularly inform the weekly meeting of Directors-General on medium-term programming of future initiatives in the context of the implementation of the Commission's work programme;
- if necessary and depending on the nature of the problem, refer cases to the weekly meeting of Directors-General, the GCOM, or any other appropriate coordination body;
- consider whether meetings of interdepartmental working parties might under certain circumstances replace written interdepartmental consultations; and – revise the current list and structure of the interdepartmental working parties and look at creating a website on their activities and setting up an electronic letter box for the use of departments so that the list of working parties can be updated on a regular basis.

Source: http://europa.eu.int/comm/reform/operation/coordin_en.pdf, p. 2.

Appendix II

It [The Commission] wants to be associated in the minds of Europe's citizens with high quality, honesty, openness and integrity. These have been the Commission's operating values since the birth of the European Union. The reform process makes a new commitment to these values, enshrining them in a new approach to management based on four principles:

Clearer responsibility

In many areas of the Commission's work, responsibility has become blurred by procedures that tend to obscure, rather than to reveal whom has actually taken a decision or approved expenditure. The reform process is remedying this by clearly defining the responsibilities of individuals at all levels, including the College of Commissioners. A clear definition of tasks also makes clear ambiguity about who is responsible for what.

Strengthened accountability

As a European Institution, the Commission is formally accountable to the citizen in various ways … At the same time the Commission's accountability is being strengthened by greater openness to public scrutiny.

Higher efficiency

The Commission has to deliver its services in the most cost-effective way. Decentralization is also increasing efficiency by clearly defining responsibilities and encouraging officials to use their own initiative.

Public and internal transparency

This word deserves clearer definition than it is often given. To the Commission it means that its procedures and actions must be open to public scrutiny. Transparency also has an internal application and requires effective communications between all levels of the administration, openness to new ideas and a readiness to accept criticism as a positive encouragement to do better. The whole reform process is dedicated to achieving these four objectives. In the interest of getting results, the Commission adopted in 2000 a comprehensive and far reaching Action Plan, comprising 98 points whose implementation is closely monitored.

Source: White Paper Reforming the Commission COM (2000) 200 final/2, 7–8.

Chapter Four

Procedural Rationality, Power, and the Bureaucratic Mode of Thinking

> Not necessity, not desire – no, the love of power is the demon of men. Let them have everything, health, food, a place to live, entertainment, they are and remain unhappy and low-spirited: for the demon waits and waits and will be satisfied.
>
> Friedrich Nietzsche, *Daybreak: Thoughts on the Prejudices of Morality*

There is currently hot debate as to what form Internet regulation should take in view of the unique characteristics of the medium. The dominant position is that the role of law should be confined to putting in place procedures enabling the participation of communities in the making of rules affecting them. This view inextricably links to the general discussion relating to the proper role of law in a highly differentiated social world, but also draws attention to the decentralized character of the Internet, which is uniquely positioned to accommodate the demand for free speech and information flows.

The aim of this chapter is to question whether new governance structures and decentralized regulation relevant to the Internet can fulfill their promise to accommodate participation and promote difference. The thesis advanced is that hierarchical power may be exercised in novel ways, as in the context of procedural rules, the theoretical tools to follow this intuition are provided by Bourdieu's notion of capital, and the focus is on the role of the European Commission in the process. In particular, the following will investigate the practical wisdom of legal texts, the operating logic of a legal field of study, and the subjective experience of legal certainty and neutrality, viewed in the context of examples drawn from various areas of Internet regulation. I will begin with architectural solutions developed by the industry, to then turn to scarce resources in the Internet with special emphasis on the domain name allocation system, and conclude with a reference to the Safer Internet Action Plan.

Proceduralization, Decentralization, and Internet Regulation

Proceduralization implies shifting into a new paradigm challenging the command and control approach to regulation. The reason for performing such a shift is partly because rule-formation becomes decentralized under the pressure of globalization, and partly because it is becoming dependent on specialized knowledge, Internet regulation being uniquely positioned to endorse both of the above justifications. The internal codes of private interests, labour law, human rights, and environmental law, are paradigms of the process of global law creation, as there is a tendency towards worldwide self-regulation producing the new living law of the world.

As for Internet regulation in particular, Teubner himself recognizes how it presents a new paradigm of regulation based on the living law of communities, as, due to its decentralized character, it has escaped the grip of state control, offering the potential for democratization and for the creation of a global civil society able to oppose globalized markets. The Internet is viewed as opening up new opportunities for re-politicization and re-individualization.[1] This is due to its decentralized character, which appears to be the model for a new form of governance, as there is no real-time transmission. This is happening since the information is not transmitted as a whole, but is broken into packets of bits, which are routed from computer to computer, to find their final destination through the most efficient path according to carrying capacity and traffic. The above process is underlied by the autonomous and independent actions of each computer, which is the sole coordinator of its actions with its nearest neighbour. It is exactly because of this unique autonomous function that when we speak of the Internet, we always stress its decentralized character.[2]

Nonetheless, the literature on Internet regulation, as developed in the US, has different theoretical underpinnings. Some commentators advance a view of strong property rights, while others argue that the technical infrastructure is in itself a means of regulating cyberspace technology. In the latter case, governmental intervention is not desirable, in view of the effectiveness of markets and social norms as regulators of individual behaviour. In other instances, the adoption of more legal regulatory measures is supported, either with a view to advance the commitment to private property, or because legal regulation is viewed as the most suitable medium to protect the interests of society, exactly because the proprietors of technical infrastructure set regulatory standards.[3]

In 1996, Barlow, co-founder of the Electronic Frontier Foundation, argued that the government should adopt a hands-off approach, as legal concepts safeguarding property, expression, and identity, may be effective in the real world, but appear to be unsuccessful on the Internet. Barlow argued that 'we believe that from ethics,

---

[1] Gunther Teubner, 'Global Private Regimes: Neo-Spontaneous Law and Dual Constitution of Autonomous Sectors in World Society?', in Karl-Heinz Ladeur (ed.), *Public Governance in the Age of Globalization* (Aldershot, 2004).

[2] Barry M. Leiner, Vinton G. Cerf, David D. Clark, Robert E. Kahn, Leonard Kleinrock, Daniel C. Lynch, Jon Postel, Lawrence G. Roberts and Stephen Wolff, 'A Brief History of the Internet By Those Who Made the History, including Barry M. Leiner, Vinton G. Cerf, David D. Clark, Robert E. Kahn, Leonard Kleinrock, Daniel C. Lynch, Jon Postel, Lawrence G. Roberts, Stephen Wolff', available at http://www.isoc.org/internet/history/ (webpage visited on 5 August 2005).

[3] There is no space here to do justice to these debates, as the present analysis is primarily concerned with the regulation of technology in the EU.

enlightened self-interest, and the commonweal, our governance will emerge'.[4] In the same spirit, Reidenberg adopted the term *Lex Informatica*[5] to argue that technology imposes a set of rules that policy makers should understand as, in the event regulation is not sensitive to them, it will fail. Therefore, technology offers a set of potentialities framing policy makers' choices. Similarly, Johnson and Post argue for a decentralized, emergent law.[6] The authors' claim is that Internet technology provides the possibility to create a self-regulated community, whose function should be premised on the notions of collective conversation and responsible participation. Therefore, Internet regulation has to be formed by virtue of voluntary observance of basic rules by network administrators, with a dispute resolution system in place to adjudicate disputes.

Finally, Lessig's argument is that cyberspace is regulated by laws, social norms, markets, and 'code' (software), with law seeking to influence the other forms of regulation (social norms, markets, and codes).[7] Lessig lays emphasis on the role of code in regulating cyberspace, but accepts that it may be altered by law, thus attributing to the latter two modalities of regulation a prominent role. Based on this understanding, Lessig embraces a pessimistic vision, as he argues that copyright and patent protections can be expanded to the point of impeding the development of new ideas on the net.[8] At the same time, he considers that legal regulation can, and should, protect creativity and innovation. Lessig's position is interesting, because he refuses to see the Internet as a space where the absence of traditional command and control rules may open the way to emancipation. The ordering of social relations can be accomplished by means of various modalities, such as code. This implies that the absence of governmental control cannot guarantee freedom and authenticity.

Foucault pointed to the ways in which power and normalization operate in disguise in the context of practices and procedural rules, involving the reinvention of new forms of control by the state. Bourdieu took this last point further to examine how legal rules tacitly reproduce dominant classifications, while simultaneously investigating the ways in which individuals unintentionally reproduce or challenge the effects of normalization. The following section will elaborate on the theoretical properties of this last point by considering the notion of capital as developed by Bourdieu, with a view to theorize issues to do with power and regulation, and thus ultimately discuss the implications of proceduralizing Internet regulation.

---

4 John Perry Barlow, 'A Declaration of the Independence of Cyberspace', (1996) at http://www.eff.org/~barlow/Declar ation-Final.html, point 10 (webpage visited on 5 August 2005).

5 Joel R. Reidenberg, 'The Formulation of Information Policy Rules Through Technology', *Texas Law Review*, 76/3 (1998): 553–93.

6 David. R. Johnson, and David. G. Post, 'Law and Borders: The Rise of Law in Cyberspace', *Stanford Law Review*, 48/2 (1996): 1367–402.

7 Lawrence Lessig, *Code and Other Laws in Cyberspace* (New York, 1999).

8 Lawrence Lessig, *The Future of Ideas: The Fate of the Commons in a Connected World* (New York, 2001).

Power, Capital, and the Interests of the European Administration

The notion of capital in Bourdieu's framework links to the concept of power, as elaborated by Nietzsche and Foucault.[9] Nietzsche sees power as pertaining human relations, distancing himself from the nineteenth-century theorists who ascribed to human nature the endeavour to maximize utility or pleasure. It underlies relations of domination; however its employment can be potentially creative when used to criticize the dominant value system, develop an independent mind, and discover one's true desires. Humans are viewed as navigating life, while elevating above the conventional in a passionate search of self-realization, and in this instance, the will to power denotes the will to discover the truth of who we are.[10]

Foucault borrows this conception of power, and builds on it to maintain that power exists in action and reaction; it is the imminent motor of activity, while constantly being reproduced in its course. In investigating the link between power and knowledge, he revealed how particular views crystallize in belief systems, while other alternative positions become unthinkable.[11] Bourdieu's conceptualization of capital and power follows the same spirit. By refusing to concentrate on the study of power in *potentia*, he is instead concerned with what power can do when exercised. The crucial question then is not *who* has power, but *in what way*, *how much*, and *why* power is exercised, as it is then that the possibility is always left open that power relations can be subjected to critique and become a locus of struggles.[12]

---

[9] The notion of power has been used in diverse ways in sociology and philosophy. For Weber, power reveals opportunities manifesting the will to resist, oppose, and impose, see Max Weber, *Basic Concepts in Sociology*, H.P. Secher (translator) (London, 1962); Max Rheinstein (ed.), *Max Weber on Law in Economy and Society* (Cambridge, 1954), 323. For Arendt, power is the opposite of violence, presenting us with the collective capacity of society to pursue common goals, see Hannah Arendt, *On Violence* (New York, 1969); Jürgen Habermas, 'Hannah Arendt's Communications Concept of Power', in Stephen Lukes (ed.), *Power: Readings in Social and Political Theory* (New York, 1986). For Habermas, it is 'communicative', and embraces the potential of engaging individuals in fruitful dialogue. In Luhmann's social systems theory, power is again 'communicative', and is understood from a functional perspective as a symbolically generalized medium of communication, operating in the context of societal evolution.

[10] Friedrich Nietzsche, *Thus Spoke Zarathustra*, R.J. Hollingdale (translator) (London, 1969); Friedrich Nietzsche, *Beyond Good and Evil*, W. Kaufman (translator) (New York, 1966).

[11] Michel Foucault, *The History of Sexuality*, R. Hurley (translator) (3 vols, New York, 1978).

[12] On this point see also Michael Hardt and Gilles Deleuze, *An Apprenticeship in Philosophy* (Minneapolis, 1993). In political science important contributors are, amongst many others, Dahl and Lukes. Lukes's three dimensional concept of power includes the power to make decisions, set agendas, and shape preferences, Stephen Lukes, *Power: A Radical Review* (London, 1974). Dahl examines how power is exercised and the kind of resources available to agents, Robert Dahl, 'The Concept of Power', *Behavioural Science*, 2/3 (1957): 201–15.

Bourdieu views power at the heart of any analysis seeking to explain action, and describes it in terms of the forms of capital people have access to, use, preserve, or maximize, in different social fields.[13] He identifies various types of capital throughout his work, for example cultural, economic, social, juridical, and symbolic capital, while he views the individual types of capital as having the potential to convert into other forms. Thus, by recognizing many different varieties of capital apart from the economic one, this concept discards an understanding of agents as engaging (only) in profit maximization activities.

In reference to *juridical capital*, Bourdieu argues that its attributes imply that every decision is based on a precedent, and that a rational approach is applied that guarantees the continuity, certainty, and objectivity of decisions. Moreover, the constitution of a field of study with a juridical element is inseparable from the monopoly of professionals over the production of the particular category of products called 'legal products'. The legal competence determines the conflicts and the specific form that these should have in order to be proper legal battles.[14]

However, Bourdieu argues that juridical capital is an objectified and codified form of *symbolic capital*, which consists of the power to shape mainstream understandings. Symbolic capital designates the symbolic power of a group or an individual,[15] with authority, knowledge, prestige, reputation, and academic degrees, being its possible forms. Therefore, the granting of an *élite* degree is a rite of institution,[16] since it differentiates those destined to occupy eminent social positions from those who will not. Still, symbolic capital is a notion that may better reveal its properties if understood as interweaving with the concepts of *symbolic violence* and *principles of division*.

If the administrative function is conceived as an important locus of the symbolic violence of the state (or, in our case, of the sum of institutions constituting the EU political system), the notion of symbolic capital implies the imposition of

---

13 Pierre Bourdieu, 'The Forms of Capital' in John G. Richardson (ed.), *Handbook of Theory and Research for the Sociology of Education* (New York: 1986), 241; Pierre Bourdieu, *Language and Symbolic Power*, G. Raymond and M. Adamson (translators) (Cambridge UK, 1991). All human actions take place within social fields, where individuals and institutions try to acquire or maximize resources (capital) specific to the particular field of study. Unfortunately, a detailed discussion cannot be undertaken here, as it falls outside the scope of the chapter.

14 Pierre Bourdieu, 'La Force Du Droit: Eléments Pour Une Sociologie du Champ Juridique', *Actes de la Recherche en Sciences Sociales*, 64/9 (1986): 3–19, translated as 'Force of Law', *Hastings Law Journal*, 38/5 (1987): 805–53, R. Terdiman (translator and introduction).

15 As Weber noted:

> those privileged through existing political, social, and economic orders never wield their power naked. They wish to see their positions transformed from purely factual power relations into a cosmos of acquired rights and to know that they are thus sanctified. Max Weber, 'The Meaning of Discipline', in Hans Gerth, and C. Wright Mills (eds), *From Max Weber: Essays in Sociology* (London, 1948).

16 Bourdieu, 'La Force Du Droit'.

principles of division upon which different social groups base their perception of what constitutes an 'insider' and an 'outsider', a 'well-educated' and 'ill-educated' person, an 'expert' and a 'layman'. Bourdieu elaborated on the notion of principles of division in *Distinction.*[17]

Moreover, the notion of symbolic violence is meant to intertwine with the concept of misrecognition. The latter notion implies the process whereby power relations come to be perceived by individuals by rendering the world reasonable, legitimizing the existing power relations to those subject to power. This approach reveals the potential of power being exercised in less visible ways, being encapsulated in what is thought to be 'normal' and 'appropriate'. Therefore, misrecognized power allows for the reproduction of the social order by setting the framework of action. Symbolic capital operates through misrecognition, as authority and the power to shape mainstream understandings is often premised on taken for granted perceptions of the social world. To illustrate this, the symbolic capital of a judge rests on the assumption that she objectively and neutrally applies the law.

To employ the latter reflections in the context of Internet regulation in Europe, it is important to note that Bourdieu, in 'Force de Droit', insists that the inhabitants of a juridical field seek to establish the legitimacy of interpretations favourable to maintaining order in the field. One of the most important strategies employed to do this is by means of linguistic strategies, which result in imposing the illusion of objectivity. Based on this reflection, the following paragraphs will argue that when regulatory law becomes a rationalist endeavour, we are trapped in observing the final product of a process. The effects of power remain disguised, and similarly, the fact that the symbolic violence of the state can still be exercised in invisible ways by the administration, remains unnoticed.

In 'Force de Droit', Bourdieu attacks Austin's argument that law has the inherent capacity to do things with words, an effect that Bourdieu terms the law's power of form, understood as in the formalization and codification capacity of the legal text. Bourdieu attacks the argument that law derives its authority by virtue of rules inherent in language as, according to him, authority interweaves with the symbolic power of the state delegated to a particular individual. Nonetheless, he accepts the importance of the written formalization of legal texts in creating the tacit faith in the basic principle of the juridical order, law's impartiality and neutrality.[18]

Proceduralization understands the administration as playing an impartial role in coordinating the engagement of interested parties in decision making, by means of engaging in the technical execution of the mandate of procedural rules. However, there is an element of formalism in the attempt to portray the administration as a technocracy merely applying the law.[19] At the same time, such an approach comes

---

[17] Pierre Bourdieu, *Distinction: A Social Critique of the Judgment of Taste*, C. Volk (translator) (Chicago and London, 1984).

[18] Ibid.

[19] See Frank I. Michelman, 'Family Quarrel', *Cardozo Law Review*, 17/5 (1996): 1163–84, where the author criticizes Habermas's thesis. On formalism and the problem of legal

close to Weber's ideal type of bureaucracy, a position also adopted by Bourdieu when describing legal rationality and the mindset of people engaging in the production and interpretation of law. However, Bourdieu adopts the Weberian view of bureaucracy, with a view to launch a critique against the tacit faith in law's impartiality and neutrality and any formalistic understanding of the function of the administration.

'Procedural rationality' and 'risk management' are underlied by formalistic presumptions in the sense that they promise neutrality, when providing for the impartial management of practical matters. On the other hand, reproducing the image of neutrality and impartiality is one of the main strategies used by administrations to pursue their interests. The logical question then is: what are the interests of the European administration? The most fundamental interest consists of accumulating and preserving symbolic capital, which implies the power to shape mainstream understandings by supporting an authoritative opinion, and in this way sustain its position as a major think tank. Nevertheless, influencing future developments is now done in indirect ways. Sustaining the belief in the neutrality and objectivity of regulatory law is crucial to achieve the above. In other words, the European Commission may be pursuing certain policy outcomes, but this is undertaken in the light of preserving forms of capital. It seeks to enhance its position as a major think tank, and remain a crucial locus of governance, and the best way to do this is by sustaining the belief in the neutrality and objectivity of law by virtue of its juridical capital, which gives legitimacy to the point of view that regulatory law is to encapsulate.

Accumulating or preserving *technocratic/informational* capital is also important for this purpose. The main quality of this form of capital consists of the ability of authorities to collect information and treat it through classification systems (for example according to sex) inscribed in law, and through bureaucratic procedures. The concentration of this form of capital is crucial, so that the juridical capital performs one of its main tasks: fitting the social world in legal categories, which ultimately implies imposing common forms of vision and division, forms of thinking, and forms of classification.[20]

However, maximizing capital is subject to minds, cognitive schemas. To give an example, maximizing juridical capital, the power to fit the social world in legal categories, may be performed in the light of *compromise*, understood as an

---

interpretation see Duncan Kennedy, *A Critique of Adjudication* (Cambridge, 1997); James Boyd White, *Justice as Translation: An Essay in Cultural and Legal Criticism* (Chicago, 1990); James B. White, *Acts of Hope: Creating Authority in Literature, Law, and Politics*, (Chicago, 1994); Georgia Warnke, *Justice And Interpretation* (Cambridge, 1993); Stanley Fish, *There's No Such Thing as Free Speech ... and it's a Good Thing, Too* (New York, 1994); Costas Douzinas, Peter Goodrich, and Yifat Hachamovitch (eds), *Politics, Postmodernity and Critical Legal Studies: The Legality of the Contingent* (London, 1994); David F. Carlson and Peter Goodrich (eds), *Law and the Postmodern Mind: Essays in Psychoanalysis and Jurisprudence* (Michigan, 1998).

20 Pierre Bourdieu, 'Rethinking the State: Genesis and Structure of the Bureaucratic Field', *Sociological Theory*, 12/1 (1994): 5–10.

anthropological category of praxis, as the previous chapter sought to illustrate. However, there are times when agents lose perspective of the fact that the legal order is their own creation, reproduced and altered by them. In this instance, the natural and social world appears self-evident and is uncontested, due to the lack of awareness of subjective influence on what appears as objective reality. For example, when 'bureaucracies create social problems by recognizing them and providing information and advice',[21] they set the agenda, as certain problems are included while others are excluded, and as such they impose a certain vocabulary framing the debate, 'present(ing) us with an ought by merely stating an is'.[22]

However, when a bureaucracy itself engages in the production of proposals and regulatory measures by applying a rational analysis in the course of undertaking the impartial management of practical issues, most of the time it tacitly accepts and reproduces the belief in the objectivity and impartiality of regulatory law, while failing to see that its decisions are the product of specific socio-historical circumstances. This is a proposition that does away with an understanding of agents as solely pursuing their interests on a rational basis. The following sections will anchor the discussion in the context of Internet regulation.

Law, Code, and Internet Regulation

Regulating the Internet is not an easy task. As it grows more and more popular, there is a widespread impression that it is a virtual Wild West, where opportunists would jump at any chance. There are various reasons for this. One of the problems concerns practices viewed as anti-competitive conduct, as it would be the case if search engine providers favoured particular sites. A different problem emerges as, since the Internet is a transnational communication medium, there is little that can be done to prevent users from arranging their illegal actions, so that they evade domestic regulations by taking advantage of foreign regulatory regimes. Even the effectiveness of European data protection laws is reduced, when personal information can be stored in offshore data havens.[23] Moreover, intellectual property rights are threatened by peer-to-peer communication systems such as Kazaa, Grokster, and Morpheus. The above link to the problem of anonymity; this does not concern the world wide web, where a host service has the means to know the content provider. Anonymity allows users to send emails to a USENET newsgroup without the recipient knowing their email address,

---

21 Ibid.

22 Ibid.

23 Michael Froomkin, 'The Internet as a Source of Regulatory Arbitrage', in Brian Kahin and Charles Nesson (eds), *Borders in Cyberspace, Information Policy and the Global Information Infrastructure* (Cambridge, 1997); Brian D. Loader (ed.), *The Governance of Cyberspace* (London and New York, 1997); Andrew Murray and Colin Scott, 'Controlling the New Media: Hybrid Responses to New Forms of Power', *Modern Law Review*, 65/4 (2002): 491–516.

because an intermediary (the anonymous remailer) has removed this information by means of a technique called encryption.[24]

Nonetheless, NGOs, business, and the European Commission seem to react in diverse ways, as to what the right way to approach the particular problems emerging in the context of the new media is. For example, with reference to the problem of anonymity, the European Commission, and in particular DG Justice and Home Affairs, argues that other key areas of public policy, such as the fight against illegal content, financial fraud, and copyright infringements, may stand in conflict with the right to freedom of expression, privacy, and data protection, which support anonymity. Therefore, the right to anonymity may be restricted, since, according to the European Convention of Human Rights, fundamental rights may be subject to certain limitations for specified reasons including the prevention of crime, with the principle of proportionality being the crucial test that any restrictive measure should pass in order to be applied.

Yet, Internet communities believe that since the Internet reveals on the one hand, the potential of free expression and exchange of ideas, and on the other hand, the possibility of greater involvement in politics, then its regulation should be left in the hands of the various communities inhabiting this virtual global city. The argument further suggests that it should be up to the users to decide for example whether and how they want to punish an unwanted intruder in a virtual chat room on the USENET system. Business groups also support self-regulation. The efforts of the International Chamber of Commerce (ICC)[25] present an example of this. Most recent efforts include the establishment of a global action plan on e-commerce, setting the conditions for the development of global self-regulation. ICC has been successful so far in having its standard on privacy marks prevail to the one developed under the auspices of the International Organization for Standardization (ISO).[26]

Nevertheless, the possibility of users' self-regulation is considered as an anathema by business actors, since it implies the potential of their intellectual property rights being infringed, and generally delaying the development of the conditions that would

[24] Encryption also refers to the encoding of plain text into non readable form, providing privacy. The receiver of the encrypted text uses a 'key' to decrypt the message, and convert it to plain text form. For the problem of encryption techniques see Manuel Castells, *The Internet Galaxy: Reflections on the Internet, Business and Society* (Oxford and New York, 2001), 181–3. Disappearing Inc. and ZipLip created self-deleting email, which encrypts users' information. Zero-knowledge Systems created a software package, which aims at providing the user with five pseudonyms, while the company itself does not have the means to know the real identity of users. Freedom encrypts email and web browsing by sending them through intermediary routers. Similar techniques are employed by Anonymizer.com and Idzap.com.

[25] ICC is the world business organization representing enterprises from all sectors in every part of the world.

[26] John Braithwaite, and Peter Drahos, *Global Business Regulation* (Cambridge UK, 2000). The ISO is a network of national standards institutes from 140 countries working in partnership with international organizations, governments, industry, business, and consumer representatives.

guarantee the flourishing of e-commerce. It is in this context that the industry strived to develop architectural solutions, as it was the case with software used to render the copying of DVDs more difficult. The problem was that this also resulted in only certain players and discs being capable of decrypting the necessary files to play a DVD.

This is why, in December 1999, a 15-year old Norwegian, Jon Johansen, who participated in the open source development of the Linux operating system, reverse-engineered the Content Scrambling System (CSS) encryption code on DVDs and emailed the decoder, called DeCSS, to the Internet. In this case, reverse engineering was used for the sake of interoperability, in order to create new software for DVD players compatible with Linux-based machines.[27] The DeCSS code spread among Linux developers on the net, as 2600 Magazine and other publishers put it on their website, with an article on it and links to other locations publishing it, but the problem was that it was also used to crack the code of DVDs to illegally copy them onto CDs.

Lessig's position is well known with regard to the above developments.[28] In particular, he argued that the various constraints built into software by their designers may be conceptualized as a form of regulation. Nevertheless, systems such as CSS make illegal copying more difficult, maybe even impractical, but not impossible. In other words, design or code proves not to be enough to regulate conduct. As such, hierarchical controls may be required to be enacted to create a 'design/hierarchy' hybrid of regulatory control.[29] This hybrid illustrates the symbiotic relationship of law and code in regulation. As the weakness of code is that it may always be decrypted or engineered, it needs an element of legal/hierarchical regulatory assistance to add strength to the design regulation.

Architectural controls are supported not only by the industry, but also by the World Intellectual Property Organization (WIPO) Treaties, as enacted within the European Union by the Directive on Certain Aspects of Copyright and Related Rights in the Information Society (Information Society Directive),[30] and in the

---

[27] Reverse engineering involves taking apart the features of a program, in order to see how it works, and how its performance can be improved. In the EU, reverse engineering is allowed for legitimate purposes (interoperability and the correction of errors). In the US the right of users to reverse engineer has been recognized in 1992 in Sega Enterprises Ltd v Accolade Inc., 977 F.2d 1510, and Atari Games Corp. v Nintendo of America Inc., 975 F.2d 832. The Linux operating system (OS) is competing with Microsoft's OS. Linux is an open source system, which means that everybody has access to its code to modify it, as opposed to the proprietary standards of Microsoft's OS.

[28] Lessig, *Code and Other Laws in Cyberspace*, 190. It is beyond the scope of this chapter to fully comment on Lessig's work on the various forms of regulation on the net. For a criticism of Lessig's work, particularly on the issue of whether law is an important regulatory mechanism in cyberspace, see David G. Post, 'What Larry Doesn't Get: Code, Law and Liberty in Cyberspace', *Stanford Law Review*, 52/4 (2000): 1439–59.

[29] Murray and Scott 'Controlling the New Media', 502, 506, and 513.

[30] Article 6 of Directive 2001/29.

United States through the Digital Millennium Copyright Act 1998.[31] In particular, Article 11 of the WIPO treaties urges parties:

> to provide adequate legal protection and effective legal remedies against the circumvention of effective technological measures that are used by authors in connection with their exercise of rights under this Treaty or the Berne Convention and that restrict acts, in respect of their works, which are not authorized by the authors concerned or permitted by law.

However, the DeCSS decoder *is* available on the net and *has* made it possible for DVD material to be put directly onto the web. Currently there are many web pages that give precise instructions as to how DVDs can be copied in users' hardware. Companies updated the encryption technology, but the Internet community produced more advanced decryption codes. Nonetheless, if one takes into account the thriving number of websites specializing in distributing decoding technology, it seems that architectural solutions, and hybrid hierarchy/design based regulatory structures, are not always successful.

To sum up, it appears that self-regulation is not the norm, but an element of hierarchical control is required to strengthen the application of design. Moreover, it may be that different self-regulatory codes of conduct of communities active in cyberworld may oppose each other (for example the free speech on the web position versus the intellectual property rights position). In other words, two different codes of conduct of two communities may be in conflict. In such a situation, we should not forget that, when a hierarchical element is introduced (as in the Information Society Directive) to strengthen architectural controls when these fail to regulate conduct, then the Directive inevitably would have to make a normative choice by means of endorsing *one* of the two positions.

The following section will take this point further by examining two different instances: domain name allocation, where a mix of hierarchical control and self-regulation was employed, and the Safer Internet Action Plan, characterized as soft law. The aim is to question the nature of the hierarchical element in hybrid forms of regulation, and to finally address the following two questions: how easy (or difficult) is it to actually separate procedural rules from norms? What is the role of the European Commission in the process of applying and interpreting the law?

Scarce Resources: Domain Name Allocation

Both DG Competition and DG Information Society of the European Commission promote the view that, although the decentralized character of the Internet epitomizes the argument for self-regulation, scarce resources and bottlenecks present a case where a mix of self-regulation and hierarchical intervention is required.[32]

---

[31] Section 1201(a)(1) and 1201(a)(2) of Digital Millennium Copyright Act 1998.

[32] Murray and Scott 'Controlling the New Media', 506 and 511.

A particular scarce resource on the Internet is the domain name allocation system. The Internet Corporation for Assigned Names and Numbers (ICANN)[33] controls the allocation in a non-hierarchical fashion, according to the demands of the community. The problem with domain names is that, although they can consist of up to 61 characters, usable domain names are almost entirely the .com top level ones. Hierarchical solutions were employed by ICANN and its predecessors, Network Solutions, in the form of domain name related dispute resolution. The need for dispute resolution was persistent in view of the problem of 'cybersquatting'. This emerges when individuals register popular domain names to subsequently sell them to the holder of the trademark.

Nonetheless, the Internet community failed to impose sanctions on these persons. Although courts could intervene in cases where cybersquatters had misappropriated another's trademark, enforcement could prove problematic due to regulatory arbitrage. Therefore, a regulatory regime was put in place, which would apply no matter what the jurisdiction of the parties is. In particular, ICANN treats the domain name space as a separate jurisdiction, and all domain name holders have the obligation to submit themselves to its arbitration procedure, which is conducted online and is characterized by low costs.

In October 1999, ICANN adopted its Uniform Domain Name Dispute Resolution Policy (UDRP).[34] Part of the registration process for obtaining a domain name includes acceptance of the UDRP, while a domain name owner can lose her rights to the domain name if she violates the Policy.[35] Paragraph 4 of the UDRP explains the mandatory administrative proceedings. Proceedings are instituted when a third party complainant asserts that the domain name owner used a domain name that is identical or confusingly similar to the complainant's mark, when the domain name owner does not have rights or legitimate interests in the name, and when the domain name has been registered and used in bad faith.[36] The UDRP lists four non-exclusive

---

[33] ICANN is a non-governmental not for profit agency. In June 1998 the US Department of Commerce released a White Paper on the administration of internet names and numbers, which aimed at transferring the administration of internet domain names and IP addresses from the US Federal Government into the hands of a private non-profit, internationally representative organization, which would be self-regulated. Governments would not intervene in its powers and structure. Instead, the private sector would form an organization based on consensus amongst members of the industry. ICANN works together with WIPO, which provides the expertise required for the development of effective procedures. On these issues see Milton Mueller, 'ICANN and Internet Governance: Sorting Through the Debris of Self-Regulation', *Info* 1/6 (1999): 477–500.

[34] http://www.icann.org/udrp/udrp-policy-24oct99.htm (webpage visited on 2 August 2005).

[35] Ibid., Paragraph 3 of the UDRP.

[36] Paragraph 4(a) UDRP.

factors to be considered in determining bad faith.[37] If *all* of the above conditions are met, the remedies sought are the cancellation of the domain name, or the transfer of the domain name to the complainant owner of the mark.[38] Nonetheless, there is strong criticism of the role of ICANN, as commentators have noted that it 'favours trade mark holders over domain name holders who fail, for whatever reason to comply with US trademark law'.[39] The so-called 'sucks' cases prove to be quite controversial. It was argued that free speech on the web was seriously curtailed, after domain names were transferred to trademark holders following arbitration.[40]

---

[37] Paragraph 4(b)(i)–(iv) UDRP.

For the purposes of Paragraph 4(a)(iii): the following circumstances, in particular but without limitation, if found by the Panel to be present, shall be evidence of the registration and use of a domain name in bad faith: (i) circumstances indicating that you have registered or you have acquired the domain name primarily for the purpose of selling, renting, or otherwise transferring the domain name registration to the complainant who is the owner of the trademark or service mark or to a competitor of that complainant, for valuable consideration in excess of your documented out-of-pocket costs directly related to the domain name; or (ii) you have registered the domain name in order to prevent the owner of the trademark or service mark from reflecting the mark in a corresponding domain name, provided that you have engaged in a pattern of such conduct; or (iii) you have registered the domain name primarily for the purpose of disrupting the business of a competitor; or (iv) by using the domain name, you have intentionally attempted to attract, for commercial gain, Internet users to your web site or other on-line location, by creating a likelihood of confusion with the complainant's mark as to the source, sponsorship, affiliation, or endorsement of your web site or location or of a product or service on your web site or location.

[38] Paragraph 4(a) of the UDRP.

[39] Murray and Scott, 'Controlling the New Media', 507, citing Michael Froomkin, 'Wrong Turn in Cyberspace: Using ICANN to Route Around the APA and the Constitution', *Duke Law Journal*, 50/17 (2000): 96–101. Also see Christopher R. Perry, 'Trademarks as Commodities: The Famous Roadblock to Applying Trademark Dilution Law in Cyberspace', *Connecticut Law Review*, 32/ 1 (2000): 1127–57, 1127, 1155–7.

[40] On these issues see Andrew Murray, 'Regulation and Rights in Networked Place', *Journal of Law and Society*, 30/2 (2003): 187–216. The author argues that normally a purely non-commercial use of the trademark for the purpose of criticism should be an absolute defence, as in this instance the arbitrator has to strike a fair balance between property rights and the right to free speech. Nevertheless, the UDRP provides a poor understanding of what constitutes a fair defence. This is because the non-commercial use defence can only be used if a trademark has not been *tarnished* (associated with obscenity) and if consumers have not been *misleadingly diverted from the trademark holder's business*. Murray argues that these two conditions substantially impoverish the fair use defence, as arbitrators found that search engines were likely to identify the '*sucks.com*' sites in response to, for example, a 'Wal-Mart' query. Internet users might then visit these sites, a process diverting potential customers from Wal-Mart. Thus, arbitrators pointed to the particularities of search engines, which, if taken into account, should lead to a different analysis than the one conducted in the physical world, see Dixons Group Plc v Mr. Abu Abdullaah, D2000-1406, (WIPO January 18, 2001). For tarnishment see L. Bently, and B. Sherman, *Intellectual Property Law*, (Oxford, 2001); Also see Mathias Strasser, 'The Rational Basis of Trademark Protection Revisited: Putting

A different problem occurred with establishing the criteria, which should underlie the trademark confusion test. For example, in Wal-Mart Stores Inc. v. Walsucks and Walmarket Puerto Rico,[41] it was decided that *walmartcanadasucks.com, wal-martcanadasucks.com, walmartuksucks.com, walmartpuertorico.com* and *walmartpuertoricosucks.com*, are confusingly similar to its trademark. In particular in point 6 of the decision the panelist found that:

> Respondent has registered the domain names 'walmartcanadasucks.com', 'wal-martcanadasucks.com','walmartuksucks.com' and 'walmartpuertoricosucks.com'. These domain names share common characteristics. In each case, Complainant's 'Wal-Mart' trademark is followed with an indication of place (Canada, Canada, UK and Puerto Rico, respectively). In *Wal-Mart v. Walmarket Canada*, it was determined that 'walmartcanada.com' and 'Wal-Mart' are confusingly similar. The Panel accepts this determination. The addition of a hyphen to form 'wal-martcanada.com' does not affect this finding. … Respondent has appended the term '-sucks' to domain names that are, in the absence of that term, confusingly similar to Complainant's mark. The addition of the pejorative verb 'sucks' is tantamount to creating the phrase 'Wal-Mart Canada sucks' (and comparable phrases with Respondent's other '-sucks' formative domain names). The elimination of the spacing between the terms of the phrase is dictated by technical factors, and by the common practice of domain name registrants. The addition of a common or generic term following a trademark does not create a new or different mark in which Respondent has rights.

Very importantly, the arbitrator held that there was strong evidence of bad faith, since the respondent registered the webpages for commercial purpose, thus he could not invoke fair use or legitimate non-commercial use permitted by paragraph 4(c)(iii) of the Policy. Similarly, some other 'sucks' cases decided (freeservesucks.com, natwestsucks.com, directlinesucks.com, dixonssucks.com and standardcharteredsucks.com) were all registered by the same respondent who asked money to return the name.[42]

Nevertheless, for natwestsucks.com, for example, to pass the confusion threshold, in point 5 of the decision the panel concluded that:

> Some will treat the additional 'sucks' as a pejorative exclamation and therefore dissociate it after all from the Complainant; but equally others may be unable to give it any very definite meaning and will be confused about the potential association with the Complainant.[43]

In this case, it appears that arbitrators stretched the UDRP criteria in order to meet the test of trademark confusion. In a different case, disquiet was raised as a result of the arbitrator's finding that 'guinness-really-sucks' is confusingly similar to the Guinness

---

the Dilution Doctrine into Context', *Fordham Media and Entertainment Law Journal*, 10/2 (2000): 331–74.

[41] *Wal-Mart Stores Inc. v. Walsucks and Walmarket Puerto Rico*, D2000-0477.

[42] Case No. D2000-0636 (Natwestsucks), Case No. D2000-0583 (Directlinesucks.com), Case No. D2000-0584 (Dixonssucks.com), Case No. D2000-0585 (Freeservesucks.com) and Case No.D2000-0681 (Standardcharteredsucks.com).

[43] Case No. D2000-0636 (Natwestsucks).

trademark.[44] Interestingly, in this case the element of bad faith was established, as the respondent was thought to have registered the disputed domain names for retaliatory purposes, because he was angered by the complainant's registration of the domain name guinnessucks.com. Therefore, the panelist accepted that the complainant made out a *prima facie* case that the respondent registered the domain names with the intention of harassing the complainant to enforce its trademark rights, and to tarnish the Guinness trademark.[45]

Criticizing the legal basis of the decisions is not enough to reveal the problems inherent in the process of arbitration.[46] Questioning who participates in the panel is crucially important for this purpose. According to Froomkin, the problem with arbitration is that ICANN allows the complainants to engage in 'forum shopping', in other words choose the arbitration provider.[47] The vast majority of disputes are being adjudicated by arbitrators from WIPO (with most of its members being practicing lawyers), and from the National Arbitration Forum based in Minnesota (with most of its members being retired judges).[48] Another provider is eResolution, based in Montreal, while the CPR Institute for Dispute Resolution is the fourth provider available to parties.

Froomkin believes that accredited registrars should select which forum will handle cases involving their domain customers. This is because, while:

---

[44] Case No.D2000–0996. In this case, the respondent has registered the domain names guinness-really-sucks.com; guinness-really-really-sucks.com; guinness-beer-really-sucks.com; guinness-beer-really-really-sucks.com guinness-sucks.com; guinnessreallysucks.com; guinnessreallyreallysucks.com; guinnessbeerreallysucks.com; guinness-beer-sucks.com; guinnessbeersucks.com. With specific reference to Paragraphs 4(i) of the UDRP, the administrative panel decided that they are confusingly similar to a trademark or service mark in which the complainant has rights. Therefore, the respondent has no rights or legitimate interest in respect of said domain names, and he has registered, and is using said domain names in bad faith. Accordingly, the said domain names should be transferred to the Complainant. As regards the conditions of 'bad faith' and 'legitimate interest' the panellist followed the line of argumentation exposed in Wal-Mart. As for the test of similarity, the panellist went on to point out that there may be some non-English-speaking readers, who may not be familiar with the word 'sucks'.

[45] Case No. D2000–0996.

[46] See for example Murray, 'Regulation and Rights in Networked Place'; Milton Mueller, Ruling the Root: Internet Governance and the Taming of Cyberspace (Cambridge, 2002); Milton Mueller, 'Rough Justice: A Statistical Assessment of ICANN's Uniform Dispute Resolution Policy', The Information Society, 17/3 (2001): 153–63; Mueller, 'ICANN and Internet Governance'.

[47] Brian McWilliams, 'Domain Arbitration Already Drawing Critics', story published on internetnews.com on 8 March 2002, including an interview with Michael Froomkin, Professor of Law, University of Miami.

[48] Empirical research on the composition of arbitration panels has been carried out by Murray, 'Regulation and Rights in a Networked Place'.

> on paper this process should be fair, I foresee a serious danger. Since plaintiffs get to choose the arbitration provider, this creates an economic incentive for companies to compete on being pro-plaintiff if they want business.[49]

The purpose of the previous analysis is to draw attention to that trivial decisions, for instance regulating the choice of arbitrator, may be crucial. This latter point will be further taken up in the following section.

Establishing the Difference between the Joint Partnership Model and the Self-Regulation Model

Pure forms of self-regulation, as in the case of having to abide by codes of conduct, are not the norm. Most of the time, some form of hierarchical assistance is required in the monitoring and enforcement stage, as in the dispute resolution mechanism introduced by ICANN, and in the Information Society Directive supporting architectural solutions developed for DVDs.[50] Nonetheless it would be wrong to consider that private interests solely support such a decentralized form of governance. For example, the European Commission plays a major role in the coordination of Internet management and in initiating consultations between itself, the private sector, and civil society. To this effect, the European Commission:

> should develop, in conjunction with ICANN, effective codes of conduct (supported by legislation as appropriate), to cover the allocation and protection of domain names, to combat fraud and cybersquatting, and to regulate access to personal data and the security and protection thereof.[51]

---

[49] Michael Froomkin, 'ICANN'S Uniform Dispute Resolution Policy: Causes and (Partial) Cures', *Brooklyn Law Review*, 67/3 (2002): 608–718, 671 and 689. Jonathan Weinberg, 'Rating the Net', *Hastings Communication and Entertainment Law Journal*, 19/2 (1997): 453–82.

[50] Encouragement by the state for industry self-regulation initiatives is sometimes labelled 'co-regulation'. As the term is being used in the current EU debate, it refers to the setting of standards by non-state actors, while monitoring and enforcement is conducted by regulatory authorities.

[51] European Parliament resolution on the Commission Communication to the Council and the European Parliament on the Organization and Management of the Internet – International and European Policy Issues 1998–2000 COM(2000) 202, point 14. During ICANN's first steps, to temper disquiet on the part of the EU as to the affinity between the US Commerce Department and ICANN, the US promised the Europeans that they would have three of the nine seats on the corporation's Interim Board. Critics in Europe have recently called the US to relinquish control over domain name allocation, and decentralize control, so that the management of country codes is undertaken by local governments and technical administrators. Moreover, the argument has been made that an international body, such as the United Nations (UN) International Telecommunication Union, should be entrusted with the task of handling basic policies over Internet addresses. The UN World Summit on the

Furthermore it is expected to promote effective alternative dispute resolution procedures to reinforce the domain name registry codes of conduct; conduct calls for a periodical evaluation of whether legislative action and self-regulatory measures have actually achieved the desired effect; aim at making the European regulatory strategies in the above areas best practice across the world Internet.

However, various commentators have noted that ICANN has failed to fulfill its promise to provide a forum for self-regulation. The White Paper produced by the US government called upon ICANN to open up the .com, .net, and .org TLDs to competing registrars and put in place a dispute resolution system together with WIPO. However, with WIPO providing the necessary expertise to develop appropriate rules of conduct to make the Internet a safer place in view of the problem of cybersquatting, simultaneously meant that a maximalist definition of intellectual property rights entered the vocabulary of ICANN. As for ICANN's board, it is true that 9 out of its 18 members were to be appointed by virtue of an election where the Internet community at large could participate. The rest were appointed by supporting organizations, such as the Address Supporting Organization, the Protocol Supporting Organization, and the Domain Name Supporting Organization.

Castells argues that the romantic vision of the Internet community, regulating itself according to its needs, was tempered by the reality of powerful lobbyists and networks influencing the election of particular candidates in ICANN's board. This is why government representatives who sit in ICANN's board expressed their disquiet when Andy Mueller was elected, as he was member of the (in)famous Chaos Computer Club in Berlin, representing Internet communities' interests.[52] Nevertheless, in 2002 ICANN suggested that there should be no more at large elections, as it considered that the experiment in global online democracy is noble, but deeply unrealistic. The online election of individual Internet users to the group's executive board was abolished.[53]

As for the dispute resolution in particular, Froomkin argues that ICANN has completely failed:

> ICANN has so far demonstrated a complete failure to monitor the activities of the dispute providers, and has taken no action when they write rules that are biased for plaintiffs. The most likely reason for that disinterest is that ICANN, which heavily represents trademark and other business interests, is not troubled by those rules, just as it was not troubled by the UDRP. The lobbies that dominate ICANN would be much quicker to demand action if the bias ran the other way, and were a rogue provider to materialize, one can reasonably expect that ICANN would be quick to take action against it.[54]

Information Society, held in Geneva (2003) and Tunis (2005), did not reach agreement on this point.

[52] Castells, *The Internet Galaxy*, 2.

[53] Instead, the members of the board of directors will be drawn from representatives of technical, business, government, and nonprofit organizations, Reuters 28 June 2002.

[54] Froomkin, 'ICANN's Uniform Dispute Resolution Policy', 671, 689, 692.

The basic point emerging from the previous discussion is that one may encounter difficulties in establishing what the difference between the joint partnership model and the self-regulation approach is. The former position understands the state as retaining greater powers extending beyond monitoring and enforcement, and as such it is one among the many actors who directly intervene in the shaping of regulation. Self-regulation may require the state to put the framework necessary to enable monitor and enforcement, which implies that regulatory authorities retain responsibility for ensuring that controls are effective, and intervene where controls fail.

However, although regulatory authorities argue that their role in the latter case is limited, in reality it is not. ICANN and the problem that emerged in relation to domain name allocation is one example that may help illustrate the latter point, as mundane decisions in reference to who the judge is in the arbitration procedure may be crucial, and it seems that national governments, WIPO, and the EU do have a say on these issues, as they are influential as to what course such decisions will take.

Monitoring and enforcement present an instance when structural patterns of thinking are encapsulated in tedious procedural rules, which may in reality be loaded with options influencing future developments. This is because, although choices were made as they presented at the time the orthodox way of doing things, this does not mean that they did not preclude the possibility of other, different, heretic ways, existing alongside.[55] These choices are encapsulated in legal rules, and if one accepts the above argument, then there can be no neutral legal rules merely confined to monitoring, enforcement, or facilitation, as a problem is never *a* problem. It is usually a multifaceted problem, and it is only one of its facets that will eventually be actualized by means of entering the monitoring stage.

An example of this is the ICANN arbitration procedure. As we saw, the European Commission thinks that supporting effective alternative dispute resolution procedures, to reinforce the domain name registry codes of conduct, is necessary. What does 'effective' mean? Should an accredited panel choose the arbitrators, or should the solution be found in allowing competition among alternative arbitration forums? The answer in the future will be one of the two alternatives, it cannot be both, and this means that one is excluded. The choice is premised not on the basis of pursuing the public good or individual preferences, but, most of the time, the administration functions on the basis of patterns of praxis reflecting the juridical element of the field, demanding a rational approach safeguarding certainty and continuity, while simultaneously reproducing tacit understandings about the role of intellectual property rights in protecting investment in view of the new global challenges.

All of these points will be followed through in the next section by virtue of another case study: the Safer Internet Action Plan, which seeks to tackle the problem of illegal and harmful content on the net. Why is 'harmful material' a problem, and what is the process behind identifying it as a problem? Moreover, how was 'harmful' defined in the preparatory and implementation stage? The following section will

---

[55] On this point see Chapter Two of this book.

seek to answer these questions, with a view to identify the taken for granted element in the answers furnished.

The Internet Action Plan and Soft Law: Setting the Vocabulary of the Debate

In January 1999, the European Parliament and the Council of the European Union adopted a multiannual Action Plan on promoting safer use of the Internet, by combating illegal and harmful content on global networks.[56] The Safer Internet Action Plan[57] (the Plan) is managed by DG Information Society and is part of the European Union's Research and Technological Development (RTD) Framework Programme.[58] It initially covered the period 1999–2002, but in March 2002 it was decided to fund the Plan with an additional budget of 13.3 million for two more years covering the period 2002–2004,[59] and in 2005 it was agreed to fund it with an additional 45 million Euros covering four more years (2005–2008).

The Plan is developed along three basic lines: it propagates the need to create a safe environment by means of self-regulation (by creating a European network of hot-lines and encouraging self-regulation based on codes of conduct), it supports the development of filtering and rating systems and the adoption of international agreements on rating systems, and finally it seeks to inform parents, teachers, and children of the potentials and drawbacks of the Internet. The Plan is closely related to the activities and priorities of the Multimedia Content and Tools Key Action (KA3) of the Framework Programme. Therefore, it presents a good example of the complex consultation process, which aims at collecting expert knowledge.

The European Commission is surrounded by myriads of committees providing advice on both the development and implementation of legislation.[60] As regards the former, independent experts, who are drawn from throughout the European Union, but do not represent the interests of any Member State or scientific institution, sit in

---

[56] Council Recommendation 98/560/EC of 24 September 1998 on the Development of the Competitiveness of the European Audiovisual and Information Services Industry by Promoting National Frameworks aimed at Achieving a Comparable and Effective Level of Protection of Minors and Human Dignity OJL 270, 48. The Recommendation followed the Communication on Illegal and Harmful Content COM(96) 487, and the European Commission Green Paper COM(96) 483 final on the Protection of Minors and Human Dignity in Information and Audiovisual Services.

[57] Dec 276/1999 of the European Parliament and of the Council of 25 January 1999 adopting the Multiannual Community Action Plan of 06 February 1999 on Promoting Safer Use of the Internet by Combating Illegal and Harmful Content on Global Networks OJL 33, 1.

[58] For the details of this plan see http://www.saferinternet.org/ (webpage visited on 3 May 2006).

[59] The proposal of the European Commission has been adopted by the EP and the Council, 'EU Moves Against Illegal and Harmful Content Online' IP/03/774.

[60] Technological Options Assessment (STOA) Programme of the European Parliament PE 167 327/Fin.St. October 1998 (PE 167 327/ Fin. St.).

expert or scientific committees. The *Comité Scientifique et Technique* (CREST) and the European Research Advisory Board (EURAB) are examples of such committees. Moreover, the same consultative role can be played by Task Forces, (whose members come from various DGs, but can draw upon external advice), and think tanks established by the European Commission, such as the Joint Research Centre.

The European Commission also convenes special 'Reflection Groups' or 'Independent Expert Panels' whose members are high-level European personalities, to advise on particular issues, such as the future macro-organization of the Framework Programme. Moreover, the Research Group of the Committee of Permanent Representatives (COREPER) also provides upstream consultation (on the development of legislation), being a high-level committee set up by the Council of Ministers, representing the interests of Member States.

The European Commission has considerable power to engage effectively in the identification of problems, as it possesses a powerful internal mechanism structured along the lines of a major think tank. Nonetheless, the implementation stage reveals more ways in which the European Commission can be influential. This point will be taken up in the following section.

Implementing the Plan: Self-regulation and the Development of Codes of Conduct

As regards the distribution of illegal content on the Internet, it is up to Member States (MS) to enforce the law, since what is illegal offline remains illegal online. The industry is viewed as playing an important role in helping reduce the circulation of illegal content (especially content such as child pornography, racism, and anti-Semitism) through self-regulation (such as codes of conduct and hotlines) in compliance with the legal system.[61]

Under this action line, the European Commission should develop guidelines for codes of conduct at the European level, build consensus for their application, support their implementation, and monitor progress. Parallel to the establishment of codes of conduct, a system of visible 'Quality-Site Labels' for Internet Service Providers (ISPs) will be developed, aiming at assisting users in identifying providers abiding to these codes of conduct.[62] ISPs will have to remove material from their servers upon request.[63]

---

[61] Green Paper on the Protection of Minors and Human Dignity in Information and Audiovisual Services COM(96) 483.

[62] Intermediate Evaluation of the Safer Internet Action Plan Volume 1, Final Report, 31 May 2001, conducted for the European Commission by Business Development Research Consultants, 18–22.

[63] As for liabilities and obligations of Internet Service providers (ISPs), according to the 1997 Bonn Ministerial Declaration, intermediaries, such as network operators and access providers, should not be responsible for content. Otherwise intermediaries would be made subject to unreasonable, disproportionate, or discriminatory rules. Therefore, third party content hosting services should not be expected to exercise prior control on content if there is no reason to believe it is illegal. The Electronic Commerce Directive (2000/31) endorsed

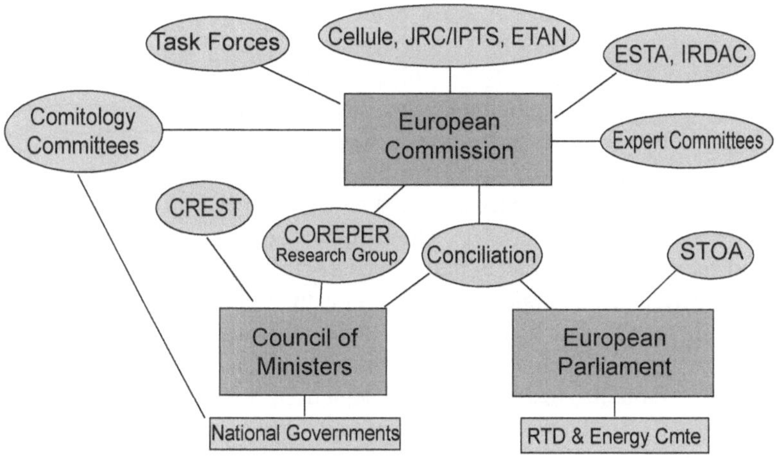

Cellule	[Cellule de Prospective (Forward Studies Unit), European Commission]
COREPER	Committee of Permanent Representatives
CREST	Comité Scientifique et Technique
ESTA	European Science and Technology Assembly
ETAN	European Technology Assessment Network
IPTS	Institute for Prospective Technological Studies
IRDAC	Industrial R&D Advisory Committee
JRC	Joint Research Centres
RTD	Research and Technological Development
STOA	Science and Technology Options Assessment, European Parliament

Figure 4.1 European Community S&T Policy 'Trialogue'

Source: Technological Options Assessment (STOA) Programme of the European Parliament PE 167 327/Fin.St. October 1998 (PE 167 327/ Fin. St.).

Clarifying the rules determining what kind of material should be removed will be subject to an independent national consortium of service providers, where membership will probably be voluntary. An example of relevant organizations is the Internet Content Rating For Europe (INCORE), whose members include broadcasters and people such as the head of the Internet Watch Foundation.[64] This group, registered in England, reviews complaints from the public and takes action by requesting Internet service providers to remove the allegedly illegal material from their servers.

this approach. Nonetheless, although the exemptions provided for may protect the ISPs from liability, they may still be made subject to a court injunction to terminate or prevent access to infringing material. Furthermore, MS may establish procedures governing the removal or disabling of access to information.

64 www.internetwatch.co.uk (webpage visited on 5 August 2005).

Developing Filtering and Rating Systems: Problems with Using Filters to Block Harmful Material

As for harmful content on the Internet,[65] the main objective of the Plan is to make content easier to identify. This can be done through a rating system, which describes the content in accordance with a generally recognized scheme (for instance, where items such as sex or violence are rated on a scale), and by filtering systems, which empower the user to select the content she wishes to receive. The European Commission funds various projects that aim at encouraging the establishment of European rating systems, and familiarizing users with their use.

There are three different kinds of filters used to block harmful content. One of the techniques is called *blacklisting*. It works on the basis of twelve categories (violence/profanity, nudity, sexual acts, gross depictions, racism/ethnic impropriety, satanic/cult, drugs, militant/extremist, gambling, questionable/illegal, alcohol/tobacco). Parents can selectively block access to any or all 12 categories by checking boxes in the program manager. However, *whitelisting* software works on the reverse principle, as it blocks out all Internet content, except expressly authorized sites.

The Platform for Internet Content Selection (PICS) is a different industry-wide standard. All sites with an Internet address must carry a PICS label, which 'tags' sites with a 'neutral' label that supports different types of information: ratings (for instance, generally evaluating language, nudity, sexual content, violence), or pointers (identifying contents according to their relevance or interest for various constituencies of users). To be viewed, the site must both carry a PICS label and be within the parameters set by parents on the home computer. Ratings can be established by content providers themselves (such as entertainment companies operating family-oriented web sites) or third parties (such as religious groups or parents' associations). Each family decides which rating systems it wishes to use, and then they choose what kind of material is acceptable by setting the parameters.[66]

Nonetheless, when the individuals who participated in the evaluation report of the European Commission[67] were asked about what they believe the current scope of the Plan is, they agreed that it does cover, and should cover, child pornography, chat

---

[65] Harmful content is both content which is allowed, but whose distribution is restricted (adults only, for instance), and content which may offend certain users. This is provided in Article 3 of the Communication to the European Parliament, the Council, the Economic and Social Committee and the Committee of the Regions on Illegal and Harmful Content on the Internet COM(96) 487, and in the Green Paper on the Protection of Minors and Human Dignity in Audiovisual and Information Services COM(96) 483.

[66] Intermediate Evaluation of the Safer Internet Action Plan Final Report, 69. In 2005 the ICRA (an international, non-profit membership organization whose members include AOL Europe, Bell Canada, BT Openworld, and others) announced the move from PICS to the W3C RDF standard. According to ICRA, the new standard allows content providers to describe more effectively the type of content published.

[67] These are people who participated or who would be interested in participating in the future in projects funded by the European Commission, Evaluation Report ibid.

rooms, violence, racist and xenophobic ideas, hate speech, and adult pornography. However, the Plan is not so strongly seen as covering satanic and cult ideas, drugs, medical information, and advertising. Yet, participants said that these areas should be included, with the possible exception of advertising. In reviewing the current scope, participants identified a number of areas, which was felt that the Plan had a remit to include (but none were especially strongly supported across all respondents): computer crime, financial scams in relation to the consumer, hooliganism, terrorism, incitement to law-break, gambling, security and hacking, email, newsgroups.[68]

The above analysis points to the particular problems surrounding the effort to produce adequate lists of categories, encapsulating consensus as to what counts as harmful material. A relevant question is whether a wide definition should be adopted and include, for instance, advertising in general. The problem linking to this concerns the difficulty inherent in any effort to fit content in suitable categories. Rating system designers have to devise rule-based systems, which would be sensitive to the complexity of content. Still, how rate a documentary on the war in Iraq, which contains descriptions of sexual violence in military prisons? Moreover, as Boyle argues, although the PICS is a:

> system touted as 'value-neutral', in practice we might believe that the PICs technology would be disproportionately used to favour a particular set of ideas and values and exclude others.[69]

In the light of this position, one could argue that similarly the Plan is not sensitive to other worldviews, such as the one supporting free speech on the web.

This is because, if for example there is a law regulating the use of the web at schools and libraries, filters may be employed as technologies of control, as the choice of filtering categories may result in blocking websites presenting information known to be of concern to people with conservative religious or political values. The Plan may set the framework of future developments, as we should not underestimate how important it is to identify a problem, set the vocabulary of the debate by collecting information on it, and set general directions according to which agents will be mobilized to find solutions to the identified problem. This is a fine example of the ways informational/technocratic capital is reproduced.

Furthermore, there is still scope for important decisions to be taken at the stage of implementation, as, for example, the term 'harmful material' can be given various definitions. For this reason, it may be very difficult to actually separate procedures from norms, as in reality procedures may frame choices and the subject matter of the discussion in such a way that it could be argued that they entail normative content. This is because they encapsulate unspoken patterns of thinking about, for example, the qualities of harmful material and the role of regulatory law.

---

68 Evaluation Report, 35–6.

69 Boyle, James, 'Foucault in Cyberspace: Surveillance, Sovereignty, and Hard-Wired Censors', *University of Cincinnati Law Review*, 66 (1997): 177–93.

Conclusions

Procedural rules are often viewed as providing the impartial management of practical matters. Nevertheless, the thesis advanced in this chapter is that the European Commission pursues its interests and sustains juridical order by giving neutral value to them. Based on the assumption that power is at the heart of action, the most fundamental interest of the European administration consists of accumulating and preserving symbolic capital, which implies the power to shape mainstream understandings, and thus sustain its position as a major think tank. This is most of the time undertaken in accordance with taken for granted patterns of thinking about, for example, the qualities of harmful material, and the nature of regulatory law. Preserving the belief in the neutrality and objectivity of regulatory law is crucial to this effect, but now, influencing future developments is done in indirect ways. To illustrate this, this chapter considered intellectual property rights, focusing on architectural solutions introduced to software by the industry, to turn to domain name allocation by ICANN, while my final case study was on the regulation of harmful and illegal content on the Internet.

Chapter Five

Ruptures in Established Practice

Never trust a person who does not like wine.

Anonymous

Common sense understandings and unspoken patterns of praxis are always potentially subject to change, as they are constantly exposed to novel experience. Therefore, the present analysis seeks to come to grips with the conditions under which knowledge encapsulated in experience may be challenged.

The argument here is that it is antagonisms between different conceptualizations of what is honourable and pleasant that underlie the evolution of the political and legal spheres.[1] Such antagonisms indicate an increase in the will and capacity to change the world, often supported by external conditions creating the need to disrupt routine.[2] The following sections will follow this intuition in the context of the proposal for a Directive on the patentability of computer-implemented inventions. This was subject to intense debate, and in the end the European Parliament rejected the common position of the Council and the proposal was withdrawn. The particular case study presents us with a characteristic instance of patterns of praxis, such as *compromise*, being subject to challenge. As explained, compromise reflects the insider/outsider taxonomy, reproducing understandings as to who is included in the circle of interdependent parties participating in law making, and as to whose voice carries weight.[3] The following sections will argue that interested parties challenged the dominant conceptualization of the insider/outsider taxonomy, upon demanding that their views are taken into account, when decisions are made. In this instance, the properties of compromise as a category of praxis were renegotiated.

External conditions, such as the continuous technological experimentation currently taking place on the net and the mushrooming of Internet communities, opened the way to challenge the conventional way to think about the role of law and property. The increasing support by academics and business organizations of alternative understandings spurred debate on the meaning of legal concepts that were beyond controversy, being reproduced in legal documents as if their connotation

---

1 Frederic Nietzsche, 'The Will to Power', (1910), Fall 1887 9 [8] [60] in *Philosophy and Truth: Selections from Nietzsche's Notebooks of the Early 1870's*, Daniel Breazeale (translator) and (ed.) (New Jersey, 1979).

2 Pierre Bourdieu and Loic Wacquant, *An Invitation to Reflexive Sociology* (Chicago, 1992).

3 See Chapter Three of this book.

should be taken for granted. This can be further attributed to the new approach in the EU, which supports the effective engagement of various interested parties in the making of decisions, in an attempt to strengthen the democratic face of the Union. Moreover, groups challenging established definitions possess expert technical knowledge (for instance, how software works), which adds weight to their opinion, since this is the kind of information that the European Commission needs in order to come up with informed legislative proposals and avoid conflicts, when a proposal for a Directive is read by the Council or the Parliament. In a nutshell, it is ruptures in the normal flow of events indicating the rise of worldviews with the capacity to change the world, which leads to the change or reconsideration of established practice by bringing it onto the conscious level. In this way phronetic patterns of praxis potentially open up to accommodate fresh experience. I say potentially, as alternatively, ruptures may result in clinging upon and supporting on the ideological level the established, by refusing to change it. However, even if phronesis opens to accommodate new experience, revolutionary visions will always comfortably settle in cognitive schemas, presenting us with new attempts to control conduct, and impose the 'right' way to conceptualize regulatory law.

A dynamic reading also requires attributing to agents multiple patterns of perception. In simple words, the proposition here is that agents have a multiplicity of roles available to them, as a result of socialization in many different settings. This understanding assumes the mobility of individuals and the formation of a new fluid concept of community, encompassing people who are, at the same time, members of various different communities and have a plurality of identities.[4] As such, structural patterns of thinking about the social world may be derived from diverse professional, national, and educational backgrounds, hence the recognition of a multiplicity of drives within us.

The Proposal for a Directive on the Patentability of Computer-Implemented Inventions: The Consultation

Patents are protected by the Paris Convention and the Trade Related Intellectual Property (TRIPs) agreement. For a patent to be granted, an invention must be new, involve an inventive step, and be capable of industrial application. Moreover, TRIPS Article 27(1) provides that patent protection can be granted to products and processes in all fields of technology, and in the same spirit Article 52(1) of the European Patent Convention (EPC), which is a non-EU agreement signed by all Member States (MS) and other countries, has been interpreted as requiring that patents can be granted for inventions, which have a technical character. The element of technical character

---

[4] Deirdre Boden and Richard Friedland, 'NowHere: An Introduction to Space, Time and Modernity', in Deidre Boden and Richard Friedland (eds), *Now/Here: Space, Time and Modernity* (Berkeley, 1994); John Urry, *Sociology Beyond Societies: Mobilities for the Twenty-First Century* (London and New York, 1999).

requires, first, that an invention belongs to a field of technology and, second, that an invention makes a technical contribution to the technological state of the art.[5]

In Articles 52(2) and (3) of the European Patent Convention (EPC) computer programs are defined as not being inventions, therefore they fall outside patentable subject matter. This is because a computer program is considered as being a solution to a mathematical problem, not having a technical character, hence copyright law may be used to protect them. For the same reasons, 'methods for doing business', 'presentations of information', and 'aesthetic creations', are not patentable.

In particular, the European Patent Convention, Article 52(2) excludes from patentability:

1. Discoveries, scientific theories and mathematical methods.
2. Aesthetic creations.
3. Schemes, rules and methods for performing mental acts, playing games or doing business, and programs for computers.
4. Presentations of information.

However, paragraph (3) provides:

> The provisions of paragraph 2 shall exclude patentability of the subject-matter or activities referred to in that provision only to the extent to which a European patent application or European patent relates to such subject-matter or activities as such.

This is where problems begin, as definitions as to what constitutes a computer program *as such* diverge, as a result of the different interpretations that may be given to terms such as technical contribution and field of technology, while at the heart of the debate is the question of whether computer-implemented inventions should be treated differently from computer programs 'as such', and thus be patentable.

The approach endorsed by the European Patent Office (EPO), which is the executive body of the European Patent Organization established by the EPC, is that, although Article 52(2) of the EPC provides that computer programs as such are excluded from patentability, 'computer-implemented inventions' are intended to be covered. According to the recent case law of the EPO, a technical contribution is performed when an invention solves an objective technical problem. For example, 'ensuring optimum exposure with sufficient protection against overloading of the X-ray tube by an X-ray apparatus incorporating a data processing unit' can be patented.[6] Moreover, 'the coordination and control by software of the internal communication between programs and data files held at different processors in a data processing system' has also been patented.[7] The latter decision has been criticized

5 EPO T854/90 [1993] OJ EPO 669. In 2000, the EPC has been amended, to explicitly include the requirement that the invention must be in a field of technology. The amended version has not yet entered into force.

6 EPO Board of Appeal, T26/86 [1988] OJ EPO 19.

7 EPO Board of Appeal, T6/83, [1990] OJ EPO 5.

heavily. Commentators have noted that, since there is always some kind of internal communication involving software and hardware, there is hardly a computer program which cannot be patented. Thus, in practice this interpretation brings Europe close to the US position, which allows software patents, as the test of 'utility' is applied, according to which business methods, algorithms, methods for doing business, can all be patented as long as they have a useful, concrete, and tangible result.

Nevertheless, the European Commission adopted a Proposal for a Directive on the Protection by Patents of Computer-Implemented Inventions in February 2002, in view of the fact that inventions using software could already be patented through the EPO or national patent offices, resulting in considerable legal uncertainty. The Directive was meant to harmonize the way in which national patent laws deal with software inventions. Some organizations representing European businesses, lawyers, established industry players, and government agencies welcomed the proposal in view of the ambiguity surrounding the patentability of software related inventions.

However, Both EuroLinux and the Economic and Social Committee of the European Community (EESC) expressed concerns that patents on computer-implemented inventions might impede the progress of innovation in the software field.[8] The latter produced in 2002 a report critical to software patentability, proposing taking into consideration the interests of small and medium enterprises (SMEs), and free/open source software companies.[9] As for the EuroLinux Alliance for a Free Information Infrastructure, this is an open coalition of commercial companies (over 200) and non-profit associations, united to promote a European software culture based on copyright, open standards, open competition, and open source software, such as Linux. Corporate members and sponsors of EuroLinux develop or sell software under free, semi-free, and non-free licenses, for operating systems such as GNU/Linux, MacOS, or MS Windows.

The Eurolinux Alliance organized a petition against software patents in Europe, which had an overwhelming response, as 1,161 valid responses were forwarded to

---

[8] Opinion of the Economic and Social Committee on the Proposal for a Directive of the European Parliament and of the Council on the patentability of computer-implemented inventions COM(2002) 92 final/2002/0047(COD). The ESC is a consultative organ, which unites experts and scientists from various fields, and drafts working papers or opinions for the codeciding organs of the European Union, such as the European Parliament and the Council of the European Union.

[9] Libre software or free software refers to the freedom to:

> redistribute copies, either with or without modifications, either gratis or charging a fee for distribution, to anyone anywhere. Being free to do these things means (among other things) that you do not have to ask or pay for permission.

See http://www.gnu.org/philosophy/free-sw.html, also see http://www.gnu.org/philosophy/free-software-for-freedom.html, (webpages visited on 11 August 2005). In respect to open source software, it may include programmes that can be redistributed and copied only for non-profit purposes (semi-free software). It may also include programmes whose redistribution or copying is completely prohibited without permission (proprietary).

DG Internal Market.[10] Interestingly, the consultation showed that the group opposing software patents (91 per cent) was numerically dominant. Nevertheless, the report prepared for the European Commission analyzing the results of the consultation, referred to the nine per cent, who supported software patents, as an economic majority.[11]

The text of the directive, as amended by the European Parliament, followed to a certain extent the spirit of the proposals of groups opposing the patentability of computer-implemented inventions. For example, Article 4a.1 concerning exclusions from patentability, as amended, stipulates that a:

> computer-implemented invention shall not be regarded as making a technical contribution merely because it involves the use of a computer, network or other programmable apparatus. Accordingly, inventions involving computer programs which implement business, mathematical or other methods and do not produce any technical effects beyond the normal physical interactions between a program and the computer, network or other programmable apparatus in which it is run shall not be patentable.

---

[10] Eurolinux argued that software patents have caused a lot of problems, as developers find it difficult to create an innovative product without infringing some patent, due to the number of features required to be implemented. Hence, the argument is that due to the peculiarities of software, it is as if the letters of the English language have been patented. This results in more and more software patent litigation cases, while many software companies and software developers are threatened to settle outside the courts, as they cannot afford litigation costs. Moreover, start-up costs increase, as new firms have to take into account that they need an in-house lawyer, or constant coordination with a lawyer/law firm, who would be able to find out whether a computer program with a technical effect is already patented, *see* European Commission DG Enterprise, *Enforcing Small Firms' Patent Rights: A Publication from the Innovation/SMEs Programme Part of the Fifth Research Programme* (Luxemburg, 2003); Nancy Gallini, 'How Well is the US Patent System Working?', *Working Paper University of Toronto*, 3/2001. Commentators have also argued that companies build large portfolios of software patents, which in fact serve the purpose of maximizing their bargaining power when striking deals, *see* Carl Shapiro, 'Navigating the Patent Thicket: Cross Licences, Patent Tools and Standard Setting in Innovation Policy and the Economy', in Adam B. Jaffe, Josh Lerner and Scott Stern (eds), *Innovation Policy and the Economy* (Cambridge MA, 2001), vol. 1; Jim Bessen, 'Patent Thickets: Strategic Patenting of Complex Technologies', Research on Innovation Working Paper, 8/2002, available at http://www.researchoninnovation.org/, (webpage visited on 11 August 2005). Finally, the findings of economic studies suggest that the impact of patents for computer-implemented inventions on the economy is ambiguous, see Jim Bessen and Eric Maskin, 'Sequential Innovation, Patents and Imitation', MIT and Harvard Working Paper Series, 00–01/2000, while Konqueror and iCab (which are shareware companies) and Opera (which is an open source company) are the only competitors of Microsoft in the market for browsers, PbT Consultants, 'The Results of the European Commission Exercise on the Patentability of Computer Implemented Inventions', *Final Report*, (2000) PRS/2000/A0-7002/E/98.

[11] PBT consultants *Final Report*, 14.

Similarly, Article 4a.2 provides that:

> Member States shall ensure that computer-implemented solutions to technical problems are not considered to be patentable inventions merely because they improve efficiency in the use of resources within the data processing system.

When the proposed Directive went back to the Council, initially it appeared that there would be no disagreement over adopting the Irish Presidency's proposal on the Directive. However, due to the Polish intervention, the vote was delayed, but finally the Council reached agreement. Nevertheless, this was subject to criticism from campaigners and members of the European Parliament, as not all the amendments introduced by the Parliament in its first reading were taken on board. When the proposal went back to the Parliament, it rejected the Council's common position in July 2005, as it considered that its views were not given sufficient weight.

The question here is, why could not the various interested parties reach agreement? Why, and to what extent, did cooperation fail?

Patterns of Thinking about Intellectual Property: The European Commission

Hobbes and Locke in the seventeenth century asserted that people have a natural right to own their creation. In the same spirit, intellectual property rights are premised on the romantic notion of inventor and author, who has a moral right in her works. Alternatively, economic theory offers a utilitarian perspective by drawing attention to the economic incentives that should be provided to inventors.[12] I do not seek here to engage in a discussion of the contingent character of notions such as *author* and *creator.*[13] I am concerned with the ways in which tacit understandings about the role of information, innovation, and regulatory law, influence action. In short, the proposition in the following paragraphs is that for DG Internal Market (primarily responsible for the preparation of the proposed directive) intellectual property rights and innovation are understood through the lenses of harmonization and market integration, when focusing on the knowledge-based aspects of the economy in Europe.

---

[12] Edwin C. Hettinger, 'Justifying Intellectual Property', *Philosophy and Public Affairs*, 18/1 (1989): 31–52; Tom G. Palmer, 'Are Patents and Copyrights Morally Justified? The Philosophy of Property Rights and Ideal Objects', *Harvard Journal of Law and Public Policy*, 13/3 (1990): 817–65; Tom G. Palmer, 'Intellectual Property: A Non-Posnerian Law and Economics Approach', *Hamline Law Review*, 12/2 (1989): 261–304.

[13] Michel Foucault, 'What is an Author?', in Paul Rabinow (ed.), *The Foucault Reader* (Harmondsworth, 1986); Mark Rose, *Authors and Owners: The Invention Of Copyright* (Cambridge MA, 1993); Brad Sherman and Alan Strowel (eds), *Authors and Origins: Essays on Copyright Law* (Oxford, 1994).

Illustrating this point requires studying the aesthetics of the language of the various legal documents produced by the European Commission, concerning in general the information society. The aim of this exercise is to discover patterns of words that are repeated and carried over from one document to the other, to finally find their way to the present one at issue, the draft directive. Such patterns of words, like rituals, are reproduced most of the time without being questioned, being symbols of authority and continuity, by means of their mere incorporation in legal texts, such as Green and White Papers, Action Plans, Directives, and Annual Reports. This would happen although the meaning of these words and patterns of words, such as 'international competitiveness', 'innovation', or 'software as such', has been subject to debate before being incorporated in a legal text in the first place.[14]

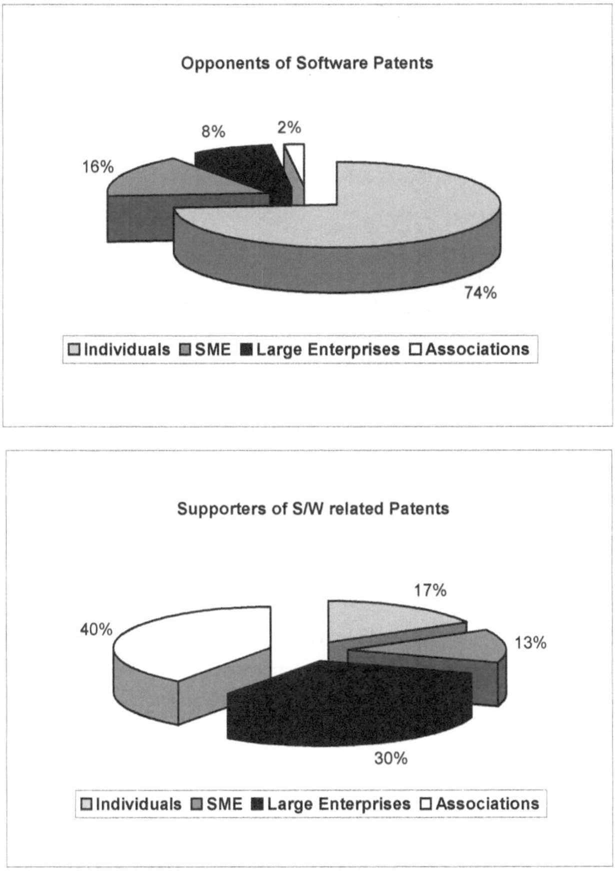

Figure 5.1 Opponents and Supporters of Software Patents: Some Statistics

[14] On innovation see Chapter Two of this book.

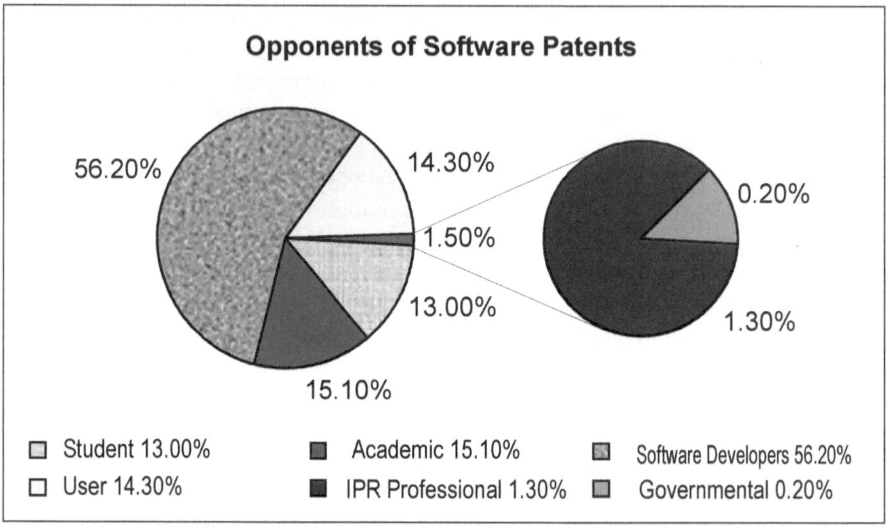

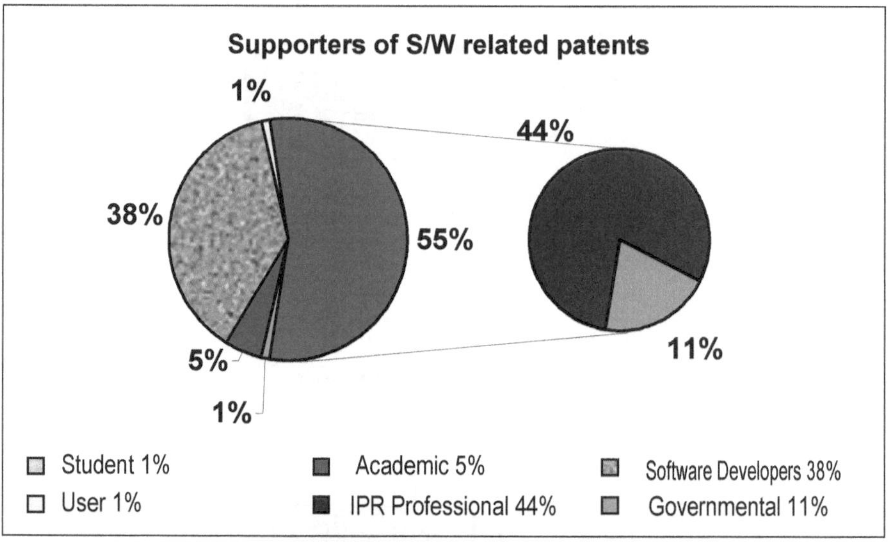

Source: PbT Consultants, 'The Results of the European Commission Exercise on the Patentability of Computer Implemented Inventions' (2000), section 4, particularly see section 4. 1, 35.

For example, the Commission's White Paper on Growth, Competitiveness, Employment,[15] stresses that information technologies and related services have the potential to 'promote steady and sustainable growth', to increase 'competitiveness', to open 'new job opportunities', and to improve the quality of life for all Europeans.

[15] White Paper on Growth, Competitiveness, and Employment: The Challenges and Ways Forward into the 21st Century COM(93), 700 final.

Then the Bangemann Report builds on the White Paper's analysis, to promote the argument for liberalizing quickly telecommunications for the sake of competing on a global level with the US and Japan.[16] Liberalization should be a priority, since being the first player to set technological standards for those who follow is crucial in the IT industry in view of the dynamic character of technological progress. For this reason, the Report calls for adopting global coordination mechanisms. Finally, a 1994 Action Plan in section III repeats that the information society promises to 'create new jobs and to promote Europe's linguistic and cultural diversity'.[17]

The introduction of the *Green Paper on Innovation*[18] deserves a direct quotation, in order to demonstrate the particular patterns of words being reproduced in all these documents:

> Innovation is vital for the viability and success of a modern economy. In this regard, Europe seems less well placed than its main competitors. It has an excellent scientific base but is less successful than other regions of the world at converting its skills into new products and market share, especially in high-technology sectors. Despite certain notable success stories, such as the French high-speed train (TGV) and the GSM mobile phone system, Europe is lagging behind in many of the new technical fields, especially information and communications technology ... It is vital to protect the fruits of innovation. In economic terms, it has been clearly established that companies with specialized know-how, which sell, branded products and patented products or processes, have a competitive advantage when it comes to maintaining or expanding their market share. We are now witnessing the globalization of our economies. At the same time, the value of what is produced lies more in the intangible investment component ... However, the patent system must under no circumstances act as a further brake on the competitiveness of European companies. Ease of obtaining patents, legal certainty, appropriate geographic coverage: these are all essential criteria for the effective protection of innovation in the European Union.

The Bangemann Report uses the same language, with 'developing a competitive European industry', promoting 'common rules' and 'international action to protect intellectual property', being the highlights:

> While there is a great deal of information that is in the public domain, there is also information containing added value which is proprietary and needs protection via the enforcement of intellectual property rights. IPRs are an important factor in developing a competitive European industry, both in the area of information technology and more generally across a wide variety of industrial and cultural sector ... [S]erious difficulties will arise if regulatory systems in different areas of the world are operating on incompatible principles, which permit circumvention or create jurisdictional uncertainties. In this global information market-place, common rules must be agreed and enforced by everyone.[19]

---

[16] Commission Report on Europe and the Global Information Society: Recommendations of the High-Level Group on the Information Society to the Corfu European Council. Bulletin of the European Union. Supplement No. 2/94 [follow-up paper for White Paper] (commonly called the Bangemann Report).

[17] Europe's Way to the Information Society – An Action Plan COM(94) 347 final.

[18] Green Paper on Innovation COM(95) 688 final.

[19] Bangemann Report, Chapter Three, section two.

In the same spirit, Frits Bolkestein, the Commissioner of DG Internal Market, repeated the position of the European Commission, when the Council voted for the Irish Presidency's compromise position after the European Parliament's first reading of the Directive:

> The Council's agreement is a big step towards getting this Directive adopted in a form, which will provide a major contribution to European competitiveness and assist the proper functioning of the Internal Market. We must reward investment in innovation if a real knowledge-based economy is to flourish in Europe … The proposed Directive seeks to harmonize the way in which national patent laws deal with computer-implemented inventions. Such inventions can already be patented by applying to either the European Patent Office (EPO) or the national patent offices of the Member States. However enforcement of patents is dealt with by national courts and, as the law may differ between Member States, the level of protection may, in practice, vary. This can represent a significant barrier to trade in patented products within the Internal Market.[20]

All these statements are underlied by one basic understanding: the commodification of information and the centrality of property rights in safeguarding the way investment is returned and innovation is promoted (although balanced by competition law). As Boyle puts it, consciously and unconsciously we are already developing the language of entitlement for a world in which information, genetic, electronic, and proprietary, is one of the main sources of wealth.[21]

The mission of DG Internal Market is to draft:

> traditional instruments regulating the market, such as harmonizing the laws of the Member States relating to industrial property rights to avoid barriers to trade. The aim is also to create unitary systems for the protection of such rights with Community-wide effect through the filing of one single application for protection (Community trade marks, designs and patents). The Internal Market DG is also increasingly concerned with ensuring that the Single Market functions properly in the Information Society and the fight against counterfeiting.[22]

In other words, the aim of the European administration is to harmonize national legislations, integrate markets, and objectively put notions such as *economy* and *property* in legal categories. The tools to achieve these are codification and objectification of practices by means of textual analysis, reliance on precedent, invention of new legal categories, and trust in legal institutions.[23] The operating parameters of the above are, formality, rule of law, and an increase in legal certainty by means of providing the tools for rational predictions of outcomes. Nevertheless, by virtue of

---

20 Press Release IP/04/659.

21 James Boyle, *Shamans, Software, and Spleens: Law and the Construction of Information Society* (Cambridge MA, 1996).

22 http://europa.eu.int/comm/internal_market/en/indprop/overview.htm (webpage visited on 11 August 2005).

23 Pierre Bourdieu, 'La Force Du Droit: Eléments Pour Une Sociologie du Champ Juridique', *Actes de la Recherche en Sciences Sociales*, 64/9 (1986): 3–19.

providing for certainty, objectivity, rationality, and continuity, certain assumptions (for instance concerning the centrality of property rights) are simultaneously reproduced, which go without saying. In other words, the administrator, in the course of drafting a legal document, views herself as disinterested and neutrally interpreting the law, failing to acknowledge assumptions about the social world reproduced therein. In this way, concepts, such as property and competition, are conceived to be unproblematic, and law is thought to be an effective tool to successfully order social relations.

Taken for granted conceptions concern not only the concept of romantic inventor, not only the utilitarian logic of economic analysis, but also other basic assumptions, such as the one that stipulates that innovation is a good thing, and that in high evolving markets firms invest heavily and need to be rewarded, as they undertake considerable risks. Uniform standards are important for this purpose, since the system has become increasingly international, and firms have to exploit their rights on a global scale.[24]

In a nutshell, it is normal for a person trained in law and having to deal with the problem of the different treatment of software between the EPO and MS, to seek to develop a solution promoting harmonization, market integration, and innovation, by means of established practice, and on the basis of the mainstream authoritative rhetoric promoting IP rights and innovation, already reproduced in a sequence of legal texts. It is then that a legal text appears objective, and the agent creating it seems disinterested, losing sight of the assumptions reproduced therein, while simultaneously regenerating basic legal conventions, such as continuity and trust in legal institutions.

In simple words, it is not easy for a civil servant working for DG Internal Market to see that protecting proprietary information may not be the only way to promote the information society. When DG Information Society was consulted by DG Internal Market, the former DG sought to include specific provisions covering interoperability. This is a concept that is fundamental in the Information Technology industry,[25] so

---

24 Interview with an administrator DG Information Society, conducted on 6 June 2004. Also see European Commission Green Paper COM(87) final; European Commission White Paper COM(93) 700 final; Recommendations of the Bangemann Group, 1994; European Commission Green Paper COM(97) 314 final; European Commission Communication COM(2003) 226 final. Between 1987 and 1997 the American copyright and patent industries increased their output at the rate of 5.8 per cent a year compared to 2.8 per cent a year for other industries, and increased the number of jobs at 4.0 per cent a year compared to 1.6 per cent in the ordinary economy. Through the 1990s knowledge based industry grew twice as fast as service industries, and four times as fast as manufacturing, see Keith E. Maskus, *Intellectual Property Rights in the Global Economy* (Washington DC, 2000).

25 The IT industry is characterized by product interoperability. The notion of product interoperability implies that a computer must be compatible with the microprocessor and any necessary peripheral hardware (such as printers, keyboards, monitors, and modems). The operating system must be compatible with the microprocessor, and the application programs must be compatible with the operating system. Only if these compatibility requirements are met will the consumer be able to use the computer. Thus, hardware and software developers' choices are driven by compatibility requirements if they want to develop a commercially

that software developers are not required to license a patent for the purpose of, for example, creating a device that can play a patented media format. However, one of the negotiators from DG Internal market strongly disagreed, the argument being that introducing such a concept would be 'contrary to the rationale of patent law', while another point of disagreement concerned the need to have strong patent protection so that 'European companies would effectively compete with US companies'.[26]

The rationale of patent law is that a monopoly period is granted to the inventor, so that she secures a return to her investment for a limited period. In return for the monopoly the inventor must disclose her invention, so that others may utilize the embedded knowledge. True, the rational of patent law requires that no unnecessary restrictions are imposed, thus, if a provision concerning interoperability is included, according to Article 30 of TRIPS this would have to not unreasonably conflict with the normal exploitation of the patent and prejudice the legitimate interests of the right holder, taking account of the legitimate interests of third parties. Moreover, we are reminded that patents are for technological inventions, and software should only be patented, where it can be shown that it is a non-obvious invention, which involves an inventive step and can be applied in the industry. In interviews with civil servants working for DG Internal Market, the legal requirements of patentability of software were meticulously explained to me. An official from DG Internal Market complained that it is exactly because interest groups do not understand legal texts that they came up with poor proposals.[27]

It appears that the same line of argumentation was adopted in the course of the consultation amongst DGs of the European Commission. In an interview with one of the *fonctionnaires* working for DG Information Society,[28] who has been directly involved in the negotiations between DG Internal Market and DG Information Society as to the aims and scope of the proposal, he described the extent to which, and the reasons why, the two services disagreed when seeking to strike the right balance between promoting innovation through the proprietary component of the patent system, and safeguarding competition, interoperability, and the interest of society in ensuring that the Internet remains an open space. It is important to note here that there is one unit in DG Information Society, whose mission is to foster the deployment of Open Source and free software, improve competition, and provide flexibility in the choice of software tools. To this effect, a working group on *libre software* was created in 1998.[29] Moreover, fostering the development and use of open

---

successful product. As a result, consumers are more likely to buy a Microsoft computer system, since they know that most current and future applications are likely to work on that system, rather than on a competing system. It follows from this point that the effect described is cyclical, and economists refer to this as the 'tipping effect', on these issues see Mark A. Lemley, 'Antitrust and the Internet Standardization Problem', *Connecticut Law Review*, 28/3 (1996): 1041–94.

26 Interview with an administrator DG Information Society, conducted on 5 June 2004.

27 Interview with an administrator DG Internal Market, conducted on 25 January 2002. The same view is expressed in PBT consultants Final Report.

28 Interview with an administrator DG Information Society, conducted on 5 June 2004.

29 http://eu.conecta.it/ (webpage visited on 11 August 2005).

source software may attract funding under the Information Society Technologies Programme (IST).

> Q. DG Internal Market had prime responsibility in preparing the text of the proposed Directive and DG Information Society was consulted. How can you describe the course of the negotiations between the two services? Was it smooth or not?
>
> A. DG Internal Market and DG Information Society had totally different points of view. The negotiations were very difficult. It was a battle between Intellectual Property Rights people and software people. Two people from the initial team from DG Information Society left the Commission. Some people from DG Internal Market were reasonable, yet looked at the legalistic picture and missed an appreciation of the social outcome and economic impact of law. In my view, we need a balance between competition and property/monopoly rights, but nowadays, patent protection is really expanding. I see the expansion of IPRs [Intellectual Property Rights] as hampering innovation, as there has not been a proper evaluation of the economic data we have.
>
> Q: DG Information Society wanted the Directive to include specific provisions safeguarding interoperability. Is this true?
>
> A: The position of the European Commission [in the proposed Directive] is normally the compromise position of transdepartmental consultation. But, the provision on interoperability was not there. After XXX [one of the chief negotiators from DG Information Society] left, I wanted to include the provision on interoperability. And this was finally accepted by DG Market.
>
> Q: Why do you think DG Internal Market promoted the particular version of the proposed Directive?
>
> A: It is important for the regulatory output of DG Internal Market: The more legal instruments are issued, the better a DG's performance is valued. Moreover, it is the people working in DG Internal Market: I think that it boils down to that they believe that an expansion of IPRs is good for innovation. However, we know that IPRs are abused. In DG Competition they also know it, with all these cross licensing agreements, firms behave like cartels. But people from DG Competition are isolated. I cannot pick up the phone and call people there. They see themselves as people who have to maintain their independency, and should not talk to interested parties, as others should not interfere with their files.

This last point links well to a discussion in the context of a different interview with a senior official at DG Competition concerning the importance of working with people with common sense.

> It is important to work with people with common sense, and they are not many. Many times, people present perfectly drafted and justified legal arguments, which are nonetheless politically impossible. People with common sense can see the implications of the legal arguments.[30]

---

[30] Interview with an administrator DG Competition, conducted on 7 June 2004.

This is because legal terms, such as the term technical contribution, which, as the following section will show, is at the heart of patent law, acquire divergent meanings in accordance with how interested parties understand the role of innovation, competitiveness, and how these can be fostered. A good legal argument is not enough to make a good proposal. The following section will take this point further.

Framing with Legal Language

At the heart of the proposal for the Directive introducing patent protection in computer-implemented inventions (interestingly, an invented term that recently enriched the vocabulary of software developers) is the concept of technical contribution. It denotes that a computer-implemented invention which makes a technical contribution to the state of the art, and which is not obvious to a person skilled in the art in the field concerned, is more than just a computer program and can be patented. Hence, the position of the European Commission is that the proposed Directive, by promoting transparency and legal certainty, would create an environment in which innovation could be most effectively protected and fostered.

Kennedy's thesis is relevant here, as he argued that the legal system, built upon the notions of property and contract, cannot regenerate itself internally, in order to come up with new concepts that would apply to new cases. This is why, legal principles are like commodities. When new cases emerge, legal practitioners are, erroneously, expected to have to draft legal arguments by means of interpreting precedent and first principles. According to this line of thinking, the argument presented has to be legally correct, otherwise a legal mistake may occur due to the lawmaker's incompetence or bad faith. However, Kennedy argues, in these problematic cases the source of the error should be found in that the rules of precedent and first principles point to multiple interpretations, which may very well be contradictory. If one accepts this, it is easy to see that in reality it is lawmakers, judges, and administrators who decide what the right interpretation of legal rules should be, deriving inspiration from 'legal, ethical, and political factors, including class interests and historical and social stereotypes, that contribute to any decision of a matter of importance in their particular culture'.[31]

The proposed Directive is a good example of how legal concepts are given divergent interpretations in the light of accepted social stereotypes. Not only DG Information Society disagreed with DG Internal Market, but also the Parliament disagreed with the Commission as to what the right definitions are. The Parliament wanted wide exclusions covering the use of patented technology for interoperability and data handling. However, the Commission and Council said that these went beyond what was required to set the right balance between rewarding inventors for their efforts

[31] Duncan Kennedy, 'The Role of Law in Economic Thought: Essays on the Fetishism of Commodities', *American University Law Review*, 34 (1985): 939–1001.

and allowing competitors to build on these inventions, therefore, the proposed exceptions could ultimately harm EU competitiveness. It appears that there is not one way to promote competitiveness, harmonization, integration, and innovation. Legal concepts relevant to patent law can be given various interpretations according to socially accepted understandings about, for example, the importance of proprietary standards, and the meaning of innovation and competitiveness.

In particular, according to the Opinion of the Economic and Social Committee of the European Parliament,[32] with the development of open and interoperable networks such as the Internet, it is important that we promote interoperability and open standards, so that freedom of expression, communication, trade, capital flows, and education are encouraged. The Opinion then addresses the question of whether the patent system is really suitable to foster the above. We see that according to this view, which comes very close to the arguments presented by EuroLinux and DG Information Society, a proprietary system will not necessarily guarantee the evolution of new technologies. Subsequently, in paragraph 3.1 the opinion goes on to criticize the legal interpretation of the notions of 'field of technology' and 'technical effect', which has been adopted in the proposal of the European Commission, as making it possible to patent any programmed computer, or programmed network, or a process implemented through the execution of a program.

> Any innovation made in this way is automatically considered 'to belong to a field of technology', even if the result is derived entirely from software operations. The door thus seems wide open to a software patent, as no programmable electronic hardware can operate without software and as the distinction between software 'by itself' and 'software producing technical results', the product of legal casuistry, is indefinable in practice as all software is made to run on a computer or an electronic component, either as a system or as an application. This extension of the scope of application of patentability could thereafter be extended without limit to software programmes and intellectual methods at successive legal rulings of the technical chambers of the EPO, irrespective of the exclusion provided for in Article 52 of the EPC.

In the same spirit, in paragraph 3.1.1 the opinion criticizes the European Commission by arguing that the text of the proposed Directive justifies the drift of the EPO's jurisprudence, when it admits that the technical effect can amount to the simple fact of a program running on a standard computer. In paragraph 3.1.2 the Opinion warns that the door may open to patenting business methods, as the EPO may in the future consider drawing an analogy between software and business methods (although currently Appendix 6 of the internal rules for examiners does not adopt this position). The Opinion further stresses in paragraph 3.7 that the European Commission should seriously take into account the fact that software is a very complex product, requiring building on previously acquired scientific knowledge, hence the importance of

[32] Opinion of the Economic and Social Committee of the European Parliament 2002/0047 (COD).

cooperation and dissemination. Therefore, the problem with patents is exactly that cooperation and free circulation of free or open source software may be hindered.

It appears that the draft directive did not seriously take into account the above-mentioned considerations. It may be because, as explained earlier, patent lawyers cannot doubt the virtues of the proprietary model upon which patent law is built, feeding into the uncontested belief that the patent system will bring economic prosperity, employment, and global competitiveness, a belief that underlines any relevant legal interpretation, according to paragraph 3.9 of the Opinion. This is why, in the same paragraph, the Opinion attacks the European Commission, as providing no adequate explanation as to how the patent system would provide better legal protection than copyright, reminding that there are conflicting economic analysis as to the effects of patent protection in the software industry.[33] After all, as an interviewee working for DG Information Society[34] pointed out, the European Commission has not taken so far open source/free software developers seriously, as 'they are considered to be "hippies" or something', promoting arguments about 'sharing and building on top of past knowledge', which certainly do not make sense to lawyers, who strongly adhere to the importance of property.

This last point is a valuable one. Developers of open source/libre software challenge one of the most important notions underpinning the legal system, that is property, and the orthodox way to view the importance of innovation and international competitiveness. It is not at all surprising that their views are not considered '*serious*', and it is equally not at all surprising that *fonctionnaires* working for DG Internal Market adopt a view that presents the orthodoxy, being followed by countries such as the US and Japan, promoting legal certainty and the production of more regulatory measures, the latter bolstering the image of a DG as being powerful. And it is normal that such regulatory measures would be produced bearing the symbols of authority and continuity, by means of the way patterns of words are repeated, based on prior texts and precedent, making a legal argument acquire the form it *should* have.

The Juridico-Administrative Rationality

The above analysis presents us with the 'juridico-administrative' way of thinking, nurtured in legal education and administrative modes of reasoning. Uncovering such modes of thinking requires, in a Foucauldian fashion, the study of rationalities operating at the time of the genesis of the particular structures at issue, in our case the European Commission.

---

33 For similar arguments see Paul A. David, Bronwyn H. Hall, Brian Kahin and W. Edward Steinmueller, 'A Critique of the Rapporteur's Explanatory Statement accompanying the JURI Report to the European Parliament on the proposed Directive on the Patentability of Computer-Implemented Inventions', (2004), available at: www.researchineurope.org/policy/critique.pdf.

34 Interview with an administrator DG Information Society, conducted on 5 June 2004.

The importance of *ordoliberalism* in the early days of the European Community in presenting a model of regulatory law based on neutral and objective procedures indirectly intervening in the economy, has already been discussed elsewhere.[35] According to it, the legal system is viewed as being required to create the conditions allowing the economic order to perform effectively, indirectly interfering in the functioning of open markets. To this effect, an economic constitution should be put in place, to safeguard basic principles such as private property and contractual freedom, while regulatory principles flow from and implement these constitutive principles. In this framework, law is viewed as in separating powers, and as in safeguarding against the abuse of private and public power, with procedural formalism and legal rationality being crucial in the process. Moreover, the European administration inherited the traits of the early days of its creation, as marked in the Franco-German influence on the institution. This is evident in, amongst others things, the idea that there is a need to create a strong, prestigious, cohesive, and autonomous from societal influences bureaucracy, with officials being educated in elite schools. Adherence to hierarchy, codification, and formalism are all elements inherited by the French influence on the institution.

Legal education and training are also important to create the effect of objectivity. A person trained in law believes in the efficacy of law, because she believes in the power of words inscribed in books, cases, and legal texts, and in their ability to help society evolve. Bourdieu, in his discussion of the neutralization effect of the juridical language, also draws attention to the grammatical persistence of passive and impersonal constructions in legal texts.[36] Everyone who has studied in a law school can recall the particular way law is taught. A legal exam is an exercise testing a student's ability to construct coherent argumentation based on continuous reference to legal texts and cases, in order to substantiate every single word of the argument if possible. A sophisticated exposition of arguments is further desired, in order to denote mastery of the national language employed. This last point is important, so as to understand how training in law directs students to think of words as cult objects, in a self-referential self-fertilizing aesthetic of legal thinking deriving meaning only from the existing legal corpus. Such a cult of words explains how legal arguments further derive authority not only from the sources they use, but also from the *form* the argument takes, from the *way* words are used, to make an argument that *looks* the way it should.

Moreover, treating and classifying information, neutrally applying the policy mandate of the Commissioner, objectively implementing legal principles, providing for the impartial management of practical issues, are all characteristic to the bureaucratic mode of thinking developed as a result of working for an organization such as the European Commission. In this instance, the need to collect information, identify problems, categorize findings in the light of the principles of independence and neutrality, manifests itself as a basic operating principle. At the same time, the

---

35 See Chapter Two of this book.

36 Bourdieu, 'La Force du Droit'.

European Commission seeks to maintain its position as a crucial locus of governance, by means of producing regulatory output following established practice and the dominant rhetoric in the field concerned, while regenerating basic conventions of the legal field of practice, such as certainty and continuity.

Bureaucracies create social problems by collecting and treating information, but expertise and the categorization of findings can never be neutral, they only formalize truth claims. Foucault reminds us that law has the power to formalize and universalize power claims, such as scientific claims, although the truth of science is conditioned upon historically contingent constructs as to how, for instance, innovation should be promoted. As discussed elsewhere,[37] there are divergent ways to foster innovation; however, it appears that DG Internal Market uses the dominant rhetoric of property rights, neglecting other views placing importance on collaboration and exchange. This is an example of how legal concepts imply the existence of choices, which have been discarded, possibilities, which failed to be actualized, as knowledge is contingent, context dependent. The narrative of administrative procedures sensitive to promoting freedom and equality holds a false promise, as, even where established with that purpose, they always involve the repression of discarded potentialities, and may result in instances of social engineering.[38] This is why, the claim to neutrality on the part of the administration should be subjected to critique, by means of deconstructing the utopia of objectivity, concentrating on how law is interpreted and practiced.[39]

Divergent Voices and Phronetic Ruptures

It appears that different Directorates Generals seem to have diverse views, as to what the 'correct' and 'authorized' interpretation of legal texts is, revealing a picture different from the one propagated by the principle of collegiality. A confrontation occurs amongst these actors, with regard to the technical competence to interpret a corpus of legal texts and collect the information necessary to conduct reliable assessments as to what kind of legislation is required and what the right execution of the mandate of law is. For example, DG Information Society and DG Research are viewed as being the most collusive with big business, in contrast to other DGs considered as more liberal. This may be attributed to that a big number of officials working for these DGs has a scientific background, having been trained as electronic or telecommunication engineers. Moreover, many of them have worked both in the industry and in national administrative systems. Therefore, they feel that they are close to lobbyists and consider themselves as mediators, as they speak the same scientific language with national groups affected by the policies of the European

[37] See Chapter Two of this book.

[38] Michel Foucault, *History of Sexuality*, R. Hurley (translator) (3 vols, Harmondsworth, 1981).

[39] Noam Chomsky and Michel Foucault, 'Human Nature: Justice versus Power', in Fons Elders (ed.), *Reflexive Water: The Basic Concerns of Mankind*, (London, 1974), 171.

Commission.[40] This is a good example of the simultaneous operation of the juridico-administrative mode of thinking alongside the more pragmatic industry oriented mindset of *fonctionnaires* of DG Information Society.

Moreover, the open source and *libre* software developers have a different understanding of the role of Intellectual Property Rights. According to this, innovation and information should be shared, allowing for technological experimentation and public discussion, especially in the case of technologies running as fast as software. They promote a vision of knowledge as being built on top of past knowledge, hence, sharing is the prerequisite for truly innovative projects. As such, they promote a different understanding of the role of intellectual property rights in modern economies. If one accepts this, then by means of promoting the creator/inventor dominant conceptualization, we may undervalue the public domain. And by giving monopoly rights to established powerful firms, we do not necessarily benefit innovation, especially in fast evolving industries.[41] For them, innovation is not only conceived as being the product of scientific research produced in laboratories but also as the result of minor modifications introduced in the course of everyday activity, with collaboration, exchange, and experimentation being crucial to this effect. Openness and communication are the foundations of the Internet, which inherited the rationale that underlied the efforts by the military to create a decentralized network, the ethos of academic research, and the counter-culture of hackers, who viewed it as a unique medium of expression and technological innovation.[42]

Yet again, not all open source developers agreed with the common position advanced by the EuroLinxu Alliance. In a joint statement of the industry directed to the members of the European Parliament, Graham Taylor, director of the Open Forum Europe seeking to promote open source, signed it acting as a representative of the Linux/Opensource world. This joint statement asked legislators to ensure that

---

[40] Laurence Jourdain, 'La Commission Européenne et la Construction d'un Nouveau Modèle d'Intervention Publique', *Revue Française des Sciences Sociales*, 46/3 (1996): 492–520, 500. One of Jourdain's interviewees said:

'I feel above all French and a specialist in my domain; this is why I feel at ease here at DG XIII (Telecommunications), as I do not have to work for the Eurocrats of DGIV (Competition) ... We come from the sector in reference to which we create policies and this why, to a certain degree, we also represent the actors of this sector.'

[41] Jerome H. Reichman and Pamela Samuelson, 'Intellectual Property Rights in Data?', *Vanderbilt Law Review*, 50/2 (1997): 51–166; Paul A. David, 'Tragedy of the Public Knowledge 'Commons'? Global Science, Intellectual Property and the Digital Technology Boomerang', Oxford IP Research Institute Working Paper, (2000), WP 04/00A; Pamela Samuelson, 'Mapping the Digital Public Domain: Threats and Opportunities', *Law and Contemporary Problems*, 66/1 (2003): 147–71. A very interesting conference on Public Domain was held by the Duke Law School resulting in a series of skeptical articles being published in *Law and Contemporary Problems* 66 (2003) Vols 1 and 2.

[42] Manuel Castells, *The Rise of the Network Society* (Oxford, 2000), 353–4; Siva Vaidhyanathan, *Copyrights and Copywrongs: The Rise of Intellectual Property and How it Threatens Creativity* (New York, 2001).

computer programs are treated as patentable inventions, taking the view that such a legislative measure would promote innovation and safeguard the interests of the open source/software libre community.

Interestingly, the reaction on the part of other organizations such as the Free Software Foundation, the Open Source Initiative, and Software in the Public Interest has been strong. He was accused of not having the credentials to represent Linux, Open Source, and Free Software developer communities, in view of the fact that he is in sharp opposition to the stance taken by the overwhelming majority of developers. Moreover, he was blamed as being a 'false' or 'misled' representative of the community.[43]

Conclusions

New governance structures and procedural law are meant to steer the activity of networks of actors, which in turn generate the raw material upon which negotiation and discussion is based. The problem in this understanding is twofold: for one thing, the steering of activity is not a neutral exercise, as the process of identifying a social problem as a legal problem is loaded with options dictated by the various scientific disciplines feeding into it. To give an example, patent protection of computer-implemented inventions assumes that patents are good for innovation, and that innovation is good for modern economies. These beliefs are not uncontested, but certainly present the orthodoxy.

For another, if one accepts the proposition that minds are socially constructed, then, understanding conflicts and problems of cooperation in forums of discussion requires directing our attention to embedded patterns of perception. In the analysis of the case study of this chapter concerning the proposed directive on the patentability of computer-implemented inventions (which failed to be adopted), it was argued that there is not a single pattern of perception for all agents in the European Commission. Structural patterns of thinking about the social world may be derived from 'lawyer thinking', and as such promote harmonization, legal certainty, and continuity. Alternatively, they may be based on professional background, and as such reproduce different understandings with regard to the legal/illegal taxonomy, closer to the needs of the industry. Moreover it may be that a vision of free information and non-proprietary standards is promoted, which can be understood if reference is made to the first steps of the development of the Internet, to see that it was actually created

---

43 It is true that the group that responded to the consultation is a very heterogeneous group with diverse economic interests and philosophical allegiances. Opposing patents for software does not preclude the possibility that software is owned; it means that software may be governed by copyright law instead. While Linux gives away software for free, the GNU license stresses the importance of ownership. However, the focus of this chapter is limited in giving an account of the ways in which the European Commission perceived the conflict, while examining the manner in which the communication amongst different worldviews is ordered by the juridical logic of the written text.

in order to promote free flows of information and speech. In the light of the above, engaging interested parties in a discussion on the basis of common shared beliefs is certainly not an easy task, in view of conflicts amongst unspoken worldviews being the product of history. In other words, cooperation is certainly not easy in the face of conflicts between law's common sense, promoting continuity and certainty, and other views challenging uncontested beliefs tacitly reproduced in legal documents.

However, this does not mean that phronesis, and the beliefs that it embraces, cannot accommodate fresh experience. For example, we saw that interest groups and DG Information Society managed to have the interoperability provisions incorporated in the proposed Directive, the European Parliament rejected the common position of the Council, as its amendments were not given appropriate consideration, and in general academic and policy debate has been spurred as to the nature and economic function of open source/*libre* software. This accomplishment can be attributed to structural reasons, such as the new approach in the EU, which supports the effective engagement of NGOs in the policy process in order to create a European civil society. It is also important that such groups have expert knowledge adding weight to their opinion, which the European Commission needs, in order to form informed decisions and avoid conflicts in the Parliament and Council. In this instance novel experience is accommodated in legal principles, having first been filtered by law's operating principles, certainty, objectivity, rationality, and continuity. To illustrate this, as discussed in chapter three of the book, compromise is an important pattern of praxis, emerging when structural conditions of interdependence generate the need to take the 'other' into account. In a fragmented world where the collection of information is vital, the establishment of expert committees and task forces, and the advancement of interdepartmental collaboration amongst the various services of the European Commission becomes crucial. In the case of the proposal for the Directive at issue, it appears that interest groups successfully managed to challenge the properties of the insider/outsider taxonomy, when demanding that their views are taken on board, a process tempered by the need to advance harmonization and public policy objectives.

Another point that implicitly emerged from the previous discussion, deserving the attention of future research, concerns the need for an individual or an organization to be a member in networks in order to promote its interests. Belonging in networks is crucial in order to participate in any discussion. The EuroLinux Alliance is very well organized, having managed to promote a petition against the proposed Directive and find supporters in the European Parliament, despite being an economic minority in comparison with the other networks of actors participating in the consultation. However, to be able to support their views, software developers had to be organized in an alliance, which promoted a unified response to the proposal. In other words, participation requires belonging in networks, which in turn advance common goals. But how common are these goals? Is it possible that a unified response normalizes divergent opinions even inside networks? Peer pressure, preserving prestige, asymmetries of power, they all underlie the process of presenting a cohesive response to externally imposed challenges. Although action based on consensus built in such networks is important, as the opposite would result in tyrannical action, can we discard the possibility that it results in normalization? This is why the important thing is to conceive forms of political participation safeguarding difference.[44]

[44] Honi F. Haber, *Beyond Postmodern Politics: Lyotard, Rorty, Foucault* (New York, 1994).

Chapter Six

Elements of a Theory of Law Making in the European Union

> O Voltaire! O humaneness! O nonsense! There is something about 'truth', about the search for truth; and when a human being is too human about it – 'il ne cherche le vrai que pour faire le bien' – I bet he finds nothing.
>
> Friedrich Nietzsche, *Beyond Good and Evil*

The previous chapters sought to cast a critical eye on our current understanding of the function of law in new governance structures. If we accept that law always reproduces understandings that go without saying (often out of date with societal developments and needs),[1] then it can never neutrally assist deliberation and communication of meaning, as it has its own life, it crystallizes particular insights as to how the objective of ordering or facilitating social life should be accomplished. It follows that if law can never be neutral and the values it promotes are context dependent, then seeking to establish consensus may imply normalization, and instead of promoting autonomy and emancipation, new forms of domination may be devised. Similarly, if agents applying and debating the law think and pursue their interests in a manner not always rational, then human communication may be hindered by unspoken prejudices and unuttered stereotypes deeply embedded in modes of perception and appreciation.

However, this is not meant to advance the view that the experiment of deliberation is hopeless. My contribution to coming to grips with the circumstances under which legal procedures may fulfill their promise to engage interested parties in the process lays in the notion of compromise. The suggestion here is that compromise is an important category of praxis regulating action, providing the theoretical tools to move away from the notions of consensus and bargaining, while incorporating the effects of power. Compromise is conceptualized as enabling the broadening of the circle of interested parties participating in the law making process, and in this instance law is viewed as encompassing a temporary balance. In other words, although law is most of the time perceived as an instance of verticality and order, compromise implies that order is always open to question, allowing for difference to be expressed.

---

[1] For instance, there are many examples of law being at odds with technological developments, such as the Internet, see Siva Vaidhyanathan, *Copyrights and Copywrongs: The Rise of Intellectual Property and How it Threatens Creativity* (New York, 2001).

In the light of the above, the present chapter seeks to locate the wider intellectual context of the theoretical concepts used in the analysis of the various chapters of the book. Nevertheless, the relevant analysis is not meant to give a detailed exposition of the complex theoretical propositions advanced by thinkers such as Habermas, Rawls, Teubner, and Foucault. Rather, the following sections will selectively discuss certain concepts, which are of particular importance to the argument of the book. The ultimate aim is to articulate elements of a theory of law making in new governance structures in the EU.

Law, the Proceduralist Paradigm, and People's Democratic Common Sense

Habermas's work presents us with an elaborate exposition of the problem of law's legitimcy. He uses elements from many different disciplines, including social theory, philosophy of language, legal theory, and philosophy of law. In simple words, Habermas argues that law is legitimate only if there is communication between the legislature and citizens in the public sphere.[2] This draws attention to the tension between facts and norms, that is between the authority of law to order social relations and citizens' shared understandings about justice. In order to overcome the difficulties created by the dual nature of law, Habermas resorts to the conceptual tools of social theory.[3]

Habermas takes on board insights from systems theory, Weber's interpretive sociology and theory of societal rationalization, and Durkheim's evolutionary sociology. The interpretive approach situates social actors as of prime importance to explaining sociological phenomena. From Durkheim we see the idea that law reflects a certain type of social organization. From systems theory Habermas borrows the idea of a social world inhabited by interelated social systems, such as the economic and administrative systems. Habermas moves to draw another important distinction, the one between system and lifeworld. The latter refers to common understandings and values constituting shared identities and developing through face to face

2 Christodoulidis notes that Habermas has gradually shifted his theoretical position in respect to the proper relationship between the notions of public sphere and law: 'In his recent "republican" tour de force – Factizitat und Geltung – his account of the demise of the critical function of the public has been "rectified" in favour of a much more optimistic theory of democracy', Emilios A. Christodoulidis, *Law and Reflexive Politics* (Dordrecht; Boston; London, 2001), p. 21. Moreover, Christodoulidis notes that the concept of public sphere as used in Habermas's work does not overlap with the public as such; rather, it includes procedures and practices and encompasses the institutional organization of public opinion, 'the rules that set up the realm of political participation as a legal constituted public sphere', Christodoulidis, ibid., p. 22. For a detailed account of the relationship amongst the notions of public opinion, public sphere, and Constitutional arrangements, see Christodoulidis ibid., Chapter Three.

3 Jürgen Habermas, *Between Facts and Norms* (Cambridge, 2004); Hugh Baxter, 'System and Lifeworld in Habermas's Theory of Law', *Cardozo Law Review*, 32/2 (2002): 474–613.

interaction over time in various social groups, such as families, communities, and social institutions.

However, Habermas contends that lifeworld should be protected from administrative rationalities and social inequality. Contrary to this Habermas observes that it is 'colonized' by systems. In respect to the role of law in particular, although within the boundaries of lifeworld it embraces shared understandings about rights and identities, these are now unduly influenced by abstract principles of formal law specific to the welfare state. This effect is termed as 'colonization', and comes under the general umbrella of 'juridification', which refers to the increase of the body of positive law in modern society, for instance with the enactment of regulations aiming at constraining the power of the executive and the endorsement of legal procedures advancing public discussion informing legislation. However, when 'juridification' results in 'colonization' it raises important questions concerning the legitimacy of law.[4] Assuming that law functions in a legitimate way only if it is informed by common understandings developed in the lifeworld, Habermas's thesis is that constitutional democracies should provide legal procedures enabling political participation and will formation by citizens, subsequently feeding into the law making process. In this sense, law has a dual nature, it is both crucial for the reproduction of the lifeworld and for system integration, as the functioning of the economic and administrative system is dependent on it. This is why law is the 'hinge'; it mediates between system and lifeworld.[5]

According to the theory of communicative action in particular, the legitimacy of law is based on discursively achieved agreement reached by affected interested parties. In an 'ideal speech situation', participants in independent public forums (located in voluntary associations, social movements, and in general processes and networks of communication in civil society) are assumed to be rational human beings, who are honest, and have perfect knowledge of their own motivations and any points of view held by the other participants. Hence the procedural character of law, as this should provide the structures of fair discussion and be the outcome of deliberation. As such, it can be both engaged with steering activity and providing the discursive modes required for the generation of rights.[6] Rights are not found in a pre-given conception of the 'good', but their determination involves the active participation of citizens, being anchored in their democratic common sense.[7] In this framework the power of initiating a legislative proposal emerges from a public use

[4] For a rich analysis on the ways the phenomenon of 'juridification' interweaves with 'colonisation' 'popular sovereignty' and the 'public sphere' see Christodoulidis, *Law and Reflexive Politics*, Chapter Three.

[5] Jürgen Habermas, *The Theory of Communicative Action. System and Lifeworld: A Critique of Functionalist Reason*, T. McCarthy (translator) (2 vols, Boston, 1987), vol. 2.

[6] Julia Black, 'Proceduralizing Regulation-Part II', *Oxford Journal of Legal Studies*, 21/1 (2001): 33–68.

[7] William Rehg, *Insight and Solidarity: The Discourse Ethics of Jürgen Habermas* (California, 1997).

of reason; 'public opinion worked up by democratic procedures cannot itself "rule", but it can point the use of administrative power in specific directions'.[8]

The practice of argumentation is based upon the *cooperative* competition for the best argument, while standards of what counts as 'good' or 'bad' argument are subject to debate. In such cooperative communication, all arguments raised should be accepted, and equal opportunities should be granted to all participants in the course of honest exchange, freed from external and internal coercion. In other words, discussion should be characterized by the force of the better argument.[9]

A concept that is of particular interest is 'rational reconstruction', which is the key to arrive at universally accepted principles, hence concerning norms that can be applied in all instances and not only in respect to a particular group of people. According to this notion, empirical research should be directed to identifying all intuitions embedded in participants' common sense, then move onto categorizing them, and subsequently construct ideal categories accommodating all such intuitions. This is an exercise aiming at assisting the better understanding of and future participation in discursive argumentation. In other words, empirical research should be concerned with making explicit implicit practices about the constitutive elements of democracy, and with constructing idealized categories guiding future practice. The normative content of such categories is due to that they already exist in participants' common sense.[10]

Therefore, a cognitive approach is adopted, as, following the tradition of Hegel and interactionists such as Mead and Garfinkel, Habermas accepts that communication is made possible on the basis of shared understandings shaping the meaning of practice. Habermas borrows from Mead the idea that by virtue of conversation humans can engage in finding fruitful solutions to problems. He further constructs the notion of communicative power based on Arendt's view of power, as encompassing the potential of reaching agreement in the course of non-coercive communication.[11] Individuals seek to reach consensus drawing on shared practice, and if no such common ground can be identified, then it is important that at least participants have entered into the cooperative endeavour of rational discourse.

---

8 Jürgen Habermas, 'Three Normative Models of Democracy', *Constellations*, 1/1 (1994): 1–10. Habermas wrote extensively on the genesis and transformation of the public sphere. Nevertheless, I will not engage in an analysis of this term, as I here seek to discuss the procedural character of deliberative democracy.

9 Jürgen Habermas, *The Inclusion of the Other. Studies in Political Theory*, C. Cronin and P. De Greiff, (translators) and (eds) (Cambridge MA, 1998); Jürgen Habermas, *Communication and the Evolution of Society*, T. McCarthy (translator) (London, 1979).

10 Terrence Kelly, 'Sociological Not Political. Rawls and the Reconstructive Social Sciences', *Philosophy of the Social Sciences*, 31/1 (2001): 3–19, 5. Research on procedural justice is useful in this respect, as Lind and Tyler suggest that the intuition favouring procedural law is not context dependent but may be characteristic to organized societies in general, Allen E. Lind and Tom R. Tyler, *The Social Psychology of Procedural Justice* (New York, 1988).

11 George H. Mead, *Mind, Self and Society: From the Standpoint of a Social Behaviorist*, (Chicago, 1967); Hannah Arendt, *The Origins of Totalitarianism* (New York, 1951).

Rawls's theory of justice, offers a different understanding of proceduralization from the liberal standpoint. It is beyond the purpose of the present analysis to discuss in detail the ongoing debate between Rawls and Habermas or all the concepts basic to Rawls's theory of justice.[12] However, the following paragraphs will concentrate on Rawls's understanding of democratic common sense, the starting point being the criticism to his notion of 'original position'.[13] Habermas's view in particular is that, despite Rawls's claims to the contrary, the original position is underpinned by substantive considerations about the good. Rawls rejects this criticism by arguing that the fundamental principles of the theory of justice are at the same time substantive *and* the result of the procedure of original position argumentation. Therefore, their content is not pre-given but the result of existing social consensus.[14] This is exactly because, Rawls argues, the fundamental concepts of the theory of justice are drawn from the political culture, democratic common sense of citizens, reflecting the community's existing concept of justice.

Kelly argues that what is interesting about Rawls's defence is that it appeals to an empirical claim. Therefore, Kelly continues, there are striking similarities between Habermas's rational reconstruction and Rawls's methodology, identifying elements of democratic common sense. The conceptualization of the procedure of original position argumentation also requires the identification of intuitions, then the formation of ideal categories, to finally construct proceduralist rules, which '... apply the idea of justification by appeal to generally acceptable reasons to the deliberations of free and equal citizens in a constitutional democracy'.[15]

However, there are still important methodological differences between the two thinkers. Rawls has been criticized as exhibiting a relativistic approach, since his reconstruction is based on the US, and in particular on writings of the liberal

---

[12] Kenneth Baynes, *The Normative Grounds of Social Criticism: Kant, Rawls, Habermas*, (Albany, 1992); Thomas McCarthy, 'Kantian Constructivism and Reconstructivism: Rawls and Habermas in Dialogue', *Ethics*, 105/1 (1994): 44–63; Jürgen Habermas, 'Reconciliation through the Public Use of Reason: Remarks on John Rawls's Political Liberalism', *Journal of Philosophy*, 42/2 (1995): 109–313.

[13] John Rawls, *A Theory of Justice*, (Cambridge MA, 1971). The 'original position' is rooted in the concept of 'social contract' as elaborated by Hobbes, Rousseau, and Locke, and as such stipulates that the principles of justice are the object of contract, which is meant to bind citizens. In the original position representatives of citizens are placed behind a 'veil of ignorance', therefore, they are considered to be unbiased. The only principles that direct decisions are the ones seeking to safeguard primary goods. In particular, Rawls's position is that representatives of citizens in the original position select two fundamental principles of justice: first, the liberty principle, which stipulates that basic freedoms, such as that the freedom of speech, should be guaranteed to all, and second, the difference principle, which justifies unequal distribution of social and economic goods on grounds of efficiency, if this is carried out in accordance with the equal citizenship and equal opportunity liberties.

[14] John Rawls, *Political Liberalism* (New York, 1996); Terrence Kelly, 'Sociological Not Political'.

[15] McCarthy, 'Kantian Constructivism and Reconstructivism', p. 48.

democratic tradition and from the output of leading institutions of constitutional democracy, such as the US Supreme Court.[16] As Kelly argues, rigorous empirical substantiation of Rawls's claims is required, as there are certainly groups of citizens who do not adhere to the basic principles of the model presented by the original position. For example, the culture of 'gangsta rap' and other marginal social groups, certainly do not follow Rawls's idealized common sense intuitions about liberal justice, as feminists, gender, and race theorists have argued.

This links to the problem of 'coherence' in Rawls's framework. In *Political Liberalism*, Rawls promotes a conception of justice as fairness, acceptable to all citizens in a liberal society. This is because it is assumed to be capable of reflecting an overlapping consensus amongst individuals with diverse views. An implication of this is that, as Dworkin argues, when organizing intuitions in a coherent set, some would have to be rejected as not being consistent with the majority of intuitions, while in Habermas's methodology of rational reconstruction it is assumed that all relevant intuitions of competent speakers must be accepted.[17] Yet, what are the ramifications of this for building consensus?[18] What are the implications for coming to grips with the concept of democratic common sense? What if an interested party holds a view deeply challenging generally accepted beliefs about the social world? Should it be included? Or should it be discarded as outrageous?

Moreover, Rawls's *Political Liberalism* has been criticized as confining justice to the existing liberal structures. The proceduralization of the public use of reason is concerned with parliamentary debates, the workings of courts, and political campaigns. However, Habermas's understanding of public reason includes independent public forums of discussion, where non-governmental organizations and networks of citizens participate.[19]

Taylor and Sandel are two of the most prominent critics of Rawls. Taylor reminds us that we do not only exist as autonomous subjects but also carry the history of our

---

[16] Terrence Kelly, 'Sociological Not Political'. See also Richard Rorty, 'The Priority of Democracy to Philosophy', in Richard Rorty, *Objectivity, Relativism and Truth* (Cambridge NY, 1991), pp. 175–96.

[17] Kelly, 'Sociological Not Political', citing Ronald Dworkin, *Taking Rights Seriously* (Cambridge MA, 1977).

[18] For a general criticism on consensus building see Jim Rossi, 'Participation Run Amok: The Costs of Mass Participation for Deliberative Agency Decisionmaking', *Northwestern University Law Review*, 92/1 (1997): 173–249; Kathryn Harrison, 'Talking with the Donkey: Cooperative Approaches to Environmental Protection', *Journal of Industrial Ecology*, 3/2 (1998): 51–72; Nicholas Rescher, *Pluralism: Against the Demand for Consensus*, (Oxford, 1993); Susan Rose-Ackerman, 'Consensus versus Incentives: A Skeptical Look at Regulatory Negotiation', *Duke Law Journal*, 43/1 (1994): 1206–20; Carry Coglianese, 'Assessing Consensus: The Promise and Performance of Negotiated Rulemaking', *Duke Law Journal*, 46/6 (1997): 255–349; Carry Coglianese, 'Is Consensus an Appropriate Basis for Regulatory Policy?', in Eric W. Orts and Kurt Deketelaere (eds), *Environmental Contracts: Comparative Approaches to Regulatory Innovation in the United States and Europe* (New York, 2000).

[19] McCarthy, 'Kantian Constructivism and Reconstructivism'.

socialization in communities. For Taylor 'the subject himself cannot be the final authority on the question of whether he is free; for he cannot be the final authority on the question of whether his desires are authentic...'.[20] Sandel's 'Liberalism and the Limits of Justice' also makes the point that Rawls's procedural model rests on an understanding of human beings as freely choosing beings.[21] Rawls responded to this critique in 'Justice as Fairness: Political not Metaphysical', rejecting this accusation. Although human beings have self-understandings, such as religious convictions, these are part of their non-public identity derived from membership in communities. Rawls then reiterates that such truths about human identity should not interfere with the expression of political practice. For instance, 'when citizens convert from one religion to another, or no longer affirm an established religious faith, they do not seize to be, for questions of political justice, the same persons they were before'.[22] Taylor insists that this view still understands human agency as self-determining, reminding us that it is not possible to separate substantial from procedural issues, and the private from the public sphere.[23]

Of particular importance for the purpose of the present analysis is Taylor's claim that human agency should be understood in the light of historically and culturally formed intuitions developed in the course of socialization. Intuitions can be made intelligible only on the basis of the contextual background, evaluative framework or horizons of significance, attributing meaning to them. Taylor draws upon Gadamer's notion of horizons to argue that we define ourselves in accordance with a social and historical background, making the social world meaningful. However, in his essay 'The Politics of Recognition' Taylor claims that in order to undertake the moral task of recognition of the self and others, we must discard both the simple understanding of the self as a social construction and as individualistic and atomistic. Instead, we need to acknowledge the dialogical nature of the self, as intertwining with the 'other', hence the importance of recognizing the difference in others and at the same time recognize our own horizons of significance, a process allowing self development.[24]

Habermas responded to Taylor's views arguing that this position contradicts the modern conception of freedom. A proceduralist understanding of rights promoting the rights of individuals should not be compromised for the sake of advancing a

---

20 Charles Taylor, 'What's Wrong with Negative Liberty', in Charles Taylor, *Philosophical Papers II: Philosophy and the Human Sciences* (Cambridge MA, 1985), p. 216.

21 Michael Sandel, *Liberalism and the Limits of Justice* (Cambridge UK, London, New York, New Rochelle, Melbourne, Sydney, 1982).

22 John Rawls, 'Justice as Fairness: Political not Metaphysical', *Philosophy and Public Affairs*, 14/3 (1985): 219–51, p. 241. However, anthropologists and sociologists of religion remind us that this view oversimplifies the complex relationship between religion and authority.

23 Charles Taylor, *Modern Social Imaginaries*, (Durham and London, 2004).

24 Charles Taylor, 'The Politics of Recognition', in Amy Gutmann (ed.), *Multiculturalism and the Politics of Recognition* (Princeton, 1994).

communitarian understanding of collective rights.[25] However, this view begs a chain of difficult questions. For some commentators, the assumption that political discourse can be truly neutral and disinterested, having been liberated from political and economic calculation, is highly problematic.[26] The problem here is the assumption that all parties have equal amounts of power in the course of deliberations.

Close to this line of criticism is the problem of institutional design that would allow the fair participation in discursive communication.[27] Moreover, research in different empirical contexts has shown that, for example, peer pressure in forums of discussion may result in parties not raising issues that they consider important but are controversial.[28] Finally, commentators question whether it is actually desirable that all issues are subject to deliberation and that all actions are justified according to the prerequisites of the ideal speech situation.[29]

However, the present analysis is not only attentive to the problems stemming from a conceptualization of individuals as autonomous subjects. As the analysis here focuses on the function of law in new governance structures, it is important to point that Habermas's framework also rests on the assumption that the administration can play an impartial role in coordinating engagement and discussion of interested parties during the stages of forming a legislative proposal and implementation. All these points require discussing the problem of rationality, objectivity, and social function of law. Habermas's and Rawls's analysis reflect the view that there is a need for a theory allowing the articulation of universal principles, as without it the result would be contextualism and relativism. Still, the view taken here is that human activity cannot be reduced to universal rules.[30] Taylor takes on board the importance of context, as in loyalties and affiliations stemming from group membership, providing the tacit background of practices and abilities. Gadamer proposes that, although our experience is anchored in different social settings, still dialogue and communication between different views of the world is possible by means of successful translation of experience, resulting in the fusion of our own horizon within the horizon of the 'other.' These ideas link to Aristotle's elaboration of the notion of *phronesis*, which points to the importance of context and practical knowledge as explanatory tools.

---

[25] Jürgen Habermas, 'Struggle for Recognition in the Democratic Constitutional State' in Amy Gutmann (ed.), *Multiculturalism and the Politics of Recognition*, (Princeton, 1994).

[26] Joanna Meehan (ed.), *Feminists Reading Habermas: Gendering the Subject of Discourse* (New York, 1995).

[27] James Bohman, 'Deliberative Democracy and Effective Social Freedom', in James Bohman and William Rehg (eds), *Deliberative Democracy: Essays on Reason and Politics* (Cambridge MA, 1997); Jack Knight and James Johnson, 'What Sort of Equality Does Deliberative Democracy Require', in Bohman and Rehg, *Deliberative Democracy.*

[28] Coglianese, 'Assessing Consensus'.

[29] For a review of these issues see Black, 'Proceduralizing Regulation-Part II'.

[30] Bent Flyvbjerg, *Making Social Science Matter: Why Social Inquiry Fails and How It Can Succeed Again* (Cambridge UK, 2001).

Yet, a sociological translation is required explaining these processes. In other words, the aim here is to employ the tools of social theory to articulate elements of a theory of lawmaking, while taking on board the importance of common sense intuitions, context and difference, power relations, and the difficulty in separating substantive from procedural issues.

Power and Context: The Regulation of Everyday Activities

The proceduralization of legal rules implies shifting into a new paradigm, challenging the command and control approach. Habermas's thesis is that law should provide the procedures and structures enabling the political participation of affected groups. Teubner's conceptualization of the social function of law is also an important source of inspiration, feeding into the decentred approach. Teubner is concerned with the harm caused by command and control rules, upsetting the conduct of autonomous social systems in a world characterized by complexity, differentiation, and communication. Regulatory failures are attributed to the insensitive intrusion of legal rules to the function of other social systems, resulting in the problematic communication of meaning, a position inspired by Luhmann's systems theory.

This is because any intervention into a different social system should take into account the internal rules regulating its function, as external 'noise' has to be first interpreted. To engage in such a reconstruction, law relies on sub-systems to furnish information, for example by means of risk assessments produced by scientific committees. Based on such information, law should indirectly steer activity rather than directly impose normative mandates, to make autonomous social systems and networks reflect upon selected social problems, in order to come up with acceptable solutions. As such, a flexible self-organizing society needs procedures generating the necessary raw material for decision making in an open-ended social milieu.[31]

However, both Teubner and Habermas situate the administration at the heart of their analysis, making the mistake to consider the exercise of juridico-administrative power as unproblematic. This is because, the movement away from command and control rules, empowering people to participate in political deliberations and relying on information to steer conduct, implies that the stages of formation of legislative proposals and implementation acquire considerable importance, more than ever before. In this instance, administrations assume an important role in providing expertise, hierarchical assistance (when required), and support for forums of discussion. Habermas and Teubner are quite explicit about this. The administration becomes an important component of the process, but its function is reduced to the technical execution of the legal mandate.

However, Foucauldian inspired analysis draws attention to that legal regulation, when understood as governance in the more general sense of ordering and controlling of social relations, need not be linked to the power concentrated in the hands of the

---

[31] Gunther Teubner, *Law as an Autopoietic System* (Oxford UK and Cambridge MA, 1993).

sovereign ruler, as manifested for instance in the power to extract levies or impose public punishment. Foucault draws attention to the daily administrative aspect of governing, involved in the accumulation of expertise and implementation of rules. This is why sovereign power is not considered to play as important a role as 'disciplinary power', which may emerge in the course of the everyday management of public affairs. The latter is dependent on scientific disciplines to furnish the knowledge claims it incorporates.[32] Surveillance, technical and operational assessments, and regulation, are the properties of disciplinary power, resulting in the production of obedient bodies. Hence, the study of government, 'governmentality', puts emphasis on the historical conditions giving birth to regulatory structures, and on regulation as involving the reproduction of social understandings.

According to this position, filters, used on the Internet to block harmful material, can be conceptualized as technologies of control. Although filters are promoted as value-neutral technological systems, in reality this is a technology that inevitably supports a particular set of ideas and values and excludes others. The very decision to treat harmful material as a regulatory problem is based on the orthodox way to think about the notion 'harmful'. Categorizing content on TV as harmful in order to monitor children's and teenagers' viewing habits implies that a set of statements, as to what is appropriate and inappropriate viewing, monitors conduct. Whilst some interest groups' practice implies the reproduction of the understanding that the web should be a free space of communication, this does not seem to present us with the dominant way to think about the Internet.

However, if we accept that law is the product of particular historical conditions, embracing claims valid under particular circumstances and for specific people, then we take away its legitimacy. The force of law should be tempered and its legitimacy is sustained by the simultaneous reproduction of the belief in the objectivity of the claims it encompasses. This is why law should deny its history. Derrida writes that the story of prohibition is a prohibited story, as law seeks to hide the source of its force.[33] If one accepts the above, then how neutral are the procedures aiming at steering activity? If one decides to employ a genealogical method to uncover the ideas underlying (and excluded in) Teubner's and Habermas's framework, one would be required to examine the notions and practices reproducing the belief in scientific objectivity, in the responsible emancipated rational agent able to regulate itself, in law's impartiality and neutrality, in the potential of consensus building

[32] The disciplinary power embraced by law involves the normalization of practices of whole populations at the everyday level. A study of such practices can be undertaken by focusing on *governmentality*, how government has been made possible as a result of demographic changes resulting in the increase of population, the numerical calculability of subjects assisted by statistics, and the emergence of the discipline of criminology, Graham Burchell, Colin Gordon and Peter Miller (eds), *The Foucault Effect: Studies in Governmentality: With Two Lectures By and an Interview With Michel Foucault* (London and Chicago, 1991).

[33] Jacques Derrida, 'The Force of Law: The "Mystical Foundation of Authority"', in Drucilla Cornell, Michael Rosenfeld, and David Gray Carlson (eds), *Deconstruction and the Possibility of Justice* (New York, 1992).

amongst agents with a free will, in the evils inherent in state control and the benefits of community control.[34]

All these different statements underpinned the understanding of new governance and new modes of legal ordering as a novel object of study. Population is again ordered and managed by means of constructing the responsible individual, who is viewed this time as having to participate in communities and networks, as if there is an ontological demand for this. Such a management of population is particularly necessary in modern societies, where governing becomes more difficult in view of the scientific and technical complexity of issues upon which political decisions have to be made, and due to the rationalization of decision making processes. Information and its provision is crucial in order to regulate conduct, and while Teubner and Foucault agree on this point, the latter author explicitly reminds us that information links to power.

Acquiring information about a population by the administration is fundamental, as it is by means of its rational management that problems are identified, assessed, categorized, and then monitored. The important step in the process of normalization is the identification of a social problem as a regulatory problem. Such normalization need not be imposed by a legal measure sanctioning conduct, as there are indirect ways to steer activity. Regulatory instruments, mediating amongst communities with the aim to make them act to solve an identified problem, may be an example of such indirect ways, as normalization is exercised in a decentralized manner, with the administration having a primary role to play in this process.

If one accepts that power structures are dispersed in a heterarchically organized legal environment, then we need to recast the problem of law's legitimacy. Habermas contends that law's claim to power should derive its legitimacy from the consent of the governed, in the process of discursive argumentation amongst equal citizens and in the light of communicative power. The force of law as a coercive instrument is tempered, as law is legitimized by virtue of deliberative democratic structures. Contrary to this, the thesis advanced here is that law, be it procedural, in the form of self-regulation, or soft law, does not only encompass the moral mandate, democratic common sense of a community, but also has it own logic, its own common sense and history reproducing power relations. In this sense, law always creates order and subsequently seeks to preserve it in the course of promoting formality, the rule of law, and legal certainty. Its force is manifested when a social problem is translated into legal categories by virtue of codification, objectification, and reliance on precedent. In other words, law creates violence in spite of reproducing the image of neutrality, objectivity, and impartiality, as it always reproduces assumptions about the social world, while simultaneously regenerating its autonomous logic of function.

---

[34] For similar thoughts on these issues also see Thomas Lemke, 'The Birth of Bio-Politics: Michel Foucault's Lecture at the Collège de France on Neo-Liberal Governmentality', *Economy and Society*, 30/2 (2001): 190–207.

The Force of Law and Participation

The main point raised in the previous discussion is that law, be it procedural, providing fair structures of discussion, or steering activity on the part of self-organizing communities such as the scientific community, always creates violence. The proposition here is that law also seeks to preserve it. This distinction reflects the difference between law as a discipline and law as a field of practice, where various institutions, such as the administration or courts, are involved in its interpretation, application, or enforcement. Law may be designed to promote deliberation and carry conceptions anchored in the democratic common sense of citizens, but the institutions engaged in interpretation and enforcement have a different set of interests: maximizing their power by means of establishing the legitimacy of interpretations favourable to maintaining order.[35]

The most fundamental interest of administrations consists of accumulating and preserving the power to shape mainstream understandings by supporting an authoritative opinion, in order to sustain their position as major think tanks. In other words, an administration is fundamentally concerned with having the power to effectively fit the social world in legal categories, which ultimately implies imposing common forms of thinking and forms of classification. To this effect, collecting information and classifying it (for example according to sex and age) in line with the law is crucial.[36]

In this framework, as in Habermas's approach, the interpretive-cognitive instance gains momentum by means of having introduced agency in the analysis. Law is conceived as a process of communication between minds and legal structures, involving the engagement in the practice of deliberation. However, unlike Habermas who promotes the concepts of communicative power and consensus, the proposition here is that the practice of law making implies entering into a relationship with the history of others, and the history of the practice. The latter implies accepting the objectifying logic of law; the former requires interacting with others who wish to maximize diverse forms of power, 'interests', and have asymmetrical resources to pursue these. However, most of the time, this is not a conscious process. Administrators and judges interpret the law in the light of *phronesis*, practical wisdom going beyond rationality.[37]

This is not meant to say that *phronesis* is the only possible strategy to be followed, although most of the times agents do what is normal to do, being reasonable and not rational, and as such no rational calculation is being involved in the course of action. However, this does not preclude the possibility that the line of action that *phronesis* suggests may be brought up on the conscious level in times of crisis, where routine is disrupted. Even in this case, the notion of interest is not defined

35 Bourdieu, 'La Force du Droit'.

36 Pierre Bourdieu, 'Rethinking the State: Genesis and Structure of the Bureaucratic Field', *Sociological Theory*, 12/1 (1994): 1–18.

37 Ibid.

in the strict economic sense but as involving everything that defines us, as being socially constructed.[38]

Kennedy suggested that the legal system, premised upon the notions of property and contract, cannot regenerate itself internally. When new cases emerge, lawmakers, judges, and administrators decide what the right interpretation of legal rules should be, deriving inspiration from historical and social stereotypes.[39] To give an example, in conserving its power, an administration would seek to adopt a view that presents the orthodoxy, being already established practice in other sectors or parts of the world, thus reproducing a set of 'common sense' understandings, such as 'innovation is good for the economy, polity, and society'. In this way, legal certainty is advanced, while the production of more regulatory measures certainly creates the image of a powerful administration. This is further enhanced by the symbols of authority and continuity, reproduced by means of the way patterns of words are repeated, based on prior texts and precedent, producing a legal argument having the form it should have. This is why law depends on who is engaged in its production. There are always asymmetries of power and divergent ways to conceptualize justice.

Is Dialogue Possible? From Consensus and Bargaining to Compromise

On the basis of the analysis in the previous section, the conclusion is that communication in the course of deliberations may turn out to be difficult, due to asymmetrical power relations, opposing interests, and divergent understandings of what a regulatory problem is and how it should be treated by agents whose actions are not always rational. Uncoerced communication is not possible, as action is always underlied by struggles of power over redefinitions. However, this is not meant to preclude the possibility that these embedded conceptions can change, or that context-dependent views can be translated to be made intelligible to someone coming from a different culture or social setting. Is such communication possible then?

This question is important, as new governance structures present us with an important challenge to the dominant model of representative democracy and vertical legal rules. However, on the one hand, in a morally fragmented society consensus may imply political normalization. On the other hand, strategic action does away with an understanding of minds as being socially bounded, to come to grips with human activity as satisfying personal expectations of happiness, discarding the process of social construction of what counts as happiness in different social settings.[40] The question then is: can we offer an alternative theory, which would be critical to the

---

38 Pierre Bourdieu, *Distinction: A Social Critique of the Judgment of Taste*, R. Nice (translator) (London, 1984), p. 477.

39 Duncan Kennedy, 'The Role of Law in Economic Thought: Essays on the Fetishism of Commodities', *American University Law Review*, 34 (1985): 939–1001, p. 941.

40 Amartya K. Sen, 'Rational Fools: A Critique of the Behavioral Foundation of Economic Theory', *Philosophy and Public Affairs*, 6/4 (1977): 317–44.

notions of consensus, rationalism, and objectivity? Can we theorize law making, while taking on board the effects of power and the contingent character of rules? Is it possible to contribute to the debate on deliberation by examining the common sense knowledge encapsulated in minds and rules? Under what circumstances, dialogue, as in the fusion of our own horizon within the horizon of the 'other', may become possible?

The thesis advanced here is that a different way to conceptualize the opening of the law making process to voices previously unheard is by means of the notion of compromise. Various authors point to the importance of articulating the difference between compromise and consensus/negotiation.[41] As the following section will elaborate, by using compromise as a conceptual tool we can think about the problem of power asymmetries, difference and context, overcoming the concepts of cooperation amongst equals. It differs from negotiation and bargaining, as it reminds us that the principles of its construction are social. It may emerge only under particular structural conditions and if mental categories of thought allow it.[42]

---

[41] Mohamed Nachi, 'Introduction: Dimensions du Compromis. Arguments pour la Constitution d'une Théorie du Compromis', *Social Science Information*, 43/2 (2004): 131–43; Olgierd Kuty and Mohamed Nachi, 'Le Compromis, Rationalité et Valeur: Esquisse d'une Approche Sociologique', *Social Science Information*, 43/2 (2004): 307–30; Christian Arnsperger and Emmanuel B. Picavet, 'More than Modus Vivendi, Less than Overlapping Consensus: Towards a Political Theory of Social Compromise', *Social Science Information*, 43/2 (2004): 167–204.

[42] For an understanding of compromise as in bargaining, and through the lenses of the rational choice model, see Richard Bellamy, *Liberalism and Pluralism. Towards a Politics of Compromise* (New York and London, 1999), p. 95; Thomas Schelling, *The Strategy of Conflict* (Cambridge MA, 1960); Jon Elster, *The Cement of Society* (Cambridge MA, 1989). Bargaining implies that agents draw on power resources external to the negotiation process, and make promises and threats for the purpose of forcing or persuading others to accept one's arguments. Compromise is the result of this process. In *Between Facts and Norms*, p. 296, Habermas argues that: 'according to the liberal view, the democratic process is effected in the form of compromises amongst interests. Rules of compromise formation are supposed to secure the fairness of results through universal and equal suffrage, the representative composition of parliamentary bodies, the mode of decision-making, rules of order and so on.' Habermas continues at p. 298: 'but the liberal model hinges not on a democratic self-determination of deliberating citizens, but on the constitutional framework that is supposed to guarantee an essentially non-political public good by satisfying personal life plans and private expectations of happiness'. However, Habermas argues that collective bargaining is nothing without communicative rationality, and similarly the willingness of the legislature to transfer powers to bargaining parties, while retaining the power to assist in coordination is not enough. Citing Spiros Simitis, 'Juridification of Labour Relations', in Gunther Teubner (ed.), *Juridification of Social Spheres* (Berlin, 1987), Habermas argues that individual self-determination can be undermined by collective bargaining, as the bargaining process reproduces bureaucratic and legal rationalities such as age limits, regulations governing part-time work, workplace safety rules. This process implies the sacrifice of the autonomy of the individual, while with communicative rationality this is preserved, see *Between Facts and*

However, the suggestion here is that compromise is one possible route of action, category of praxis, regulating the process through which a legal argument is crystallized. Humans are complex and fragmented beings, having manifold identities, multiple phronetic frameworks. As such, compromise functions alongside other phronetic categories, such as law's common sense to fit the social world in legal categories; or common sense understandings brought by interests groups participating in law making, as structural patterns of thinking about the social world may be derived from various professional, national, and educational backgrounds. Finally common sense understandings may be embedded in the various disciplines (for instance biotechnology and criminology) feeding into legal structures.

However, when compromise emerges, agents engage in concerted action and cooperation and not individual maximization of power, and law temporarily objectifies truth claims bound to change again.

Compromise and Law Making

Compromise does not involve a point where different self-interests converge in the process of strategic bargaining and in the light of exogenous power resources. It discards the possibility of difference being accommodated in the notions of consensus and communicative power. Instead, it takes on board the understanding that agents involved in the law making process are not the sole creators of their action, as we 'seize, in the act of perception, something, which outruns perception itself'.[43] We carry the history of our socialization, we reproduce the fragmentation of our upbringing, we act on the impulse of experience, reflecting the practical dimension of knowledge. The wisest of decisions are not the result of following rules and theoretical principles; instead they manifest the capacity to use in different contexts knowledge accumulated in the process of experiencing life. Claiming that action can be fully justified before its initiation holds a false promise, as it is almost certain that its ramifications will supersede the logic of the theoretical principles applied.

Similarly, legal structures carry their own history and intrinsic logic. Consensus and strategic bargaining oversimplify the complexity of human action and downplay the normative importance of legal rules, for the sake of allowing the articulation of a general explanatory framework. The belief in the possibility of arriving at universal principles, discovered by interested parties involved in deliberations, neglects the horror that lays in the assertion of the universality of human values, potentially opening the way to totalitarianism and egoistic closure towards difference. In other words, consensus on universals values, instead of promoting a happy democratic society, encloses the possibility of exclusion in the light of the blind faith in the

Norms, p. 412. However, also see p. 108, where Habermas accepts that regulated bargaining and compromise, conducted on the basis of fair principles, may be acceptable.

[43] Henri Bergson, *Essai sur les Données Immédiates de la Conscience* (Paris, 1936).

virtues of the one truth. Strategic bargaining, by means of the concept of profit maximization, sacrifices the importance of context in the name of predictability.

Instead, compromise, understood in the light of a phronetic approach stressing the importance of common sense knowledge, brings to the foreground the possibility of uncovering the different kinds of unspoken practical knowledge, encapsulated in legal documents aiming at promoting deliberation, and embedded in the mental taxonomies of interested parties participating in deliberations. It sheds light on the significance of conceptualizing the law making process as enabling the formation of flexible legal concepts bound to change again, being perceptive to difference and new normative mandates. It is regulated by the logic of formal law to create continuity, certainty, and trust in legal institutions in the light of accepted first principles, precedent, and the need to provide the tools for the rational prediction of outcomes.

According to Simmel compromise is at the heart of any effort to live together with others, as it is by means of it that social organization becomes possible. Simmel conceptualized compromise as the way to escape the authority of single definitions as to what counts as common good and what is politically desirable. Compromise loses its derogatory meaning by means of accommodating an understanding of social obligations as always embracing the possibility of acting differently.[44] Following Bergson's analysis,[45] Simmel contends that there are indeterminate potentialities in everyone. Each individual could have become something different from what she actually became. In this way, action opens up to accommodate contingency, and agents are consciously aware of alternative possibilities, hence the obligation to engage in compromise.

It then becomes a category of praxis, in such situations where the validity of alternative views of the social world is acknowledged, and there is an obligation to also consider them. Individuals have a responsibility to respect the 'other', and as such, compromise enables a pluralist conception of justice, committing to an understanding of modern society as having to accommodate difference in the notion of order.

Still, how do we learn to take the 'other' into account? According to MacIntyre, this would not be feasible, in view of that individualism has been elevated to the status of religion. In particular, he uses the notion of *phronesis* to challenge the possibility of changing behavioural patterns of attitude on the basis of a rational process. Instead, change of behaviour can be brought about as a result of the adoption of practices oriented towards acknowledging our dependence on others.[46] This can

---

44 Georg Simmel, *The Sociology of Georg Simmel,* K.H. Wolff (translator) and (ed.) (New York, 1950); Georg Simmel, *Conflict*, K.H. Wolff (translator) (Glencoe, 1955); Kuty and Nachi, '*Le Compromis, Rationalité et Valeur*'.

45 Henri Bergson, *Matter and Memory*, N.M. Paul and W.S. Palmer (translators) (New York, 1990).

46 Alasdair MacIntyre, *Dependent Rational Animals: Why Human Beings Need the Virtues* (London, 1999), pp. 155–6.

be accomplished only in a society where social norms, developed in the course of socializing in families and communities, would foster relationships based on giving. In this instance, families and communities function as a political space between the private and the public realm. Following the same line of thinking, the proposition here is that there is something else that pre-exists and makes possible the emergence of the notion of compromise as a category of thought. The will to compromise, as in taking the 'other' into account, is not the result of rational calculation of costs and benefits in the course of a bargaining process; instead it is socially constructed in social settings, where members are interdependent.

We do not compromise because we want, but because we need to, and whether there is a need to compromise is subject to structural factors. Structural reasons refer to a state of interdependence. Only if we need the 'other', or to put it more accurately, only if we think we need the 'other' will compromise emerge, sacrificing personal ends, while taking into consideration other alternative views for the sake of acting jointly. There are two important ramifications of this proposition: first it implies the existence of a relationship of interdependence with strong ties; second, the notion of power always resides in such relationships.

Compromise and Power

Men on a ship are surrounded by water, with heavy seas reminding them of their isolation and distant smells of the existence of safe harbours. They have to cooperate despite differences and personal disagreements. They have to coexist, as mistakes are fatal. Nevertheless, coexisting on a ship means being part of a team, and this may in turn result in coming closer with people one would initially may have even disliked, for the simple reason that she needs others to effectively produce outcomes.

To follow this intuition in the context of the process through which a legal argument is crystallized in a proposal produced by the administration, the thesis advanced here is that, in an increasingly differentiated world, where furnishing information about local needs is crucial in order to form informed decisions, compromise may become an important category of praxis. However, it is relations of interdependency that give rise to compromise. Such relations may be identified where a plethora of institutions and agents are involved in decision making, and there is a need to collect information from as many sources as possible and cooperate with many other individuals. In other words, in order to uncover relations of interdependency, it is important to consider whether it is essential to recognize the 'other', in the light of the need to produce outcomes in the process of law making.

The concept of compromise accepts the importance of context. Contrary to the notion of consensus, it seriously takes into account the effects of power. Opposite to the civic republican tradition, it discards the possibility of one common collective good. It then becomes a cognitive lens, when a legal proposal becomes less about saying the right thing, and more about reflecting a temporary balance bound to change again. Despite the gloss of individualism in the image of autonomous parts of society collaborating to pursue common ends, in practice the need to compromise in order to achieve results is often witnessed. As the state needs interest groups, networks, and experts to furnish information, and since tasks performed by the administration become specialized and the responsibility of various individuals or departments, law often reflects a compromise position ordered by the force of the written text to temporarily objectify practices and simultaneously ensure legal certainty and continuity.

In this instance, compromise implies that members of a society are held together by the fact that their functions are interrelated. In other words, specialization and the autonomous function of agents, networks, and social systems does not necessarily result in emancipation but may amount to depriving them of their autonomy by means of making them an integral part of a whole.[47] Interdependence, by means of entailing dependency, acquires a derogatory meaning, as it implies the compromise of individuality. However, its status is elevated, by means of simultaneously attributing to interdependence the possibility of generating concerted action.

Yet, it is not that such concerted action is characterized by the realization that common goals are to be attained after a cost-benefit analysis takes place, when rational agents recognize that it is to their advantage to collectively pursue their individual interests.[48] As Durkheim taught us, it is the sacred ritual of oath that makes possible the emergence of contract. From the same theoretical vantage point, social relations in a state of interdependence are regulated by social norms, reproducing communal bonds and belonging. When our own needs are inextricably bound up with the needs of others, interaction is characterized by that participants express themselves in ways reflecting what is thought to be a 'proper' way of expression, conforming to expectations, and compromising their individuality.[49] Dignity, pride, and reputation are important variables in the process of conforming to expectations, resonating in the effort to pursue acceptance and belonging. In such a situation, concerted action and compromise, as in the recognition of the 'other', may emerge.

Empirical research should be directed to uncovering relevant structures. For instance, empirical research concerning patterns of praxis regulating the making of a legal proposal by an administration, should study modes of interaction inside it, amongst officials, and between departments and interest groups. Moreover, the relevant study should be attentive to modes of collaboration in shared files, rules and practices governing promotion, appraisals, and mobility, practices concerning the creation of a good reputation, and the processes of consultation and implementation. The focus of the relevant research should be on establishing relationships of interdependence, as then individual plans and goals are compromized, in the face of the need to both gain recognition by the community and achieve outcomes.

---

[47] This idea is expressed in Emile Durkheim, *The Division of Labour in Society* (New York, 1933).

[48] James Coleman, 'The Rational Reconstruction of Society', *American Sociological Review*, 58/1 (1993): 1–15.

[49] Erving Goffman, *The Presentation of Self in Everyday Life* (London, 1990).

In this instance, legal procedures regulate issues such as the choice of topics, and how opposing views should be treated. They also entail understandings as to who should participate in the law making process and as such, compromise as a category of praxis interweaves with the notion of power and reflects the insider/outsider taxonomy, reproducing understandings as to who is included in the circle of interdependent parties. Nietzsche and Foucault conceive power as pertaining human relationships: it is everywhere, it is the motor of action, it involves action and reaction. Similarly, power relations are found in any state of interdependence. This is because, in this case compromise implies tacit understandings as to who should be included in the process of law making and whose voice carries weight. In other words, it regulates who is included in the circle of people expected to work together rather than against each other, and in this instance interdependency loses its derogatory meaning. Being in a group, even if this is defined as a loose network of interdependent parties, such as various Directorates Generals of the European Commission, committees, and advisory groups, seeking to find an acceptable solution to a legal problem, reflects tacit understandings about the properties of being an 'insider' and requires sustaining a self-image expected by the other members of the group, conforming to expectations as to what is thought to be a proper way of expression.

I have two final observations to make: first, it is important to repeat that compromise is one possible course of action amongst others, such as the maximization of interests, whose construction is social. Moreover, linking *phronesis* to power is not meant to trap agency and legal structures in the melancholia of irreversible relations of domination. The phronetic approach is often criticized as introducing constraints, trapping free agents and rendering impossible the conceptualization of creative change. In reply to this criticism, I sought to introduce an understanding of *phronesis* that comes to grips with social reality as experienced reality, fluid, relative, and immanent, encapsulated in flexible concepts, reinterpreted in the light of constant communication between minds and structures, between agents' common sense and law's common sense, and amongst different modes of experience. In this way social reality is conceived as a process that involves perpetual interaction of objective and subjective forces, with knowledge revealing its plural character.

To this effect, the book engaged in a dynamic reading of the operation of *phronesis*, by means of attributing to agents multiple patterns of perception, with compromise being one of them. Another suggestion was that it is important to seek to come to grips with the conditions under which knowledge encapsulated in experience may be challenged. The proposition was that it is the increase in the will and capacity of interested parties to change the world, supported by external conditions, which may result in the renegotiation of the properties of common sense understandings.

Conclusions

As the state has become more complex, heterogeneous, and fragmented, state law and parliamentary democracy have been challenged as to their capacity to promote social justice. In response to this criticism it has been suggested that the democratic character of governance structures should be deepened, by employing new techniques seeking to enhance participation. In this framework, the role of state law should be confined to putting in place fair procedures, enabling the participation of communities in the making of rules affecting them. Hence, new modes of legal ordering are conceived to be the way to escape the gripping effect of command and control rules.

It appears that our traditional understanding of the function of state law is being transformed. This is because it is also concerned with facilitating and promoting the direct inclusion of affected parties, while retaining the role of establishing the general conditions of negotiation. In other words, the study of law requires recognizing its dual nature in new governance structures, as in ordering and compromising, objectifying and negotiating, stabilizing and accommodating. Then, the study of law should be prepared to come to grips with both the process of debating and implementing legal rules and the product of this process, encapsulated in the final legal text; having the effect of objectifying practices, and creating stability and certainty.

Our current understanding of the function of new modes of legal ordering resonates with the belief in the responsible emancipated subject. It also assumes that legal structures can effectively and neutrally promote facilitation, mediation, empowerment, and inclusion. The focus of the book was on formulating a critique of this understanding. It progressively theorized law making in new governance structures in the EU, while being attentive to the ideas of domination, inequality, and difference. To this effect, it suggested the exploration of the importance of practical wisdom, common sense knowledge. The thesis advanced is that this approach may help us articulate useful insights by drawing attention to the different kinds of unspoken practical knowledge encapsulated in legal documents aiming at promoting deliberation. Moreover, the focus is on the cognitive frames of interested parties, applying legal principles, and participating in new governance structures. The proposition here is that, if one accepts that law can be conceived as the product of communication between agents and structures, and amongst different social fields, then the notion of practical wisdom can act as a catalyst to reconceptualize the quality of this interaction and to answer questions as to the possibility of introducing legal procedures, enabling the effective communication of meaning, as articulated by autonomous systems, networks, and groups, having their own codes of conduct regulating their behaviour.

The hope of this work is to become a prolegomenon towards the development of a theory of law making in new governance structures, attentive to the ideas of common sense knowledge, power, and compromise. In modern multicultural societies, where the topical question concerns the possibility of engagement and dialogue, the need to reflect on the substance of procedural law becomes imperative. In this instance, theory meets practice; legal theory encounters political theory; social theory engages in a dialogue with anthropology; and law contemplates upon the historical conditions of its existence. There is much work to be done to this direction.

Bibliography

Secondary Sources

Ackerman, Susan R., 'Consensus versus Incentives: A Skeptical Look at Regulatory Negotiation', *Duke Law Journal*, 43/1 (1994): 1206–20.

Ahmad, Syed, 'Smith's Division of Labour and Rae's "Invention": A Study of the Second Dichotomy with an Evaluation of the First', *History of Political Economy*, 28/3 (1996): 95–107.

Arendt, Hannah, *The Origins of Totalitarianism*, (New York: Harcourt, 1951).

Arendt, Hannah, *On Violence*, (New York: Harcourt, Brace & World, 1969).

Arendt, Hannah, *Crises of the Republic*, (New York: Harcourt Brace, 1972).

Arendt, Hannah, *The Human Condition*, (Chicago: University of Chicago Press, 1998).

Αριστοτέλης, *Ηθικά Νικομάχεια*, (3 τόμοι, Αθήνα: Κάκτος, 1992).

Arnsperger, Christian and Picavet, Emmanuel B., 'More than Modus Vivendi, Less than Overlapping Consensus: Towards a Political Theory of Social Compromise', *Social Science Information*, 43/2 (2004): 167–204.

Audretsch, David B., Baumol, William J. and Burke, Andrew E., 'Competition Policy in Dynamic Markets', *International Journal of Industrial Organization*, 19/1 (2001): 613–34.

Babbage, Charles, *On the Economy of Machinery and Manufactures*, (London: Frank Cass & Co, 1963).

Bachelard, Gaston, *Le Nouvel Esprit Scientifique*, (Paris: Presses Universitaire de France, 1941).

Balkin, Jack M., 'The Promise of Legal Semiotics', *Texas Law Review*, 69/3 (1991): 1845–58.

Baynes, Kenneth, *The Normative Grounds of Social Criticism: Kant, Rawls, Habermas*, (Albany, New York: State University of New York Press, 1992).

Bazard, Amand, Barrault, Emile and Enfantin, Prosper, *The Doctrine of Saint-Simon: An Exposition; First Year, 1828-1829*, G. Iggers, (translator) (New York: Schoken Books, 1972).

Beck, Ulrich, 'The Truth of Others: A Cosmopolitan Approach', *Common Knowledge*, 10/3 (2004): 430–49.

Bellah, Robert, Madsen, Richard, Sullivan, William, Swindler, Ann and Tipton, Steven, *Habits of the Heart*, (Berkeley: University of California Press, 1996).

Bellamy, Richard, *Liberalism and Pluralism: Towards a Politics of Compromise*, (London: Routledge, 1999).

Bellier, Irène, 'La Commission Européenne: Du Compromis Culturel à la Culture du Compromis', *Revue Française des Sciences Sociales*, 46 (1996): 431–52.

Bellier, Irène, 'La Commission Européenne: Hauts Fonctionnaires et Culture du Management', *Revue Française d'Administration Publique*, 70/1 (1994): 253–62.

Bergson, Henri, *Essai sur les Données Immédiates de la Conscience*, (Paris: Presses Universitaires de France, 1936).

Bergson, Henri, *Matter and Memory*, N. M. Paul and W. S. Palmer, (translators) (New York: Zone Books, 1990).

Bessen, Jim and Maskin, Eric, 'Sequential Innovation, Patents and Imitation', *MIT and Harvard Working Paper Series*, 00–01/2000.

Bessen, Jim, 'Patent Thickets: Strategic Patenting of Complex Technologies', *Research on Innovation Working Paper*, 8/2002.

Black, Julia, 'Proceduralizing Regulation-Part I', *Oxford Journal of Legal Studies*, 20/4 (2000): 597–614.

Black, Julia, 'Proceduralizing Regulation-Part II', *Oxford Journal of Legal Studies*, 21/1 (2001): 33–68.

Blumer, Herbert, *Symbolic Interactionism: Perspective and Method*, (Englewood Cliffs NJ: Prentice-Hall, 1969).

Boden, Deidre and Friedland, Richard (eds), *Now/Here: Space, Time and Modernity*, (Berkeley: University of California Press, 1994).

Bohman, James and Rehg, William (eds), *Deliberative Democracy: Essays on Reason and Politics*, (Cambridge: MIT Press, 1997).

Bogdan, Robert and Taylor, Stephen J., *Introduction to Qualitative Research Methods: The Search for Meaning*, (New York: John Wiley and Sons, 1984).

Bourdieu, Pierre, *Distinction: A Social Critique of the Judgement of Taste*, R. Nice, (translator) (London: Routledge, 1984).

Bourdieu, Pierre, 'La Force du Droit: Eléments pour une Sociologie du Champ Juridique', *Actes de la Recherche en Sciences Sociales*, 64/9 (1986): 3–19.

Bourdieu, Pierre, 'Habitus, Code et Codification', *Actes de la Recherche en Sciences Sociales*, 64/9 (1986): 40–44.

Bourdieu, Pierre, *The Logic of Practice*, R. Nice, (translator) (Cambridge UK: Cambridge University Press, 1990).

Bourdieu, Pierre, *Language and Symbolic Power: The Economy of Linguistic Exchanges*, G. Raymond and M. Adamson, (translators) (Cambridge: Polity & Blackwell, 1991).

Bourdieu, Pierre, 'Rethinking the State: Genesis and Structure of the Bureaucratic Field', *Sociological Theory*, 12/1 (1994): 1–18.

Bourdieu, Pierre and Wacquant, Loic, *An Invitation to Reflexive Sociology*, (Chicago: University of Chicago Press, 1992).

Boyle, James, *Shamans, Software, and Spleens: Law and the Construction of Information Society*, (Cambridge: Harvard University Press, 1996).

Boyle, James, 'Foucault in Cyberspace: Surveillance, Sovereignty, and Hard-Wired Censors', *University of Cincinnati Law Review*, 66 (1997): 177–93.

Braithwaite, John and Drahos, Peter, *Global Business Regulation*, (Cambridge UK: Cambridge University Press, 2000).

Bramsted, Ernest, K. and Melhuish, John K. (eds), *Western Liberalism: A History in Documents from Locke to Croce*, (London: Longman, 1978).

Brewer, Anthony, 'Economic Growth and Technical Change: John Rae's Critique of Adam Smith' *History of Political Economy*, 23/1 (1991): 1–12.

Burchell, Graham, Gordon, Colin and Miller, Peter (eds), *The Foucault Effect: Studies in Governmentality: With Two Lectures By and an Interview With Michel Foucault*, (Chicago: University of Chicago Press, 1991).

Brubaker, Rogers, Loveman, Mara and Stamatov, Peter, 'Ethnicity as Cognition', *Theory and Society*, 33/1 (2004): 31–64.

Cambrosio, Alberto, Keating, Peter and Mackenzie, Michael, 'Scientific Practice in the Courtroom: The Construction of Sociotechnical Identities in a Biotechnology Patent Dispute', *Social Problems*, 37/3 (1997): 275–93.

Carlberg, Russell, 'The Persistence of the *Dirigiste* Model: Wireless Spectrum Allocation in Europe *à la Francaise', Federal Communications Law Journal*, 54/2 (2001): 130–63.

Carlson, David F. and Goodrich, Peter (eds), *Law and the Postmodern Mind: Essays in Psychoanalysis and Jurisprudence*, (Michigan: Michigan University Press, 1998).

Castells, Manuel, *The Internet Galaxy: Reflections on the Internet, Business and Society*, (Oxford and New York: Oxford University Press, 2001).

Castells, Manuel, *The Rise of the Network Society*, (Oxford: Blackwell, 2000).

Catephores, George, 'The Imperious Austrian: Schumpeter as Bourgeois Marxist', *New Left Review*, 205/1 (1994): 3–30.

Cerulo, Karen A. (ed.), *Culture in Mind: Toward a Sociology of Culture and Cognition*, (New York: Routledge, 2002).

Christiansen, Thomas, 'Tensions of European Governance: Politicized Bureaucracy and Multiple Accountability in the European Commission', *Journal of European Public Policy*, 4/1 (1997): 73–90.

Christodoulidis, Emilios A., *Law and Reflexive Politics*, (Dordrecht; Boston; London: Kluwer, 2001).

Cini, Michelle, *The European Commission. Leadership, Organization and Culture in the EU Administration*, (Manchester: Manchester University Press; New York: St. Martin's Press, 1996).

Cini, Michelle, 'Organizational Culture and Reform: The Case of the European Commission under Jacques, Santer', *EUI Working Paper EC*, (1996/00/25).

Clavin, Patricia, *The Great Depression in Europe, 1929–1939*, (Basingstoke: Macmillan, 2000).

Coglianese, Carry, 'Assessing Consensus: The Promise and Performance of Negotiated Rulemaking', *Duke Law Journal*, 46/6 (1997): 255–349.

Comaroff, Jean and Comaroff, John, *Of Revelation and Revolution: Christianity, Colonialism, and Consciousness in South Africa*, (Chicago: University of Chicago Press, 1991).

Comaroff, Jean and Roberts, Simon, *Rules and Processes: The Cultural Logic of Dispute in an African Context*, (Chicago: University of Chicago Press, 1981).

Cornell, Drucilla, Rosenfeld, Michael and Carlson, David G. (eds), *Deconstruction and the Possibility of Justice*, (New York and London: Routledge, 1992).

Craig, Paul and Búrca, De Grainne, *EU Law: Text, Cases, and Materials*, (Oxford: Oxford University Press, 2003).

Czech, Brian, *Shoveling Fuel for a Runaway Train: Errant Economists, Shameful Spenders, and a Plan to Stop Them All*, (Berkeley: University of California Press, 2000).

Dahl, Robert, 'The Concept of Power', *Behavioural Science*, 2/3 (1957): 201–15.

D'Andrade, Goodwin R., 'The Cultural Part of Cognition', *Cognitive Science*, 5/3 (1981): 179–95.

David, Paul, 'The Computer and the Dynamo: A Historical Perspective on the Productivity Paradox', *The American Economic Review Papers and Proceedings*, 80/2 (1990): 355–61.

David, Paul A., 'Tragedy of the Public Knowledge 'Commons'? Global Science, Intellectual Property and the Digital Technology Boomerang', *Oxford IP Research Institute Working Paper*, (2000) WP 04/00A.

De Ruggiero, Guido, *The History of European Liberalism*, (Gloucester: Peter Smith, 1981).

Delgado, Richard, 'When a Story is Just a Story: Does Voice Really Matter?', *Virginia Law Review*, 76 (1990): 95–111.

DiMaggio, Paul J., 'Culture and Cognition', *Annual Review of Sociology*, 23/1: (1997) 263–87.

Douzinas, Costas, Goodrich, Peter and Hachamovitch, Yifat (eds), *Politics, Postmodernity And Critical Legal Studies: The Legality Of The Contingent*, (London: Routledge, 1994).

Dunlop, John T., *Dispute Resolution: Negotiation and Consensus Building*, (Dover: Auburn House, 1984).

Durkheim, Emile, *The Division of Labor in Society*, G. Simpson, (translator) (New York: The Free Press, 1933).

Edwards, Geoffrey and Spence, David (eds), *The European Commission*, (London: Longman, 1997).

Egeberg, Michael, 'Organization and Nationality in the European Commission Services', *Public Administration*, 74/3 (1996): 721–35.

Ehrlich, Eugen, *Fundamental Principles of the Sociology of Law,* W.L. Moll, (translator) (Cambridge: Cambridge University Press, 1936).

Elders, Fons (ed.), *Reflexive Water: The Basic Concerns of Mankind. A Series of Television Debates*, (London: Souvenir Press, 1974).

Elliott, John E., 'Marx and Schumpeter on Capitalism's Creative Destruction: A Comparative Restatement', *Quarterly Journal of Economics*, 95/1 (1980): 45–68.

Elster, Jon, *The Cement of Society*, (Cambridge: Cambridge University Press, 1989).

Estrin, Saul and Holmes, Peter M., *French Planning in Theory and Practice*, (London: Allen and Unwin, 1983).

Eucken, Walter, *The Foundations of Economics: History and Theory in the Analysis of Economic Reality*, (London, Edinburgh and Glasgow: William Hodge, 1950).

Featherstone, Kevin, 'Jean Monnet and the Democratic Deficit in the European Union', *Journal of Common Market Studies*, 32/2 (1994): 149–70.

Fish, Stanley, *There's No Such Thing as Free Speech ... and It's a Good Thing, Too*, (New York: Oxford University Press, 1994).

Fitzpatrick, Peter, *The Mythology of Modern Law*, (London and New York: Routledge, 1992).

Fitzpatrick, Peter, *Modernism and the Grounds of Law*, (Cambridge: Cambridge University Press, 2001).

Flyvbjerg, Bent, *Making Social Science Matter. Why Social Inquiry Fails and How It Can Succeed Again*, (Cambridge UK: Cambridge University Press, 2001).

Foucault, Michel, *The Archaeology of Knowledge*, A.M. Sheridan-Smith, (translator) (London: Tavistock, 1972).

Foucault, Michel, *History of Sexuality*, R. Hurley, (translator) (3 vols, Harmondsworth: Penguin, 1984).

Franz, Robert, 'The Statistical History of the German Banking System', *Miscellaneous Articles on German Banking*, US Senate Document 508, (Washington DC, 1910).

Freeman, Jody, 'Collaborative Governance in the Administrative State', *UCLA Law Review*, 45/1 (1996): 18–98.

Froomkin, Michael, 'ICANN'S Uniform Dispute Resolution Policy: Causes and (Partial) Cures', *Brooklyn Law Review*, 67/3 (2002): 608–718.

Gadamer, Hans-Georg, *Philosophical Hermeneutics*, (Berkeley: University of California Press, 1976).

Gadamer, Hans-Georg, *Reason in Age of Science*, (Cambridge: MIT Press, 1986).

Gadamer, Hans-Georg, *Truth and Method*, (New York: Continuum, 1994).

Galanter, Marc, 'Justice in Many Rooms: Courts, Private Ordering, and Indigenous Law', *Journal of Legal Pluralism*, 19/1 (1981): 30–42.

Gallini, Nancy, 'How Well is the US Patent System Working?', *Working Paper University of Toronto*, 3/2001.

Geertz, Clifford, *Local Knowledge: Further Essays in Interpretive Anthropology*, (New York: Basic Books, 1983).

Gerber, David J., *Law and Competition in Twentieth Century Europe: Protecting Prometheus*, (Oxford: Clarendon Press; New York: Oxford University Press, 1998).

Gerth, Hans H. and Mills, Wright, C. (eds), *From Max Weber: Essays in Sociology*, (London: Routledge, 1948).

Goffman, Erving, *The Presentation of Self in Everyday Life*, (London: Penguin Books, 1990).

Grimm, Dieter, 'Does Europe Need a Constitution?', *European Law Journal*, 1/3 (1995): 282–302.

Gulliver, Peter H., *Disputes and Negotiations: A Cross-Cultural Perspective*, (New York: Academic Press, 1979).

Gurvitch, George, *Sociology of Law*, (London, Kegan Paul, Trench, Trubner & Co., 1947).

Gutmann, Amy (ed.), *Multiculturalism and the Politics of Recognition*, (Princeton: Princeton University Press, 1994).

Haber, Honi F., *Beyond Postmodern Politics: Lyotard, Rorty, Foucault*, (New York: Routledge, 1994).

Habermas, Jürgen, *Communication and the Evolution of Society*, T. McCarthy, (translator) (London: Heinemann, 1979).

Habermas, Jürgen, *The Theory of Communicative Action: System and Lifeworld: A Critique of Functionalist Reason*, T. McCarthy, (translator) (2 vols, Boston: Beacon Press, 1987).

Habermas, Jürgen, *The Structural Transformation of the Public Sphere: An Inquiry into a Category of Bourgeois Society*, T. Burger, (translator) (Cambridge: MIT Press, 1989).

Habermas, Jürgen, 'Reconciliation through the Public Use of Reason: Remarks on John Rawls's Political Liberalism', *Journal of Philosophy*, 42/2 (1995): 109–313.

Habermas, Jürgen, *The Inclusion of the Other. Studies in Political Theory*, C. Cronin and P. De Greiff, (translators) and (eds) (Cambridge: MIT Press, 1998).

Habermas, Jürgen, *The Postnational Constellation: Political Essays*, (Cambridge: MIT Press, 2001).

Habermas, Jürgen, *Between Facts and Norms*, (Cambridge UK: Polity Press, 2004).

Harrison, Kathryn, 'Talking with the Donkey: Cooperative Approaches to Environmental Protection', *Journal of Industrial Ecology*, 3/2 (1998): 51–72.

Heclo, Hugh and Wildavsky, Aaron, *The Private Government of Public Money: Community and Policy inside British Politics*, (London: Macmillan, 1981).

Hettinger, Edwin C., 'Justifying Intellectual Property', *Philosophy and Public Affairs*, 18/1 (1989): 31–52.

Hirsch, Susan F. and Lazarus-Black, Mindie (eds), *Contested States: Law, Hegemony and Resistance*, (New York: Routledge, 1994).

Hirschman, Albert O., 'Social Conflicts as Pillars of Democratic Market Society', *Political Theory*, 22/2 (1994): 203–18.

Hunt, Alan, 'The Ideology of Law: Advances and Problems in Recent Applications of the Concept of Ideology to the Analysis of Law', *Law and Society Review*, 19/1 (1985): 11–37.

Jaffe, Adam B., Lerner, Josh and Stern, Scott (eds), *Innovation Policy and the Economy*, (Cambridge: MIT Press, 2001), vol. 1.

Johnson, David. R. and Post, David. G., 'Law and Borders: The Rise of Law in Cyberspace', *Stanford Law Review*, 48/2 (1996): 1367–402.

Jourdain, Luis, 'La Commission Européenne et la Construction d'un Nouveau Modèle d'Intervention Publique', *Revue Française des Sciences Sociales*, 46/2 (1996): 496–520.

Kahin, Brian and Nesson, Charles (eds), *Borders in Cyberspace, Information Policy and the Global Information Infrastructure*, (Cambridge: MIT Press, 1997).

Katzenstein, Peter J., *Small States in World Markets: Industrial Policy in Europe*, (Ithaca: Cornell University Press, 1985).

Kelly, Michael (ed.), *Critique and Power. Recasting the Foucault/Habermas Debate*, (Cambridge: MIT Press, 1994).

Kelly, Terrence, 'Sociological Not Political. Rawls and the Reconstructive Social Sciences', *Philosophy of the Social Sciences*, 31/1 (2001): 3–19.

Kennedy, Duncan, 'The Role of Law in Economic Thought: Essays on the Fetishism of Commodities', *American University Law Review*, 34 (1985): 939–1001.

Kennedy, Duncan, *A Critique of Adjudication*, (Cambridge: Harvard University Press, 1997).

Kuhn, Thomas S., *The Structure of Scientific Revolutions*, (Chicago: University of Chicago Press, 1962).

Kurzweil, Raymond, *The Age of Intelligent Machines*, (Cambridge: MIT Press, 1990).

Kuty, Olgierd and Nachi, Mohamed, 'Le Compromis, Rationalité et Valeur: Esquisse d'une Approche Sociologique', *Social Science Information*, 43/2 (2004): 307–30.

Kymlicka, Will, *Multicultural Citizenship*, (New York and Oxford: Oxford University Press, 1995).

Ladeur, Karl-Heinz (ed.), *Public Governance in the Age of Globalization*, (Aldershot: Ashgate, 2004)

Landau, Ralph and Rosenberg, Nathan (eds), *The Positive Sum Strategy: Harnessing Technology for Economic Growth*, (Washington DC: National Academy Press, 1986).

Landes, David S., *The Unbound Prometheus: Technological Change and Industrial Development in Western Europe from 1750 to the Present*, (Cambridge UK: Cambridge University Press, 1969).

Lemke, Thomas, 'The Birth of Bio-Politics. Michel Foucault's Lecture at the Collège de France on Neo-Liberal Governmentality', *Economy and Society*, 30/2 (2001): 190–207.

Lemley, Mark A., 'Antitrust and the Internet Standardization Problem', *Connecticut Law Review*, 28/3 (1996): 1041–94.

Lessig, Laurence, *Code and Other Laws in Cyberspace*, (New York: Basic Books, 1999).

Lessig, Laurence, *The Future of Ideas: The Fate of the Commons in a Connected World*, (New York: Random House, 2001).

Lévi-Strauss, Claude, *Structural Anthropology*, C. Jacobson and B. Schoepf, (translators) (2 vols, New York: Basic Books, 1963).

Levy, Roger, 'Critical Success Factors in Public Management Reform: The Case of the European Commission', *International Review of Administrative Sciences*, 69 (2003): 553–66.

Lind, Allen E. and Tyler, Tom R., *The Social Psychology of Procedural Justice*, (New York: Plenum, 1988).

Loader, Brian D. (ed.), *The Governance of Cyberspace*, (London and New York: Routledge, 1997).

Lukes, Stephen, *Power: A Radical Review*, (London: Macmillan, 1974).

Lukes, Stephen (ed.), *Power*, (New York: New York University Press, 1986).

MacCormick, Neil, 'The Maastricht-Urteil: Sovereignty Now', European Law Journal, 1/3 (1995): 259–66.

MacIntyre, Alasdair, *Dependent Rational Animals: Why Human Beings Need the Virtues*, (London: Duckworth, 1999).

MacLeod, Roy M. (ed.), *Technology and the Human Prospect*, (London: Frances Pinter, 1986).

Martin, Luther H., Gutman, Huck and Hutton, Patrick H. (eds), *Technologies of the Self: A Seminar with Michel Foucault*, (London:: Tavistock, 1988).

Maskus, Keith E., *Intellectual Property Rights in the Global Economy*, (Washington DC: Institute for International Economics, 2000).

McCarthy, Thomas, 'Kantian Constructivism and Reconstructivism: Rawls and Habermas in Dialogue', *Ethics*, 105/1 (1994): 44–63.

Mead, George H., *Mind, Self and Society: From the Standpoint of a Social Behaviorist*, (Chicago: University of Chicago Press, 1967).

Meehan, Joanna (ed.), *Feminists Reading Habermas: Gendering the Subject of Discourse*, (New York: Routledge, 1995).

Mény, Yves, Muller, Pierre and Quermonne, Jean-Louis (eds), *Politiques Publiques en Europe*, (Paris: L'Harmattan, 1995).

Michelman, Frank I., 'Family Quarrel', *Cardozo Law Review*, 17/5 (1996): 1163–84.

Mueller, Milton, 'Rough Justice: A Statistical Assessment of ICANN's Uniform Dispute Resolution Policy', *The Information Society*, 17/3 (2001): 153–63.

Mueller, Milton, *Ruling the Root: Internet Governance and the Taming of Cyberspace*, (Cambridge: MIT Press, 2002).

Murray, Andrew and Scott, Colin, 'Controlling the New Media: Hybrid Responses to New Forms of Power', *Modern Law Review*, 65/4 (2002): 491–516.

Murray, Andrew, 'Regulation and Rights in Networked Place', *Journal of Law and Society*, 30/2 (2003): 187–216.

Nachi, Mohamed, 'Introduction: Dimensions du Compromis: Arguments Pour la Constitution d'une Théorie du Compromis', *Social Science Information*, 43/2 (2004): 131–43.

Nachi, Mohamed, 'The Morality in/of Compromise: Some Theoretical Reflections', *Social Science Information*, 43/2 (2004): 291–305.

Nietzsche, Friedrich, *Beyond Good and Evil*, W. Kaufman and R.J. Hollingdale, (translators) (New York: Vintage, 1966).

Nietzsche, Friedrich, *The Will to Power*, W. Kaufmann and R.J. Hollingdale (translators), W. Kaufmann, (ed.) (New York: Random House, 1967).

Nietzsche, Friedrich, *Thus Spoke Zarathustra*, R.J. Hollingdale, (translator) (London: Penguin, 1969).

Nugent, Neil (ed.), *At the Heart of the Union. Studies in the European Commission*, (Basingstoke: MacMillan, 2000).

Orts, Eric W. and Deketelaere, Kurt (eds), *Environmental Contracts: Comparative Approaches to Regulatory Innovation in the United States and Europe*, (New York: Kluwer Law International, 2000).

Page, Edward G., *People Who Run Europe*, (Oxford: Clarendon Press, 1997).

Palmer, Tom G., 'Intellectual Property: A Non-Posnerian Law and Economics Approach', *Hamline Law Review*, 12/2 (1989): 261–304.

Palmer, Tom G., 'Are Patents and Copyrights Morally Justified?: The Philosophy of Property Rights and Ideal Objects', *Harvard Journal of Law and Public Policy*, 13/3 (1990): 817–65.

Patterson, John and Teubner, Gunther, 'Changing Maps: Empirical Legal Autopoiesis', *Social and Legal Studies*, 7/4 (1998): 451–86.

Patton, Michael Q., *Qualitative Evaluation and Research Methods*, (California: Sage, 1990).

PbT Consultants, 'The Results of the European Commission Exercise on the Patentability of Computer Implemented Inventions', *Final Report* (2000) PRS/2000/A0-7002/E/98.

Perry, Christopher R., 'Trademarks as Commodities: The Famous Roadblock to Applying Trademark Dilution Law in Cyberspace', *Connecticut Law Review*, 32/1 (2000): 1127–57.

Peterson, John and Sharp, Margaret, *Technology Policy in the European Union*, (Basingstoke: Macmillan, 1998).

Pildes, Richard H. and Sunstein, C.R., 'Reinventing the Regulatory State', *University of Chicago Law Review*, 62/3 (1995): 1–129.

Polanyi, Michel, *Personal Knowledge: Towards a Post-Critical Philosophy*, (London: Routledge, 1958).

Polanyi, Michel, *The Tacit Dimension*, (New York: Doubleday Anchor, 1967).

Posner, Richard, *Economic Analysis of Law*, (New York: Aspen, 1998).

Post, David G., 'What Larry Doesn't Get: Code, Law and Liberty in Cyberspace', *Stanford Law Review*, 52/4 (2000): 1439–59.

Quinn, Naomi, 'Culture and Contradiction: The Case of American Reasoning About Marriage', *Ethos*, 24/3 (1996): 391–425.

Rabinow, Paul (ed.), *The Foucault Reader*, (Harmondsworth: Penguin, 1986).

Radice, Lisanne, *Beatrice and Sidney Webb: Fabian Socialists*, (London: Macmillan, 1984).

Rae, John, *The Sociological Theory of Capital: A Complete Reprint of the 'New Principles of Political Economy'*, (New York and London: Macmillan 1905).

Rawls, John, *A Theory of Justice*, *(*Cambridge: Harvard University Press, *1971*).

Rawls, John, 'Justice as Fairness: Political not Metaphysical', *Philosophy and Public Affairs*, 14/3 (1985): 219–51.

Rawls, John, *Political Liberalism*, (New York: Columbia University Press, 1996).

Rescher, Nicholas, *Pluralism: Against the Demand for Consensus*, (Oxford: Clarendon Press, 1993).

Reichman, Jerome H. and Samuelson, Pamela, 'Intellectual Property Rights in Data?', *Vanderbilt Law Review*, 50/2 (1997): 51–166.

Reidenberg, Joel R., 'The Formulation of Information Policy Rules Through Technology', *Texas Law Review*, 76/3 (1998): 553–93.

Rheinstein, Max (ed.), *Max Weber on Law in Economy and Society*, (Cambridge: Harvard University Press, 1954).

Rice, Elizabeth, 'On Cultural Schemata', *American Ethnologist*, 7/2 (1980): 152–71.

Richardson, John G. (ed.), *Handbook of Theory and Research for the Sociology of Education*, (New York: Greenwood Press, 1986).

Roberts, Simon, 'After Government? On Representing Law Without the State', *Modern Law Review*, 68/1 (2005): 1–24.

Rorty, Richard, *Contingency, Irony, and Solidarity*, (Cambridge: Cambridge University Press, 1989).

Rorty, Richard, *Objectivity, Relativism and Truth*, (Cambridge: Cambridge University Press, 1991).

Rose, Mark, *Authors and Owners: The Invention Of Copyright*, (Cambridge: Harvard University Press, 1993).

Rosenberg, Nathan, *Technology and the American Economic Growth*, (New York: Harper and Row, 1972).

Rosenberg, Nathan, *Inside the Black Box: Technology and Economics*, (Cambridge: Cambridge University Press, 1982).

Rosenberg, Nathan, *Exploring the Black Box: Technology, Economics and History*, (Cambridge: Cambridge University Press, 1994).

Rossi, Jim, 'Participation Run Amok: The Costs of Mass Participation for Deliberative Agency Decisionmaking', *Northwestern University Law Review*, 92/1 (1997): 173–249.

Roy, Katrik and Sideras, Jörn (eds), *Domestic Institutions and Empowerment in an Integrating World Economy: A Global Perspective*, (Cheltenham UK: Edward Elgar, 2004).

Salvadori, Massimo, *The Liberal Heresy: Origins and Historical Development*, (London: Macmillan, 1977).

Samuelson, Pamela, 'Mapping the Digital Public Domain: Threats and Opportunities', *Law and Contemporary Problems*, 66/1 (2003): 147–71.

Sandel, Michael, *Liberalism and the Limits of Justice*, (Cambridge, London, New York, New Rochelle, Melbourne, Sydney: Cambridge University Press, 1982).

Sandholtz, Wayne, *High-tech Europe: The Politics of International Cooperation*, (Berkeley: University of California Press, 1992).

Schelling, Thomas C., *The Strategy of Conflict*, (Cambridge: Harvard University Press, 1960).

Schumpeter, Joseph A., *Capitalism, Socialism and Democracy*, (London: Allen & Unwin, 1965).

Searle, John, *Intentionality: An Essay in the Philosophy of Mind*, (Cambridge: Cambridge University Press, 1983).

Sen, Amartya K., 'Rational Fools: A Critique of the Behavioral Foundation of Economic Theory', *Philosophy and Public Affairs*, 6/4 (1977): 317–44.

Sherman, Brad and Strowel, Alan (eds), *Authors and Origins: Essays on Copyright Law*, (Oxford: Clarendon Press, 1994).

Shore, Chris, *Building Europe: The Cultural Politics of European Integration*, (London and New York: Routledge, 2000).

Simmel, Georg, *The Sociology of Georg Simmel*, K.H. Wolff, (translator) and (ed.) (Glencoe: Free Press, 1950).

Simmel, Georg, *Conflict*, K.H. Wolff, (translator) (Glencoe: Free Press, 1955).

Simon, Jonathan, 'Ideological Effects of Actuarial Practices', *Law and Society Review*, 22/4 (1988): 771–800.

Smith, Adam, *The Wealth of Nations*, (London: Penguin Books, 1999).

Starr, June and Collier, Jane F.J. (eds), *History and Power in the Study of Law: New Directions in the Study of Legal Anthropology*, (Ithaca, New York: Cornell University Press, 1989).

Stevens, Anne and Stevens, Handley, *Brussels Bureaucrats? The Administration of the European Union*, (Basingstoke: Palgrave, 2001).

Stevenson, John and Cook, Chris, *Britain in the Depression*, (London and New York: Longman, 1996).

Strasser, Mathias, 'The Rational Basis of Trademark Protection Revisited: Putting the Dilution Doctrine into Context', *Fordham Media and Entertainment Law Journal*, 10/2 (2000): 331–74.

Strathern, Marilyn (ed.), *Audit Cultures: Anthropological Studies in Accountability, Ethics and the Academy*, (London: Routledge, 2000).

Tamanaha, Brian Z., *A General Jurisprudence of Law and Society*, (Oxford: Oxford University Press, 2001),

Taylor, Charles, *Philosophical Papers II: Philosophy and the Human Sciences*, (Cambridge: Cambridge University Press, 1985).

Taylor, Charles, 'Précis of The Sources of the Self', *Philosophy and Phenomenological Research*, 54 (1994): 185–6.

Taylor, Charles, *Philosophical Arguments*, (Cambridge: Harvard University Press, 1995).

Taylor, Keith, *The Political Ideas of the Utopian Socialists*, (London: Frank Cass, 1982).

Teigas, Demetrius, *Knowledge and Hermeneutic Understanding: A Study of the Habermas-Gadamer Debate*, (Lewisburg, London and Cranbury NJ: Bucknell University Press, 1995).

Teubner, Gunther, 'Substantive and Reflexive Elements of Modern Law', *Law and Society Review*, 17/2 (1983): 239–85.

Teubner, Gunther, *Autopoietic Law: A New Approach to Law and Society*, (Berlin: de Gruyter, 1987).

Teubner, Gunther, 'How the Law Thinks: Toward a Constructivist Epistemology of Law', *Law and Society Review*, 23/5 (1989): 727–57.

Teubner, Gunther, *Law as an Autopoietic System*, (Oxford and Cambridge: Blackwell, 1993).

Urry, John, *Sociology Beyond Societies: Mobilities for the Twenty-First Century*, (London and New York: Routledge, 1999).

Vaidhyanathan, Siva, *Copyrights and Copywrongs: The Rise of Intellectual Property and How it Threatens Creativity*, (New York: New York University Press, 2001).

Vandenberghe, Frédéric, 'The Real is Relational: An Epistemological Analysis of Bourdieu's Generative Structuralism', *Sociological Theory*, 17/1 (1999): 32–68.

Ward, John R., 'The Industrial Revolution and British Imperialism, 1750–1850', *The Economic History Review*, 47/1 (1994): 44–65.

Warnke, Georgia, *Justice and Interpretation*, (Cambridge: MIT Press, 1993).

Weber, Max, *Basic Concepts in Sociology*, H.P. Secher, (translator) (London: Owen, 1962).

Weiler, Joseph H.H., 'The Transformation of Europe', *Yale Law Journal*, 100/8 (1991): 2403–83.

Weiler, Joseph H.H., 'Does Europe Need a Constitution? Reflections on Demos, Telos and the German Maastricht Decision', *European Law Journal*, 1/3 (1995): 219–58.

Weiler, Joseph H.H., 'To Be a European Citizen – Eros and Civilization', Working Paper Series in European Studies Special Edition, Spring 1998.

Weinberg, Jonathan, 'Rating the Net', *Hastings Communication and Entertainment Law Journal*, 19/2 (1997): 453–82.

Weir, David R., 'Life under Pressure: France and England, 1670–1870', *Journal of Economic History*, 42/1 (1984): 27–47.

White, James B., *Justice As Translation: An Essay In Cultural And Legal Criticism*, (Chicago: University of Chicago Press, 1990).

White, James B., *Acts Of Hope: Creating Authority In Literature, Law, and Politics*, (Chicago: University of Chicago Press, 1994).

Yngvesson, Barbara, 'Making Law at the Doorway: The Clerk, the Court and the Construction of Community in a New England Town', *Law and Society Review*, 22/3 (1988): 409–48.

Zuckert, Catherine H., *Postmodern Platos: Nietzsche, Heidegger, Gadamer, Strauss, Derrida*, (Chicago: University of Chicago Press, 1996).

Printed Primary Sources

Action Plan: Europe's Way to the Information Society COM(94) 347.

Commission of the European Communities Report on Europe and the Global Information Society [1994]: Recommendations of the High-Level Group on the Information Society to the Corfu European Council. Bulletin of the European Union. Supplement No. 2/94

Commission of the European Communities Report by the Inspectorate-General 'Designing Tomorrow's Commission – A Review of the Commission's Organization and Operation' (1999).

Commission of the European Communities 'An Administration at the Service of Half a Billion Europeans: Staff Reforms at the European Commission, State of Play', Spring 2002.

Commission of the European Communities, *Reform Progress Review*, COM (2003) 40/2.

Commission, DG Enterprise, *Enforcing Small Firms' Patent Rights. A Publication from the Innovation/SMEs Programme Part of the Fifth Research Programme*, (Luxemburg, 2003).

Communication from the Commission to the Council, the European Parliament, the Committee of Regions and the Economic and Social Committee on Illegal and Harmful Content on the Internet COM(96) 487.

Communication from the Commission to the Council, the European Parliament, the Committee of Regions and the Economic and Social Committee on the Competitiveness of European Enterprises on the Face of Globalization – How It Can Be Encouraged COM(98) 718.

Communication from the Commission to the Council and the European Parliament on Europe's Environment: What Directions for the Future? The Global Assessment of the European Community Programme of Policy and Action in Relation to the Environment and Sustainable Development COM(1999) 543.

Communication from the Commission on Impact Assessment COM(2002) 276.

Communication from Vice President Kinnock to the European Commission on Guidelines on Mobility SEC 2002 146.

Communication from the Commission on 2004 Environmental Policy Review COM(2005) 17.

Council Recommendation 98/560/EC of 24 September 1998 on the Development of the Competitiveness of the European Audiovisual and Information Services Industry by Promoting National Frameworks aimed at Achieving a Comparable and Effective Level of Protection of Minors and Human Dignity OJL 270, 48.

Council Regulation (EC) No 1260/1999 of 21 June 1999.

Council Regulation (EC) No 104/2000 of 17 December 2000.

Council Regulation (EC) No 2371/2002 of 20 December 2002.

Dec 276/1999 of the European Parliament and of the Council of 25 January 1999 adopting the Multiannual Community Action Plan of 06 February 1999 on Promoting Safer Use of the Internet by Combating Illegal and Harmful Content on Global Networks OJL 33, 1.

European Parliament Resolution on the Commission Communication to the Council and the European Parliament on The Organization and Management of the Internet – International and European Policy Issues 1998–2000 COM(2000) 202.

Green Paper on Innovation COM(95) 688.

Green Paper on the Protection of Minors and Human Dignity in Information and Audiovisual Services COM(96) 483.

Green Paper on the Community Patent and the Patent System in Europe COM (97) 314.

Opinion of the Economic and Social Committee on the Proposal for a Directive of the European Parliament and of the Council on the Patentability of Computer-Implemented Inventions COM(2002) 92/2002/0047(COD).

Technological Options Assessment (STOA) Programme PE 167 327/Fin.St.

Union Syndicale Fédéral, The Reform: Working Paper of the USF of 7 March 2000 on the Advisory Document of 18 January 2000.

White Paper on Growth, Competitiveness, and Employment: The Challenges and Ways Forward into the 21st Century COM(93) 700.

White Paper on Reforming the Commission COM(2000).

Index

action
  and Bourdieu, Pierre 65, 66
  and consensus 105
  and context 36
  native patterns of 46
  and phronesis 3, 4
  and power 64
  and practical reason 34
  and tacit understandings 90
administration
  and common sense 78, 119
  and compromise 55, 58, 123, 124
  and decentralized law making 6, 8
  and information 53
  and interaction 42, 53, 55, 124
  interests of 64, 66, 67, 84, 94, 118
  and mobility 49
  and Monnet, Jean 25, 27
  and national affiliations 57
  and neutrality 10, 66, 67, 101, 102 114, 115
  and normalization 117
  and power 32, 66, 115, 117, 118, 119
architectural solutions 61, 70, 71, 76, 84
Aristotle 3, 34, 114
authority
  definitions of 122
  of law 108
  and power 37
  of the subject 113
  and symbolic forms 35, 65, 66, 100, 101, 119
  of written text 56, 91, 101

Babbage, Charles 12, 13, 14
bargaining 5, 37, 46, 51, 107, 119, 120, 121, 123
Bourdieu, Pierre
  and action 65
  and bureaucracy function of 68
  and capital 61, 64
    juridical, symbolic 65
    technocratic/informational 67, 83
  and deliberation 119
  and habitus 34, 35
  and legitimizing power 66
  and linguistic strategies 66
  and misrecognition 66
  and neutrality 101
  and objectivity 66
  and power 64, 65
  and principles of division 65
  and rationalism 5
  and symbolic violence 65, 66
  and training in law 101

Castells, Emmanuel 77
civil society 1, 10, 62, 76, 105, 109
cognitive 4, 8, 29, 33, 35, 36, 37, 55, 58, 67, 86, 110, 118, 123, 126
common market 24, 25, 27
common sense
  and change 85
  and compromise 120, 121, 122, 126
  and consensus 5
  and Habermas, Jürgen 109, 110
  and law 105, 117, 118
  and phronesis 3, 4, 121, 122, 125, 126
  and Rawls, John 111, 112
  reproduction of 119
  and social practices 36
communication
  between minds and structures 35, 118, 125, 126
  and dialogue 5, 7, 31, 114
  and Habermas, Jürgen 108, 109, 110, 114
  and the Internet 116
  meaning of 5, 7, 107, 114, 115, 126
  and power relations 115, 119
competition law 11, 23, 94
compromise
  and action 123
  and belonging 124

and capital 67
as a category of praxis 5, 56, 58, 85, 121, 125
and consensus/negotiation 120, 121, 123
and context 121
and deliberation 6, 107, 121
and difference 37, 122
and the insider/outsider taxonomy 85, 125
and interaction 124
and interdependence 56, 105, 123, 124, 125
and law making 55, 56, 58, 107, 120, 121, 122
and patterns of thinking 12
and power 6, 7, 107, 120, 123, 125
and Simmel, Georg 122
subject to change 85, 125
consensus
and action 105
and compromise 5, 107, 119, 120, 121, 123
and free will 7, 117
and Habermas, Jürgen 2, 110
and innovation policy 22
and knowledge 102
and market integration 25
and the Monnet Plan 26
and normalization 107, 121
and phronesis 114, 118
and Rawls, John 2, 111, 112
and the Single European Act 28
and values 121
continuity 4, 5, 56, 65, 78, 91, 95, 100, 102, 104, 105, 115, 119, 122, 124

decentralized governance structures 58
decentralized law making 6
deliberation 2, 4, 5, 6, 30, 107, 109, 111, 114, 115, 118, 119, 120, 121, 122, 126
deliberative democracy 2
democratic deficit 8, 9, 11, 22, 29, 30, 32
democratic demos 29
Derrida, Jacques 116
dialogue 4, 5, 12, 31, 32, 43, 46, 47, 50, 64, 114, 119, 120, 126
difference 5, 32, 61, 106, 107, 113, 115, 120, 121, 122, 126
dispute resolution 63, 72, 75, 76, 77, 77, 78
division of labour
and Babbage, Charles 13
inside the European Commission 56
and Marx, Karl 17
and Ray, John 14
and Smith, Adam 12, 14
and technological innovation 14
domain name allocation 6, 61, 71, 72, 78, 84
domination 5, 7, 8, 32, 64, 107, 125, 126
Durkheim, Emile 37, 108, 124

economic progress 12, 14
economic theory 11
Keynesian 19
neo-classical 16, 21
and Schumpeter, Joseph 20
Electronic Frontier Foundation 62
enforcement 2, 3, 6, 11, 45, 72, 76, 78, 93, 94, 118
enlightenment 11, 30, 31
esprit de corps 38
ethical 4, 30, 98,
ethnomethodological 34, 36, 37
Eucken, Walter
and the economic constitution 23
and ordoliberalism, 23
European Commission
and activity based management 50
and Annual Management Plan 50
and anthropological research 36
and appraisal 50, 51, 55, 124
and the Bangemann Report 93
cabinet of the President of 38, 39, 40, 41, 42, 46, 51, 52, 53, 57
and career development 50
and the cognitive approach 36
and the College of Commissioners 46, 47, 51, 53, 60
and comitology 2, 54
and committees 2, 3, 25, 38, 54, 58, 79, 80, 105, 115
and compromise 6, 55, 56, 57, 58, 85, 105, 124
and the Council 40, 51, 53
and the culture of cooperation 58
and Delors, Jacques 49, 51
and democratic deficit 29
Directorate General (DG) of 38, 39

and division of labour 56
and the environmental dimension 44
and the European Parliament 40, 53
and exchanging information 52, 53
and file allocation 39
and forms of capital 67
and the Green Paper on Innovation 93
and internal notes 45
and interservice consultations 39, 43, 46, 47, 96, 124
and the Jean Monnet approach 27
and the Kinnock communication 48
and legal certainty 56, 61, 93, 94, 98, 100, 117, 124
and the Legal Service 39
and legal training 101
and the liberalization of telecommunication markets 11, 28, 93
and market integration 22, 90, 94, 99
and meetings 53
and mobility 48, 49, 55, 57, 124
and open source and free software 96
President of 39, 46
and the principle of collegiality, 40, 46, 102
and proceduralization 2
and professional background 102
and promotion 49, 50, 51, 55, 57, 124
and the Proposal for a Directive on the Protection by Patents of Computer-Implemented Inventions 85, 88, 89, 90, 94, 96, 96, 98, 99, 100
and the Reform by the Prodi Commission 36, 43, 49, 51
and the Reform Progress Review 50
and regulating scarce resources 71
and regulatory output 53, 56, 58, 97, 102
and the Secretariat General 39
and Staff Regulations 2004 50
and structural patterns of thinking 104
and subsidiarity 45
and the Union Syndicale Fédérale 51
and the White Paper on Growth, Competitiveness, Employment 92
experience
and action 121
communication of 114
and genealogy 9, 11
and legal texts 5
and phronesis 3, 4, 117, 125
and schemas 34, 36, 37
subject to change, as 7, 85, 105
translation of 114
expertise 11, 22, 26, 27, 28, 32, 48, 49, 102, 115, 116

facilitation 3, 8, 78, 126
formal law 1, 109, 122
formality 56, 94, 117
Foucault, Michel
and administrative rationality 100
and genealogy 31
and governmentality 116
and information 117
and normalization 6, 63
and power 32, 63, 64, 125
and rationality 5
and social engineering 102
freedom to trade 12

Gadamer, Hans Georg 113, 114
Garfinkel, Harold 34, 36, 110
Geertz, Clifford 35
German historical school 16
globalization 11, 61, 93
Goffman, Erving 34, 55
governmental intervention 23, 62
great depression 16, 19

Habermas, Jürgen
and administrative neutrality 114, 115
and the cognitive approach 110
and communicative action 109, 110
and the concept of demos 30
and consensus 110
and ideal speech 109
and law's legitimacy 108, 109, 117
and participation 109
and procedural law 2, 109
and rational reconstruction 110
and system/lifeworld 108, 109
and Taylor, Charles 113
Heclo, Hugh and Wildavsky, Aaron 49
hierarchy 38, 39, 40, 42, 47, 49, 51, 53, 55, 70, 71, 101
historical analysis 5

impartiality 6, 7, 66, 67, 68, 116, 117
inclusion 2, 6, 8, 126
industrial revolution 12, 13, 18, 19
information society 11, 45, 70, 71, 76, 79, 91, 93, 94, 95, 97
innovation
  and the chain-linked model 21
  and collaboration 100, 103
  and competitiveness 91, 98, 99
  contingent construct, as a 102
  and the Green Paper on Innovation 93
  and investment 95
  and law 9, 10, 11, 17, 18, 19, 20, 21, 22
  and market integration 90
  political economy of 7, 10, 12, 14, 16, 17
  and property rights 94, 96, 97
intellectual property rights 6, 10, 31, 68, 71, 77, 78, 84, 90, 93, 97, 103
interaction 5, 21, 33, 34, 35, 36, 37, 38, 45, 58, 89, 109, 110, 124, 125, 126
interdependence 5, 56, 105, 123, 124, 125
interest intermediation 11, 27, 28, 31
Internet
  and anonymity 68, 69
  and communities 62, 69, 71, 77, 85
  and copyright law 63, 69, 70, 71, 87, 88, 100
  and cybersquatting 72, 76, 77
  and dispute resolution 63, 72, 75, 76, 77
  and domain name allocation 6, 61, 71, 72
  filters 2, 82, 83, 116
  and harmful content 78, 79, 82
  and Internet Service Providers, liabilities of 80
  and patent law 85
  and power 84
  and property 85
  and soft law 79
  and technologies of control 83
  and trademark law 72, 73, 74, 75
Internet Corporation of Assigned Names and Numbers 2, 6, 72, 73, 75, 76, 77, 78, 84
interoperability 70, 95, 96, 97, 98, 99, 105
interviews 37, 38, 43, 55, 96

Kennedy, Duncan 98

legal certainty 4, 5, 56, 61, 93, 94, 98, 100, 104, 117, 119, 124
legal pluralism 1
legitimacy 5, 6, 29, 30, 35, 48, 66, 67, 109, 116, 117, 118,
Lessig, Lawrence 63, 70
lex informatica 63
liberalism 11, 14, 16
living law 62
local knowledge 2, 6

market integration
  and the common market 25
  and Monnet, Jean 26
  and ordoliberalism 24
  and the Single European Act 27
Marx, Karl 17, 18, 20
Marxism 16
Monnet, Jean
  and the Coal and Steel Community 24
  and the Monnet Plan 25, 26
  and the technocracy discourse 22, 25, 26

networks 1, 3, 6, 10, 53, 54, 55, 59, 77, 79, 99, 104, 105, 106, 109, 112, 115, 117, 124, 126
neutrality
  and the administration 10, 101, 102
  and law 6, 7, 32, 61, 66, 67, 84, 116, 117
new governance 1, 6, 61
  and administrative rationality 114
  and compromise 5, 119, 126
  and context 7
  and democratic deficit 31
  and the function of law 1, 3, 4, 5, 104, 107, 126
  genealogy of 9, 10
  and the Internet 61
  and the management of population 117
  and participation 2, 3, 31
  and power 31
  and the responsible individual 117
Nietzsche, Friedrich
  and the political 5
  and power 3, 64

objectification of practices 56, 94
objectivity, and law 4, 7, 10, 32, 65, 66, 67, 68, 84, 95, 101, 102, 105, 116, 117
ordoliberalism 11, 22, 23, 32, 101

participation
and difference 31, 105, 106
and Habermas, Jürgen 109
and law making 2. 3. 6. 9, 10, 21,32, 61, 63, 109, 110, 114, 115, 118, 126
patent law
and competition law 97
and competitiveness 96
and computer programs 87
and copyright law 87, 88
and the EuroLinux Alliance 88
and the European Patent Convention (EPC) 86, 87
and the European Patent Office 87, 99
and field of technology 86
and innovation in the software field 88
and interoperability 96
and justifications 90
and open source software 88, 100
and patentability
of computer-implemented inventions 2, 86, 88, 89, 90, 94, 99
and technical character 86
and technical contribution 86, 98
and the Trade Related Intellectual Property agreement 86, 96
peer to peer communication systems 68
phronesis
and action 4
and administrations 118
and context 114
and schemas 34
and the study of law 3
subject to change, as 86, 105, 125
potentialities 9
power
and action 64
asymmetries of 114, 119
and authority 35, 37
and compromise 6, 7, 107, 120, 123, 125
and deliberation 114, 115
disciplinary 7, 116
and the function of administrations 56, 61, 63, 65, 66, 67, 84, 102, 115, 118, 119
hierarchical 61
and law making 4, 5, 7, 32
legitimizing of 66
and practice 31, 37, 63
and regulation 56, 63, 102, 116
and truth 5
practical knowledge 4, 34, 114
practical wisdom 4, 8, 61, 118
procedural rationality 61, 67
procedural rules 2, 61, 63, 66, 71, 78, 84
proceduralization 1, 2, 5, 61, 66, 111, 112, 115
property rights 6, 10, 22, 31, 62, 68, 71, 77, 78, 84, 90, 93, 94, 95, 97, 102, 103
Proposal for a Directive on the Protection by Patents of Computer-Implemented Inventions 85, 88, 89
and the Council 90, 94
and the European Parliament 89, 99
and the Opinion of the Economic
public consultation on 89
and Social Committee 99, 100

Rae, John 14
Rawls, John
and coherence 112
and consensus 2, 112
and democratic common sense 111
and Habermas, Jürgen 111
and the original position 111
and proceduralization 111
and the public/private sphere 113
and relativism 112
reason 4, 31
reputation 38, 40, 42, 43, 47, 51, 52, 53, 55
reverse engineering 70
risk management 67
Rosenberg, Nathan 18
rule of law 56, 94, 117
ruptures 7, 9, 85, 86, 102

Safer Internet Action Plan 61
Sandel, Michael 113
schemas 34, 35, 37, 55, 57, 67
Schuman, Robert 24

Schumpeter, Joseph 19, 20, 21
Self-regulation
and architectural solutions 71
and business 69
and communities 63, 69
and the Information Society Directive 71
and intellectual property rights 67
and Internet 62, 63, 69, 71, 79, 80
and the Internet Corporation of Assigned Names and Numbers 77, 78
and the joint partnership model 76, 77, 78
and power relations 117
and proceduralization 2
and soft law 79, 80
and software code 71
Single European Act 27
Smith, Adam 12, 13, 14
social constructivist 33
social norms 1, 3, 6, 62, 63, 123, 124
soft law 71, 79, 117
software 10, 63, 70, 82, 84, 86, 87, 88, 89, 91, 95, , 96, 97, 98, 99, 100, 103, 104, 105
symbolic violence 10, 65, 66

tacit knowledge 7, 21, 22, 34, 36
taxonomies 7, 122
Taylor, Charles
and Gadamer, Hans Georg 113
and the politics of recognition 113
technological fences 2, 6
technological innovation *see innovation*
Teubner, Gunther
and administrative power 115, 117
and information 117
and the Internet 52
and neutrality 116
and proceduralization 2, 108, 115
Trade Related Intellectual Property agreement 86, 96
tradition 3, 12, 30, 31
treaties of Rome 24, 25, 27

universal rules
and consensus 121
and human activity 114
and phronesis 4

Weber, Max 67, 108
Weiler, Joseph 30, 31